Table of Contents

For I dipped into the future, far as human eye could see,
Saw the Vision of the world, and all the wonder that would be;

Saw the heavens fill with commerce, argosies of magic sails,
Pilots of the purple twilight, dropping down with costly bales;

Heard the heavens fill with shouting, and there rained a ghastly dew
From the nations' airy navies grappling in the central blue;

Far along the world-wide whisper of the south wind rushing warm,
With the standards of the peoples plunging through the thunderstorm;

Till the war drum throbbed no longer, and the battle flags were furled
In the Parliament of man, the Federation of the world.

— Tennyson, *Locksley Hall*, 1842

Preface

Well, of course this book will show you how to go online. And of course it will show you all the wonderful things you can do once you get there. Indeed, I personally guarantee that this book will change your life. I'd even go so far as to say that if you don't want your life changed, put this book back on the shelf for someone else to find—someone with a more adventurous soul.

Adventurous? Yup. Adventure is what the online world is all about. Yes, yes, yes—we've all heard of people who exchange electronic mail ("e-mail") with co-workers and colleagues. Some of us even know people who send and receive faxes from their computers. But e-mail and faxes are all these people do. And that's not "going online."

Not in my book, anyway.

Going online is Captain Jean-Luc Picard standing on the bridge of the Federation starship *Enterprise*, and, as the camera dolleys in for a close-up, saying, "Let's see what's out there!" Cut to computer graphics of the *Enterprise* soaring off and winking into warp drive. Fade to black. Bring up music and roll credits.

A keyboard is not a starship. But both can be used in the same way. Both are tools of commerce, communication, and exploration.

Online is Online is Online

When did the "online" in the phrase "going online" become a noun? No one knows, but it has certainly happened in the last few years. Today it is not uncommon in the industry to hear someone say, "Online is the solution to many of our information problems." By which the speaker means, "the databases and other resources available to you once you go online are the solution to ..."

It's too soon to tell whether *online* will become the noun we all use to refer to the information superhighway or the Electronic Universe. But *online* certainly takes less time to say, and that is a major point in its favor.

It makes no difference what brand or model of personal computer you use. Nor is CPU power or your machine's vintage of much significance. If you've got a computer of any sort, you are only a few steps away from entering a universe that's just as deep and broad—and just as exciting—as any explored in any episode of *Star Trek.*

Welcome to the Electronic Universe!

It's an *Electronic Universe* in which messages and information streak across the continent or around the world at the speed of light. It's a place where you can find a fact or find a job, play a game, publish a poem, meet a friend, pay your bills, or do thousands of other things without ever leaving your home or your office.

The Electronic Universe, in short, is a realm of myriad opportunities destined to forever alter the way each of us lives, works, and plays. And it is here—waiting for you—today!

This book will show you how to tap in. It will show you where the goodies are and how to avoid the junk, regardless of whether you go online for work or for pleasure. It will build a foundation of understanding—a matrix that will show you where everything fits. And it will do so as quickly and easily as is humanly possible.

Passionate Pilot

If you haven't guessed by now, the Electronic Universe is one of my passions. I very much want to share it with you. I want you to *feel* the power, to *feel* the joy, to *feel* the interaction and soul-to-soul communication—all while avoiding the mistakes I myself have made over the years.

I've been sailing the online seas since 1979, and through my books (*The Complete Handbook of Personal Computer Communications, How to Look it Up Online, The Master Guide to FREE Software, The Information Broker's Handbook,* etc.), magazine articles, and communications columns (*PC Magazine* and *Home Office Computing*), I have introduced literally hundreds of thousands of people to the wonders of the online world.

I know the good, and I know the bad. And, after you've read this book, you will too.

At that point you will undoubtedly agree that the Electronic Universe or Information Superhighway or "Cyberspace"—call it what you will—has the potential to transform our lives as profoundly as radio and television transformed the lives of our parents and grandparents.

Today, we are all "pilots of the purple twilight." We are all participants in a "Vision of the world." And if the Internet and the Electronic Universe are not the beginnings of a "Parliament of man, the Federation of the world," I don't know what is.

Eight Parts, a "Cookbook," and an Appendix

The Electronic Universe encompasses such a large area that it's best to break it up into small, easily digestible bits. That's why *The Little Online Book* is divided into eight parts, one "cookbook," and an appendix:

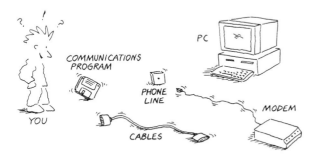

Part One, "Up and Running", lays the foundation for understanding everything you need to know about the actual process of going online. The chapters here teach you how to drive the car and keep it running smoothly, regardless of your destination.

Part Two, "Who Ya Gonna Call?", will give you the kind of straight-from-the shoulder insights and advice you need to choose the online system—or systems—that's right for you.

Part Three, "Bulletin Boards, the Internet and Other Online Services", introduces you to the wild and exciting world of bulletin board systems (BBSs). There are tens of thousands of them, and most of them are free. Find a system in your local calling area, and you can go online at no charge any time you wish.

Part Four, "Reaching Out and Touching Someone", surveys the vast array of person-to-person or person-to-group communications options that are available to everyone with a modem and a computer. Whether it's e-mail, real-time chat, computer-based fax, the Internet, or something else, the chapters in this part will help you choose the right tool for the job.

Part Five, "Special Interest Groups (SIGs)", introduces you to the true essence of the online experience—special interest groups (SIGs). Electronic information, database searches, online library card catalogues—all are wonderful, but all pale in comparison to a brace of really good special interest groups. Why search a database for expert opinion when you can use a SIG to actually *ask* an expert? The chapters in Part Five will show you how to find, join, participate in, and take full advantage of these wondrous resources—regardless of your topic of interest.

Part Six, "Games Unlimited!", is in this book because all work and no play makes Jack and Jill boring dinner companions. You simply haven't lived until you have killed an opponent seven states—or seven thousand miles—away in interactive, real-time, get down/get dirty combat online. The weapons and arena can be anything from Spitfires and Messerschmidt fighters in the

skies over London to death spells, magic, and fire orbs in the mystical land of Ogg. Just don't let them gang up on you!

Part Seven, "FREE Software and Other Files", gives you the skills you need to locate and obtain files online, and to deal with them once you've got them on your hot little disk. Transfer protocols (ZMODEM, Kermit, etc.) and compression programs (LHA, PKZIP, StuffIt, etc.) are the two biggest roadblocks in this area. The chapters here will flatten the roadblocks and have you handling files like a master.

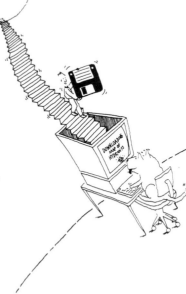

Part Eight, "Information at Your Fingertips", demonstrates the unbelievable *power* of online communication. That's *power* as in money—made because you found out something that let you underbid your competitor, or not lost because you learned something that let you avoid a pitfall. It's also *power* as in knowledge—about the company that wants to hire you, about the person who wants to become your business partner or your spouse.

And, of course, it's information for daily living. Whether it's news, weather, sports, or Roger Ebert's movie reviews, or information on some symptom or drug drawn from medical journals—you can get it online, and you can get it today. The chapters in this part of the book will show you how.

"The Online Cookbook" is included to boost sales of this book by, among other things, showing you how to *use* the Internet.

Thanks to Vice President Al Gore and his "information superhighway," the Internet is a very hot topic. In 1993, it was the subject of at least two *New Yorker* cartoons, and as we are constantly told, that magazine is super-hip, thanks to editor Tina "Vanity Fair" Brown these days. I'd be a fool not to include Internet coverage, wouldn't I?

Well, yes. But not for the reasons you might think. My goal in this, as in all my books, is to give you the straight story. It's a sad fact, but whether from ignorance or by design, many computer books lie to their readers. You can find today any number of books extolling the virtues of the Internet and purporting to tell you how to use it. (Just look at the computer book best-seller lists.)

But the reality is that the Internet is chaos incarnate. It is anything but easy to use, and all the cute drawings and terminally clever asides in a book cannot change that fact. The truth is that unless you're a UNIX wizard, it is damned near impossible to locate or obtain what you want on this "network of networks" that seems to link every computer or computer network in the entire world into one gigantic mass of electronic spaghetti.

Unless you have this cookbook.

Like so many things computer, using the Internet can be reduced to a few essential commands and concepts. This cookbook renders those items from the blubber you'll find in most other books. It clarifies, filters, and de-glazes, presenting just the essence of the subject. But you will find that this is just the essence you need to quickly, easily, and cheaply tap the Net for whatever your appetite demands. (You will also find some really handy quick-reference sections to help you use the leading consumer services such as CompuServe and America Online.)

Money-saving Coupons and Glossbrenner's Choice

The cost of going online has plummeted faster than a booster rocket falling back to earth. But every little bit of savings helps. At the back of this book you will find an array of coupons designed to save you money

on your hardware and your software and—most important of all—on your subscriptions to online services.

There aren't enough hours in the average person's day to take advantage of all available online systems. And most of us would be reluctant to pay monthly subscription fees to more than two or three services.

The chapters in Part Two are designed to help you select the system or systems that best meet your needs. The coupons in the back of the book are intended to make sampling a given system as easy and as cost-free as possible. I've assembled these coupons by contacting my long-time friends in the industry, and believe me,

they *all* want your business! So give them a shot. Thanks to these coupons, you've got nothing to lose but time, and that can be a good investment.

As for Glossbrenner's Choice (GBC), it is a boutique shareware distributor offering what I personally feel is the very best program in each category of software for users of IBM-compatible and DOS/Windows machines. (This section of the book also includes some disks that can be used on Macintosh computers.)

Much of what GBC offers can be found and downloaded online. The chapters in Part Seven of this book will give you all the skills you need to do exactly that. But you've got to know where to look for a particular program. And oftentimes, it is simply faster and cheaper to order a disk containing precisely the programs you want. GBC was created to fill that need; Visa and MasterCard, accepted, of course.

Ready, Set, Communicate!

If I were your tour guide for the Uffizi Palace Museum in Florence, I might have a red umbrella or other standard to raise at this point to summon you all around for some last-minute instructions before we enter.

I don't have such a standard, but please consider it raised. I will be speaking to you directly in each of the chapters that follow. But this is my last opportunity to talk to everyone as a group.

My advice is simple: Regardless of your past experience in the Electronic Universe, please take the time to page through the chapters in Part One before you do anything else. These chapters really do lay the foundation you need to understand any piece of communications hardware or software and any online system. And once you have understanding, you can get comfortable with any online situation or system in no time.

Message Me!

"Knowledge is proud that he has learn'd so much; Wisdom is humble that he knows no more," said the metaphysical poet William Cowper ("Cooper") in 1785.

Big deal.

The only reason I know this quote is that it was on a banner in the Robert A. Taft Junior High School library in Canton, Ohio, where I wasted many an hour in my youth.

Still, there's something to it. Specifically, I hope I'm wise enough to be humble that I know no more about the Electronic Universe. So, if you've got a tip, a trick, or something to say, use the technology! You can reach me on MCI Mail at AGLOSSBRENNER; on CompuServe at 70065,745; and via the Internet at ALFRED@DELPHI.COM. (I'm on many other systems as well, but MCI Mail, CompuServe, and Delphi are the ones I check every day.)

I cannot promise to respond. Indeed, I almost certainly will not have time to do so. But I do promise to read each and every word you send. And, if I can find a way to use one of your unique tips, tricks, or whatever in a book or a magazine column, I will do my best to give you credit.

Author and reader interaction. It's just one of the many life-expanding possibilities that is open to you, once you go online. You and I and everyone else involved in this adventure are going to change the world. And anyone who doubts that fact will be left in the electronic dust.

If you're an experienced user, be proud of what you have learned. Just as we all are. But be honest and admit that none of us knows it all. There just may be a few things in Part One that will surprise—and help—you. In any case, what can you lose by flipping and scanning a few pages?

If you are a brand-new user, reading the chapters in Part One is more important still. I promise you that we will all have a lot of fun. But at the same time, I cannot deny that Part One is the meat and potatoes portion of the book. Get its information under your belt, and you will enjoy the dessert all the more.

Tickling the Keys

There is one other procedural matter to take care of, and that's keys, commands, and mouse clicks. I don't believe in clogging a book's arteries with elaborate fonts and typesetting devices to signify computer commands. When a specific key is referred to, you will know it, as in "Hit your F1 key."

As for key *combinations*, if I say, "Do an Alt-F1," I mean for you to hold down your Alt key and then hit your F1 key. Finally, if I say, "Key in `help`," I mean that you should type in the word *help* and hit your Enter key. The actual command to be typed appears in a different, monospaced font, and "keying in" always means hitting your Enter key to complete the command.

Mouse clicks are easy. A single click, as in "Click on the Files menu button," means to move your pointer to the designated spot and click your left mouse key once. A double-click merely means to click the left mouse key twice in quick succession.

Okay. Everyone ready? Then let's dig in. Let's get it on.

Let's get online!

one

Why Go Online?

Okay, okay. You've got a right to ask. "Why go online?"
Why bother buying a modem—if you don't already have
one—and hooking your computer up to the telephone?
I don't blame you one bit for asking, "What's in it for me?"

The quick answer is sheer, unadulterated joy!

Forget about features and benefits and fancy explanations. Going online is *fun!*

It is and always has been the *best* reason for buying, renting, or learning to use a personal computer. It's what makes all the other stuff you've got to put up with worthwhile.

After all, you can write letters with a typewriter, balance your checkbook with a pocket calculator, and keep track of information with a card file. But the only way to talk to or tap the brains and collective wisdom of 20 million people is to go online. And you need a computer—any make, any model—to do it.

I can hear you already: "To do what, exactly?" Well:

1. To correspond with relatives and friends at any time of day or night, from any location on Earth.

I'm not kidding. With electronic mail, or "e-mail," time and distance don't matter. You send when you want to send, and they receive when they want to receive. E-mail is like an answering machine for your

mailbox.

And guess what: You can send pictures and sound, too. Won't grandma be proud to see little Jessie's latest drawing appear on her computer!

2. To meet and make new friends.

"Online" is a people place. No matter what you're interested in, you'll find scores of others who like the same things you do, who have experienced the same problems, or, better still, who have the answers to your questions.

There are groups devoted to music, photography, astronomy, cars, aviation, wine, cancer care, chess, comics, cooking, and court reporting. Yes, court reporting.

Other groups focus on collectibles and crafts, Democrats and Republicans, Rush Limbaugh, diabetes and disabilities, the environment, Europe, genealogy, gardening, and sex. Oh yes, sex—but for adults only.

If you're interested in creative writing or journalism (which often amounts to the same thing), living history, missing children, the geniuses at Mensa, coin and stamp collecting, camping, pets, Rotarians, sports, students, travel, or trains, there's a group for you. There's even an entire network devoted to seniors.

And what I've included here is just the tip of the iceberg!

3. To get free—yes, FREE!—software.

You can get clip art for your company newsletter, sound files for your multimedia speakers, and programs to edit sound files or to alter graphic images. You can also find word processors, spreadsheets, spell checkers, fonts (lots and lots of fonts), game programs, and much, much more.

All of it can be delivered over the phone to your computer, whenever you want it, free. Once you go online, you may never need to *buy* software again!

4. To give your kids an electronic edge in education.

The perfect encyclopedia article to help with that report is only a few keystrokes away once you're online. You'll have access to photos and graphics, *Time* magazine, and *U.S. News and World Report*. Plus you can contact online, realtime, certified tutors to

Play Where in the World is Carmen Sandiego? *on Prodigy, one of the consumer online services.*

help your kids with their homework assignments. And you can play educational games like *Where in the World is Carmen Sandiego?*

5. To play games.

How'd you like to climb into the cockpit of a Spitfire, a Corsair, or a Sopwith Camel and head out to face the Red Baron or whoever else happens to be flying this evening? (Your opponents may be located all over the world.)

Fly with your joystick, fire with its buttons. Hear the thrum of the engines through your speakers and the ping of the bullets as your opponent catches you with a barrel roll maneuver.

There are lots of shoot-'em-up-type games online. But perhaps you'd rather hurl magic spells at ogres and evil wizards as you and your motley band of friends make your way through an enchanted land? Or perhaps you'd like to play a "simple" game of blackjack or poker against others who are in the online casino tonight?

Truly, when it comes to games, the fun online just keeps on coming!

Here's what you can expect when playing Air Warrior *on General Electric's GEnie, a consumer online service.*

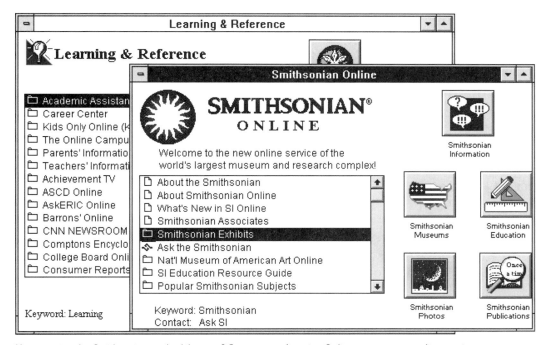

You can visit the Smithsonian or the Library of Congress on America Online, a consumer online service.

6. To tap the libraries of the world.

What do you want to know? There's a very good chance that you can find the information you seek using your personal computer and modem.

What *kind* of information? Well, just about anything that's been published in a newspaper, magazine, or scholarly journal; transcripts of leading television and radio programs; and almost anything published by the United States government.

You can also find corporate directories, Yellow Pages, White Pages, credit reports, and public records; the complete works of William Shakespeare, John Milton, and Virginia Woolf; and the Library of Congress—the list of readily available online information sources goes on and on.

Truly, it is only a slight exaggeration to say that everything you want to know is either already available online or soon will be!

7. For financial gain.

That's right, to make more money! As noted, online is fundamentally about people. And people always have things they want to buy or sell or trade. That's how cities and towns came to be, after all.

Many companies have made technical information and files of frequently asked questions (and answers) available online.

A modem lets anyone with something to buy or sell announce that fact to the world—the online world, at least. And that facilitates things enormously. Thanks to the power of computers, you can scan for just those announcements from people with antique duck decoys to sell, or for notices about classic cars (or parts for them), out-of-print books, limited edition lithographs, or whatever. And you can use e-mail to contact the seller and negotiate a deal.

It almost goes without saying that just about any piece of stock, bond, or other financial information can be found online as well, usually with no more than a 15-minute delay when the markets are open.

8. To stop being put on "Hold."

If you have ever tried to contact a hardware or software vendor for help in making their product work, you know all about the voice-mail mazes they put you through and about being put on "hold" for what seems like hours.

It just may be that online holds the answer to this frustration. Many companies have made technical information and files of frequently asked questions (and answers) available online. In the computer world, this is called "online support." But you and I can think of it as instant "HELP!"

Basically, if you've got a modem and you need help using some leading brand of hardware or software, your first step should not be calling the company's "customer support" number. Your first step should be checking for online "support," either through a commercial service or via a bulletin board operated by the company. (These terms will be explained later, so don't worry.)

9. To stay up-to-date on important news—automatically.

You can go online to set up your own customized news clipping service. Suppose you can tell an online service to automatically scan the Associated Press newswire or some other news source for stories about a particular company or topic? Suppose the service will automatically place matching stories in your electronic mailbox for you to read the next time you sign on?

Then, my friends, you've got something. News as news is cheaper via radio and TV. But a fully automated, computerized clipping service is something to go online for!

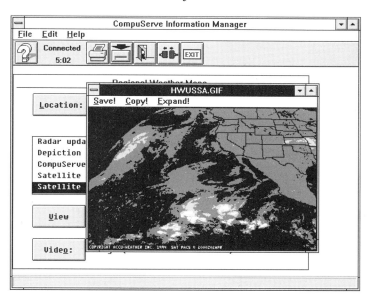

Continuously updated radar weather maps are only a mouse click away on CompuServe, a consumer online service.

10. To be in the know should Vice President Al Gore happen to be at your next cocktail party.

I'm serious! Al Gore may not be there, but no thinking person these days can escape the "Information Superhighway" or news and magazine stories about it.

You may find that it is worth buying this book and going online simply to say that you have been there.

```
┌──────────────────────────────────────────────────────────────────┐
│                                                                    │
│        THE DELPHI INTERNET SPECIAL INTEREST GROUP                  │
│            Helping you connect to everywhere!                      │
│                                                                    │
│        Walt Howe (WALTHOWE), INTERNET SIG Manager                  │
│      Andy Eddy (VIDGAMES), Assistant Manager (Library, Mac)        │
│                                                                    │
│    Internet SIG Menu:                                              │
│                                                                    │
│    About the Internet      Help                                    │
│    Conference              Exit                                    │
│    Databases (Files)                                               │
│    EMail                   FTP                                     │
│    Forum (Messages)        Gopher                                  │
│    Guides (Books)          IRC-Internet Relay Chat                 │
│    Register/Cancel         Telnet                                  │
│    Who's Here              Utilities (finger, traceroute, ping)    │
│    Workspace               Usenet Newsgroups                       │
│                                                                    │
│    Internet SIG>Enter your selection:                             │
│                                                                    │
└──────────────────────────────────────────────────────────────────┘
```

You can explore the Information Superhighway with the Internet Special Interest Group on Delphi, a consumer online service.

Conclusion

I have done my best in this book to include the information and coupons you will need to go online as easily, as painlessly, and as cheaply as possible. I cannot quite say that "If you do not have a modem, one will be provided for you," but I can direct you to coupons that will make the modem you buy quite inexpensive. And I have done my best to make sure that this book makes it possible for you to sample most of the leading online services for very little or no money.

So, basically, you've got nothing to lose. And, in my humble opinion (IMHO), you've got an entire electronic universe to gain!

So, What Do I Need to Do All this Great Stuff?

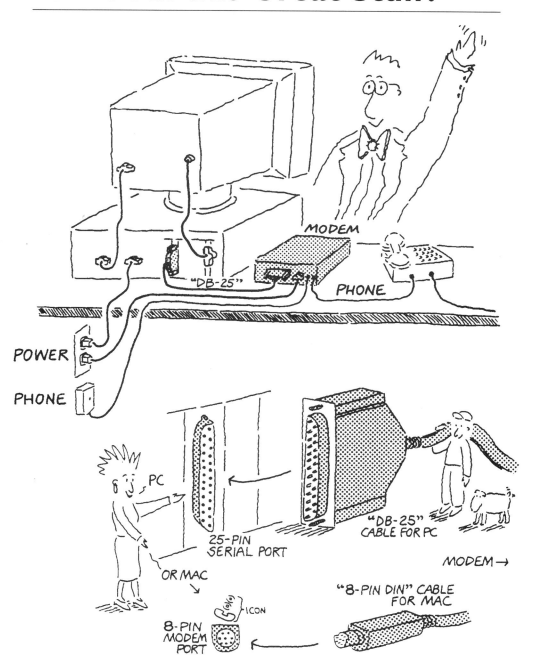

2

*Going online—getting your computer to "talk" on the telephone—is very simple these days. All it takes is a computer, a little device called a **modem**, and communications software. And, oh, yes, a telephone.*

When you get everything connected and load your **comm program,** you'll be able to dial the phone by tapping keys at your computer. The distant phone will ring once or twice and then pick up. Next you'll hear a lot of beeps and static-y noises that would make good sound effects for a science fiction movie.

After a moment, all will be silent. You will probably be asked for an account number and password next. It all depends on who you're calling. But very soon you'll see something like "Welcome to CompuServe!" or "Now Connected to the Big Bad BBS! Welcome!" or some other welcoming message. This screen is usually called a **greeting screen,** and seeing it is a sure sign that you are indeed online.

Nothing in computing is more exciting than this the first few times you do it. And each time you sign onto a different service, it's like opening a birthday present, since you never know what you'll find.

---

modem
Short for "modulator/demodulator." Modems are needed to convert the kind of signals computers use internally into a form that can be sent and received over the telephone lines.

comm program
Also called a "terminal program," this kind of software basically channels your keystrokes out the back door and into the modem. Communications software also displays text that comes in over the phone lines and modem on the screen, and, at your option, records it in a file on your hard disk. Those are the basic functions of comm programs, but most packages offer many, many more features.

greeting screen
As its name implies, a greeting screen is simply the first screen you are shown when you connect with an online service. Most greeting screens do include a word of welcome. Many also include a menu of initial options and possibly a "banner" noting items of special interest.

Making the Right Connections

In this chapter, I'm going to assume that you already have a modem and a communications program. If that's not the case, skip ahead to the next two chapters for my advice on what to get. Then come back here when you're ready to put everything together.

The first thing you need to know is that there are two main types of modems: internal and external.

If you want to make all the right connections, the first thing you need to know is that there are two main types of modems: internal and external. Internal modems are mounted on an add-on card inside your computer.

If you look at the back of your computer and see two telephone jacks, it's a pretty sure bet that your computer has an internal modem. If you see only a single phone jack back there, you may have an internal modem or you may be looking at a connector for a local area network (LAN). That brings up an important point: If you are using a computer at work that is part of a network and you're not a computer whiz, don't do anything without first consulting your network manager.

As for external modems, you used to be able to say that you can't miss them since they're the big, flat boxes with the blinking lights sitting next to your computer. These days, however, external modems can be as small as a deck of playing cards. If you are in doubt, just look at the back of your computer and trace down every cable that connects to it.

Other Crucial Connections

If you have an internal modem, all you have to do is connect its phone jack to the phone jack on the wall. The necessary phone cable will almost certainly have been supplied with the modem. It will terminate with a male "RJ-11" modular plug on each end and will be identical to the kind of phone extension cord you find at Radio Shack or AT&T Phone Centers.

The only way you can mess up is if you've got two jacks at the back of your computer, and you pick the wrong one. Some internal modems give you a jack to plug into your telephone as well as a jack to connect the modem to the wall. Look closely to see if they are labeled. If not, consult your modem manual. Or just experiment!

If you have an external modem, you've got three connections to make. First, there is the cable that connects your modem to your computer. For most computers (except Apple Macintoshes), this is a flat **ribbon cable,** each end of which has what's called a "D-shell 25-pin connector." The connectors get their name from the fact that they are shaped like an elongated D and have 25 gold pins or holes. The term "DB-25" is also often used.

> **ribbon cable**
> *The term applied to most flat computer cables. Such cables usually carry data or computer signals, and they typically include 25 or more separate wires.*

The only way you can make a mistake here is if you look at the back of your system and see more than one place to plug in such a cable. The problem is that printers are often connected to computers using the same kind of plugs.

The trick to know is that a connector offering 25 *sockets* at the back of your computer is almost certainly a parallel printer port, while a connector offering 25 *pins* at the back of your computer is almost certainly a communications port.

If your computer is an Apple Macintosh, look for the connector at the back of your machine with a telephone handset icon. That is the modem port. The required plug is a round "DIN" connector, and the cable is also round, not flat. As long as you told your computer store that you were buying your modem for use with a Macintosh, the proper cable should have been supplied with the unit.

The two other connections needed to hook up an external modem are easy. You will need to make sure it is plugged into an electrical outlet, and that it has been connected to the telephone wall jack. Finally, make sure that the modem is turned on.

How Can I Tell If It's Working?

Since an internal modem draws its power from your computer and since it has no external lights, the only way to tell if it is working and if you've made all the right connections is to load your comm program and do a little test. Most external modems have lights, so you can at least tell if they are turned on or not. But, by and large, you must load your software to test them, too.

The quickest way to test everything is to load your comm program and then get into **terminal mode.** See your program's documentation or online help information for details.

Once in terminal mode, anything you type will be sent to the modem. Going into terminal mode is like opening a channel from your keyboard to your modem, with the results being displayed on the screen.

The quick way to make sure that all connections are correct and that everything is working as it should is to type in AT and hit your Enter key when in terminal mode. (Some modems will only accept capital letters for AT.) If you see "Okay" or "OK" appear on your screen after you do this, it is a sure sign that your computer is able to converse with your modem.

Basically, that means that everything is fine on your end and that your hardware and software are ready to go online. If you have never been online before, see Chapter 8, "Online in an Instant!" for some really neat and useful—and free!—numbers to dial.

> **terminal mode**
> *All computer communications are designed around the old mainframe model in which you had one big computer and lots of scattered "terminals" used to access it. A terminal has always been nothing more than a keyboard and a display screen. (No disk drive, CPU [central processing unit], memory, or anything else.)*
>
> *Today, if you want to talk to most systems, your software must be able to make your highly intelligent and extraordinarily capable computer appear to be just a plain old dumb terminal, as far as the system you are calling is concerned.*
>
> *Terminal mode is thus the lowest common denominator in computer communications. When you are a "terminal," no one expects you to be able to do anything more than send, receive, and display text.*

What If I Don't Get an "Okay?"

You'll find more extensive troubleshooting tips later in this book. But at this point, if you key in AT and do *not* see "Okay" or words to that effect, your computer is *not* talking to your modem.

The first thing to do is to check all of your cables and connections:

- Is everything firmly and properly seated?
- Is everything plugged into the correct spot?
- If you have an external modem, are you sure it is turned on?
- If you have an internal modem, can you check to see that its card is firmly seated in your system's motherboard?

Remember, now, this is strictly between your modem, your computer, and your communications software. The telephone connection has nothing to do with whether or not you get an "Okay."

If everything checks out, and you still don't get an "Okay" when you key in AT, the next thing to check is the "comm port" your software is talking to. This isn't much of a problem in the Macintosh world. But, as many users of IBM-compatible systems know, DOS and Windows are designed to use up to four communications ports: COM1 through COM4.

The hardware items most likely to use a comm port in an IBM-compatible machine are printers, mice, and modems. Printers aren't usually a problem since most are connected to what are called **parallel printer ports.** But a mouse can be a different story.

---

parallel printer port
When it comes to receiving data from your IBM-compatible computer, printers aren't much different from modems. Like a modem, many printers can be set to accept data "one-bit-at-a-time," or "serial," fashion. In that case, you hook them up using the same kind of communications or serial port used for a modem.

Most printers, however, work faster if you can hook them up to a parallel—"eight-bits-all-at-once"—port. Remember what I said earlier, your parallel printer port will almost certainly have 25 sockets, while your comm port will offer you 25 pins.

A mouse can be connected to an IBM-compatible system in one of two ways. It can either use a special mouse port on an add-on card that is connected directly to the computer's main circuit pattern or "bus." Or it can plug into a communications "serial" port, which is to say, COM1 through COM4.

Now here's the rub. Most communications programs automatically assume that your modem is connected to COM1. Thus, if your mouse (or printer) are plugged into COM1, you will have to make a small change in your software. You will have to tell it that your modem is on COM3 or whatever.

In short, if you don't get the big "Okay" when you key in AT, and if you are sure your cables are properly connected, check your software manual to learn how to tell the program to talk to a different communications port. Change the setting and try the "AT" test until you get an "Okay."

Now What?

There's kind of a strange law in effect regarding personal computers: These machines *can* be devilishly complicated beasts—even the supposedly "simple" Macintosh. After all, they are designed to do anything you want, regardless of who "you" might be. So they offer more options and possibilities and settings than most normal people will ever need or want to know about.

But essentially they work. With little or no effort, most people can hook a computer to a modem and go online. Especially if they follow the crystal-clear instructions given here. And if there is some weird little twist that is causing things not to work, there are usually plenty of people to call for help.

There is thus every reason to assume that, if you have a modem and a comm program and a computer and a telephone, you are now ready to go online. So your next step is a skip—as in "skip ahead to Chapter 8, 'Online in an Instant!' to apply your new-found power."

Don't Despair!

There's an old saying that a chain is only as strong as its weakest link. The computer communications corollary is that the more links needed to make a connection, the more things that can go wrong.

When you don't get an "Okay," it is very easy to fly into a state in which you try everything and nothing seems to work. I have been there more often than I will ever admit. I have spent hours trying to get something to work, only to discover in the end that the cable I was using had a broken wire or its plug had a loose pin.

My advice is this: If you have followed the steps outlined in this chapter and you still don't get an "Okay" from your modem when you type in AT and hit your Enter key, call for help. Ask your friends, your favorite computer guru, your brother-in-law, your computer salesperson—anyone.

Do not suffer in silence. If you're a novice and you can't seem to make it work, call for help. Immediately. Don't waste your time trying to puzzle things out yourself.

After all, your mother didn't raise you to be a computer engineer, did she? All you want to do is get online as quickly and painlessly as possible. And there are lots of friends, neighbors, co-workers, and computer sales personnel who can easily help you do just that. So ask!

How to Buy a Modem

3

THE "BAUD-HOG 288" BOASTS
A BLAZING 28,800 BPS,
PERFECT FOR FAMILY STROLLS
DOWN THE INTERNET....YOU WANT
THE BEST FOR YOUR KID, RIGHT?
....NO?....OKAY, MY FRIENDS,
HERE'S THE "SKINFLINT 24,"
SLUGGISH BUT HEY, GETS THE
JOB DONE, RIGHT?....

If you are reading this chapter, you are doing so either
because you do not yet own a modem, or because you
are so entranced by my subtle writing style that you

*would read anything I'd written—much as I would glad-
ly have listened to Laurence Olivier or Richard Burton
read anything, from Keats to the Manhattan phone
book.*

You shall not read in vain!

In the decades to come, when everything has been converted to fiber optics, modems will no longer be necessary. But at this point in time, and for many years ahead, we will all need modems to translate internal computer signals into a form that can be sent and received over common telephone wires.

Fortunately, if you have a desktop computer, buying a modem these days couldn't be easier. Simply do this: *Buy the fastest external data/fax modem you can afford.* That means a modem that complies with the international V.34 standard of 28.8 Kbps for data communications and that can also handle speeds of up to 14.4 Kbps for fax ("Kbps" means "kilobits per second"). And it probably means spending about $180. The international body responsible for such things finally approved the V.34 standard in June 1994.

Prior to this official approval, modem makers had to make an educated guess at what the standard would look like, calling it "V.Fast." Many hedged their bets by making their units fully upgradable to the official standard. Still, until units that don't meet the official V.34 standard right out of the box disappear from the market, a bit of caution is in order. You don't want to get stuck with a non-upgradable modem that can only talk at 28.8 Kpbs with another unit made by the same company.

If $180 is more than you care to pay, your next best bet is a "14.4 Kbps/V.32bis external data/fax modem" for about $90. In fact, it's hard to see how you can go far wrong with a modem like that, even if you can afford a more expensive model.

Finally, if you're still not sure about this whole online thing, spend $50 for a "9600 bps/V.32" modem ("bps" means "bits per second"). Being able to communicate at 9600 bps has a major impact on the ease with which you can use an online system. There is simply no point in buying anything slower.

A 9600 bps unit will serve you in good stead for the next year or so, as online services upgrade their equipment to accept even faster speeds. Indeed, while the nation's bulletin board systems (BBSs) have long offered 14.4 Kbps connections, few consumer online services do so at this writing. By the time they do, and you're ready to upgrade to a faster modem yourself, prices will surely have fallen.

That about covers it. You do not have to know what the terms mean to use a modem.

Modems Have Become Commodities!

The reason I can be so succinct is that modems have become commodities. All modems these days are "Hayes-compatible," or "AT command set-compatible," which means the same thing. Though a brand name can be important in terms of quality and warranty, it really doesn't mean much any more when it comes to the basic features.

Other than price, the main points of difference in modems these days center around:

- Physique (internal or external)
- Top data speed
- Fax capability

A Preference for Externals

As you may have noticed, I recommend external modems. This is a personal preference. The fact is that the guts of both an external and an internal modem from the same company are often identical.

What I like about external modems is that they almost always include about a dozen little lights to tell me what's going on. I hit my Enter key, for example, and the "SD," or "send data," light flashes. So I know that at least my computer is successfully talking to the modem. Some external modems these days have gone lights one better and offer liquid crystal displays that really keep you informed.

Internal, card-mounted units that you insert into a slot inside your computer work just as well. But, like all add-on cards, internal

A Software Bonus

Many modems these days ship with communications software, so you really can get just about everything you need in a single package. The software may not be spectacular, but it will certainly include the main features you need to get online.

In no case, however, should you base your purchase decision on whether or not the modem comes with a comm program. Full-featured, full-powered communications packages for every make and model of computer are available for a song. Well, not a "song," actually, but most shareware comm programs can be had on disk for about $5. (Please see the "Glossbrenner's Choice" section at the back of this book for more information.)

One other tip: Ask the person you buy your external modem from whether the modem comes with a cable to plug it into your computer's serial port. If it doesn't, you might as well order such a cable then and there. The cost will be about $12 or less. Internal modems do not need such a cable.

modems add heat to the insides of your computer, an important consideration if your 486 or Pentium gives new meaning to the term "hot new chip."

Also, like all add-on cards, an internal modem can be used with only one type of computer. An external unit, in contrast, can be connected to an IBM one moment, to a Macintosh the next, and to some kind of laptop computer later on. All it takes is the right cable or cables.

When to Go Internal In my opinion, there are only two instances when an internal modem makes sense. The first is for laptops, notebooks, or other types of portable computers. An internal modem adds to the system's weight, but it means one less gadget to remember to take with you.

The main drawback is that you may find that your choice is limited to units made by your computer manufacturer. Credit-card size PCMCIA (Personal Computer Memory Card International Association) modems are another solution, but they tend to be very expensive. And, as always with laptop and notebook computers, there is the question of battery life and electrical power. My advice is to discuss your needs with your dealer and with your laptop- and notebook-using associates to see what they recommend.

The second instance in which I'd suggest an internal modem is when dealing with an older IBM-compatible machine that does not have a "16650A UART." The UART is the Universal Asynchronous Receiver/Transmitter chip that turns your computer's internal bit configurations from parallel to serial formation. Basically, it is the heart of your computer's communications port.

Older models can't keep up with speeds beyond 9600 bps. So if you want to go faster, you've got two choices. Replace your current serial communications card with a 16650A card and plug in an external "14.4" or "28.8" modem. Or get an internal, card-mounted modem that *includes* the faster UART you need.

Top Data Speed

And speaking of speed: As you may have noticed, it is measured in "bits per second," or "bps," though you will hear the term "baud" often—and incorrectly—used. As speeds have increased, the term "Kbps" for "thousands of bits per second" has begun to be used more frequently. Thus "14,400 bps" is the same as "14.4 Kbps."

So how fast is fast? Well, ten bits are needed for each alphanumeric character. And a typed, double-spaced page of text equals about 1820 characters. So a speed of 14.4 Kbps means you can send a ten-page college paper anywhere in the world in about 13 seconds. That's how fast is fast!

And What About Fax?

Finally, you will notice that I recommended a data/fax modem. Why? Well, I'll tell you.

The bottom line is that getting fax capability costs no more (or only a pittance more) than getting data transmission alone. And the benefits

100K in 35 Seconds!

My strong suggestion that you get the fastest modem you can afford is more than a "greed for speed." It is pure practicality, given the way things are going in personal computing and in the online world.

The key word is *graphics*. Because of graphics, screen fonts, and the like, programs for Windows and the Mac tend to be rather large. In addition, online systems themselves are rapidly becoming more and more "graphical," with real-time pictures and images playing an ever- increasing role.

The result in both cases is that a relatively large number of computer bits and bytes (a byte is eight bits) must be transmitted from them to you. So the faster, the better!

Here, for example, is a quick comparison of how long it takes to transmit a file or an image that occupies 100K (100,000 bytes):

Speed	Transmission Time
2400 bps	7 minutes
9600 bps	1 minute, 45 seconds
14.4 Kbps	1 minute, 10 seconds
28.8 Kbps	35 seconds

The actual times will vary depending on the quality of your connection and how many other people are being served by the host computer at the same time. But you can see why "faster is better."

can be so great that even if you already own a fax machine, buying a high-speed data modem that can also send and receive faxes is a no-brainer.

This is because, with a fax modem, you can send any file you've got on disk in your computer. And the results on the receiving end will be sharper and clearer than if you had printed out the file and sent it via a conventional fax machine.

Similarly, when you receive a fax via your fax modem, it gets stored on disk as a graphics file. That means you can easily forward it to someone else or alter and add to it using a graphics or paint program.

How to Buy—or Obtain—a Comm Program

You've got a computer. You've got a modem. And you've got a telephone. The final component is a communications software program, which you probably already have too, most likely because it came with your modem.

If, by some strange quirk of fate, you do not have a comm program, the answer to the question posed by this chapter's title is: Don't *buy* a comm program! At least not yet.

In the first place, if your plan is to use only online services like Prodigy and America Online (AOL), the software you need comes with your subscription. In fact, you've got to use their software, even if you have a comm program of your own.

Second, full-powered shareware communications programs are a dime a dozen. Well, not a dime exactly—you'll have to pay about $5 to get a copy on a disk—but they are cheap, and you're not obligated to pay any more unless you like and regularly use the program. That's what the shareware concept is all about. Most importantly, shareware comm programs are generally every bit as good as the commercial kind. (See the "Glossbrenner's Choice" section at the back of this book for more details.)

A Severe Case of "Featuritis"

The reason comm programs are so abundant is that the basic communications function is really quite simple. So simple, in fact, that only about six lines of programming are required to take your system online. (See the accompanying sidebar for a bit of BASIC fun.) This essential simplicity of function is the reason that comm programs long ago came down with what Xmodem creator Ward Christensen first called "featuritis."

Clearly, if absolutely anybody can create a comm program, the only way to make your product stand out is to add more and different features. Never mind that most people will never in a million years use even 75 percent of these features. Never mind that larding all of these features into the product makes it infinitely more complex and its manual infinitely denser than it needs to be.

The bottom line is that every comm program these days has more than enough power to satisfy your needs (unless you've got some very strange needs, indeed). Thus, it's hard to go far wrong, regardless of which comm program you choose.

A Bit of BASIC Fun:
The Smallest Comm Program Ever

Listed below is just about the shortest, simplest communications program ever for DOS-based computers. The program will work with QBASIC, IBM BASIC, GW BASIC, and just about every other flavor of the BASIC programming language sold for DOS machines. All it does—all any comm program does, essentially—is initialize your communications port, send whatever comes in that port to the screen, and send whatever you type at the keyboard out the port to the modem.

First, key in `basic` or `qbasic` or whatever is needed to load your version of BASIC. Then type in the program as shown below:

```
10 OPEN "com1:2400,E,7,1" FOR RANDOM AS #1
20 OPEN "scrn:" FOR OUTPUT AS #2
30 LOCATE , , 1
40 IF NOT EOF(1) THEN PRINT #2, INPUT$(1, 1);
50 B$ = INKEY$: IF B$ <> "" THEN PRINT #1, B$;
60 GOTO 40
```

Save the program to disk as COMM.BAS. Then run the program. If your modem sends you an "OK" when you key in `AT`, you will know that the program is working properly.

I suggest you key in `ATDT` and then dial one of the numbers cited in Chapter 8, "Online in an Instant!" If you want a copy of anything appearing on the screen, enter a Ctrl-PrintScreen to toggle on the print-screen function. A Ctrl-C or Ctrl-Break will get you out of the program and back to BASIC, from which you can key in `system` to return to DOS.

Just the Essentials, Please

Because comm programs can have so many features, I'm going to focus on the truly essential ones and what they will mean to you once you go online. This information will save you a great deal of time since it will alert you to what's really important in your comm software and manual. (The next chapter will save you even more time, since it will show you how to set up almost any comm program without even reading the manual!)

Let's start with the general and move to the specific. Let's imagine that you have an account on CompuServe and want to be able to sign on and check your mail. Ideally, you simply key in `cis` at the DOS prompt or double click on an icon in Windows or on the Mac. This activates the software, which automatically dials the system and logs you on.

Once you are connected, you want to be able to capture the text of your e-mail and any other text to a disk file for editing, viewing, and printing later, after you're offline. If you are using a feature and a lot of text appears, it can also be very helpful to be able to "backscroll" text that has apparently disappeared from the screen.

Once you become an online addict, you will also appreciate the ability to generate frequently used commands by hitting a single "macro" key or key combination. (Macros are explained a little further on in this chapter.) And, of course, you will want to be able to "upload" (transmit) and "download" (receive) files using an error-checking protocol.

That's about it, really. The only essential feature I've left out is a "dialing directory" that lets you record frequently used numbers and dial them with a single keystroke—or tell a program to dial a group of numbers in sequence until it gets an answer. This "attack dialing" feature is especially useful when tapping bulletin board systems (BBSs), since it lets you cycle to the next BBS number on your list if the last one proved to be busy. (See Chapters 19 through 23 for more about bulletin board systems.)

The Benefits of a Single Comm Program Life is too short to spend much of it mastering multiple communications programs. Yet that is what the various online services would have you do. With Prodigy and AOL you have no choice, as I noted earlier.

But CompuServe offers its CompuServe Information Manager (CIM) for various brands of computers, and there are shareware equivalents like TAPCIS and ATO. (In fact, *PC Magazine* has counted nearly 20 different programs designed to access just CompuServe.) GEnie offers its Aladdin program. MCI Mail and Dow Jones News/Retrieval have their various "front-end" programs. And the list goes on.

This is perfectly fine. It's nice that everyone's being so considerate and making it as easy as possible for you to use their system. But consider this: How would you feel if you had to master five different word processing programs—each of which did exactly the same things, but in a different way, with a different set of commands—to read and edit five different documents?

I wouldn't like that at all. If I've got to use Prodigy's software to access Prodigy and AOL's software to access America Online, so be it. The services are good, and the software is good. But they're different from everything else I use, so perhaps I won't use Prodigy and AOL so much.

Personally, I like being able to bounce from CompuServe to MCI Mail to Delphi to Dow Jones News/Retrieval to GEnie to NewsNet to Dialog and to any BBS on the planet using the *same* communications program. In my case, the program of choice is ProComm Plus.

Since I use ProComm Plus for all of these services, I know that, regardless of the service, if I want to upload a file, I hit my PgUp key, and if I want to download a file, I hit the PgDn key. Those are the keys ProComm Plus uses for those functions.

If you want to truly explore the electronic universe, then you're going to need a general-purpose comm program capable of accessing almost any online service or system.

You might feel the same way about CrossTalk, Smartcom, Microphone, White Knight, Qmodem, or any of the other leading commercial and shareware offerings for DOS and Macintosh machines.

The point is this: If you plan to use one and only one online service, then it might make sense to obtain and thoroughly master that service's front-end communications program. But if you want to truly explore the electronic universe, then you're going to need a general-purpose comm program capable of accessing almost any online service or system.

Getting Specific About Features

If you're a DOS or Windows user, turn to the back of this book to the "Glossbrenner's Choice" section. Get the software; beat the heck out of it, testing it every way you can; and if you like it, send the person who wrote it the requested shareware registration fee. Or consider getting one of the leading commercial programs. If you are a Macintosh user, call Educorp, one of the leading distributors of Mac shareware. Order Disk #4910 (Zterm and StuffIt). The cost is $6.99, plus $4.00 for shipping and handling.

Resources

Educorp
800-843-9497

Regardless of the program you use, here are the features to zero in on. These are the features you will need for just about any online service or system:

1. Script files

Script files let you automate virtually every aspect of an online session. Software packages offering this capability have their own programming or "script" language. But many come with sample scripts that you can adapt by substituting your own account number and password.

Unless you're a born programmer, you should use scripts primarily to automate the sign-on process. That ought to make it possible for you to key in `cis` or `mci` or to double click on an icon, or whatever, and automatically be logged onto a service.

If you want something that will automatically check your mailbox and/or pick up messages addressed to you in your favorite Special Interest Group (SIG) areas, don't spend time creating a comm program script from scratch. Either adapt a sample script supplied with the program or use a front-end program for your chosen service (CompuServe Information Manager or TAPCIS, GEnie's Aladdin, Delphi's D-Lite, etc.).

2. Capture buffer

In computer talk, a buffer is just an area of memory set aside as a temporary "holding tank." A comm program capture buffer can be opened and closed at will, to preserve incoming text. When the buffer gets full, the comm program normally saves its contents in a file on disk. Your program will usually ask you for a file name to use when you first open the capture buffer.

3. Scroll recall

If you're online at 9600 bps or faster, you cannot possibly read all the text that scrolls up your screen. That's why it is essential to be able to hit a key to put everything on "hold" and use your arrow keys or mouse to scroll back to look at the text that has disappeared from the screen.

4. Macros

The term "macro" is short for "macro-expansion." It simply means that you can load a series of keystrokes into a single key or key combination.

From then on, whenever you strike that key or key combination, the entire keystroke series you have loaded will appear. Macros are very useful online if you find that you tend to do the same things in each session.

5. Dialing directory

A comm program's dialing directory is a phone book that operates like a telephone that lets you record frequently dialed numbers—Mom and Dad, Joe's Tomato Pies, Miss Julie's Chinese, etc.—and assign them to a menu item number.

Once you record a phone number, you can tell your program to dial it with a single mouse click or keystroke. Just select the desired menu item.

Better still, you can usually tell the program to put several dialing directory numbers in a queue and dial each in turn until it gets an answer. Or you can tell it to repeatedly dial a single number until it has success. This is an essential feature for anyone interested in "working the boards" (regularly tapping bulletin board systems), since many popular BBSs are often busy.

6. Uploading and Downloading

Sending and receiving files is one of the pillars of the online world. ASCII text files are no problem, since you simply open your capture buffer and have the distant system type out the file. But binary "machine language" files, like programs, graphics files (.PCX, .GIF, .JPG, etc.), and compressed archive files (.ZIP, .SIT, etc.), cannot be transmitted without a special "protocol." (ASCII and binary files are discussed in detail in the next chapter.)

A "protocol" is simply a procedure both sender and receiver agree to follow to transfer files. The Xmodem protocol is the lowest common denominator here. It is not the best one available, but most remote systems offer it as an option. Far, far better is the Zmodem protocol.

So Xmodem and Zmodem support are something to look for. Other protocols exist, as we will see in Chapter 41, but if you've got these two, the only other one that really counts is the CompuServe B+ or Quick-B protocol, if you are a CompuServe user.

Basically, Xmodem is acceptable; Zmodem is the best; and, with the exception of the CompuServe Quick-B protocol, nothing else matters very much. (There are ways to add CompuServe Quick-B support to most comm programs. See the "Glossbrenner's Choice" section at the back of this book for details.)

7. Highest speed
How fast can your comm program go? This gets complicated, so don't worry about what it means. But basically, for optimal throughput, your comm program should be able to send and accept data at 57.6 Kbps. Most comm software will support a top speed of at least 57.6 Kbps, but it is worth checking all the same.

Conclusion
As I said earlier, many modems these days come with comm programs, so you might not need to do anything. On the other hand, you do not have to be satisfied with what your modem maker supplies. There are lots of alternatives.

If everyone at work uses a particular program, look into buying a copy. That way, if you have any questions, there will be lots of people to ask. If your co-workers have no preference, consider starting with a shareware program. As with cars, there's nothing like an extended test drive, and that's what shareware programs offer.

Whatever you decide, it is difficult to make a major mistake. Worst case, you'll spend time learning a program you don't like and later have to spend a little time learning a different program. In general, though, all comm programs can do what needs to be done.

Before charging off to go online with whatever software you happen to have, however, you might want to peruse the next chapter. It has been especially designed to save you bundles of time by showing you how to set up *any* comm program without reading its manual!

The Basic Settings
of *Any* Comm Program

HERE'S YOUR BOTTLENECK:
LOW BAUD RATE.

KER-PLUNK!

BINARY
DATA STREAM

If you've been successful getting online with your current modem and comm program, feel free to skip this chapter.

For the time being.

There's no point in reading this chapter, for instance, if you are using only Prodigy or America Online, since both of those services require you to use their own software. But if you do much communicating, sooner or later you will need the information presented here.

The most important thing you need to know is that the two most common comm program settings are 7 data bits, even parity, and 1 stop bit (7/E/1); and 8 data bits, no parity, and 1 stop bit (8/N/1).

A setting of 7/E/1 is the lowest common denominator and should work with any online service. If you use this setting and make sure your "baud" rate matches that of the online service or network number you are calling, you shouldn't have any problem communicating.

Standards for All Makes and Models

I'm going to assume that you have a modem of some sort and that it is properly connected. And, since so many people use Microsoft Windows, I'm going to use the Terminal program that comes with Windows as my example.

Please remember, however, that whether you use a Macintosh, an Amiga, a DOS machine, or an old Apple II or CP/M computer, all the communications settings discussed here apply to you as well. Somewhere in every piece of communications software for every computer you will find a way to enter and record these settings.

Why? Because for communications to work at all, there must be universally accepted standards. Your computer can do whatever it likes within the confines of its own system unit. But once it starts talking to other computers, everything must obey the same standards. Otherwise, no communications could take place.

The Windows Terminal Program

If you have Windows, load it now and double click on the Terminal icon in the Accessories group to load the Terminal program. This program is

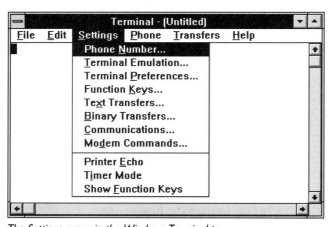

The Settings menu in the Windows Terminal program.

appropriately named, for it is the fundamental goal of every comm program to make a computer appear to the outside world like a dumb terminal attached to a mainframe computer. That's the lowest common denominator and the reason why comm programs are also called "terminal emulation" or "terminal" programs.

If you are not using Windows, load whatever communications software you plan to use. Then see if you can figure out what must be done to enter your "communications settings" or "communications parameters." Once you find the right feature, you will discover that it tracks quite nicely with what you are about to learn here.

When you click on the Settings option in Windows Terminal, you will see a drop-down menu like the one shown in the figure "Terminal (Untitled)." Mouse down to the Communications option and click, and you will see a screen like the one in the figure "Communications."

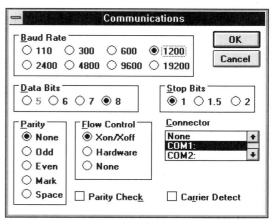

The main Communications settings screen in the Windows Terminal program.

The Belly of the Beast

Uh-oh. What have you gotten yourselves into here? "Baud Rate," "Data Bits," "Flow Control?" You can almost hear: "Bauds and bits and flows, oh, my ... bauds and bits and flows ..."

Fortunately, it's not as bad—or as "baud"—as it seems. The cardinal rule of online communications is this: The settings on your system and the one you want to talk to must match.

Practically speaking, this means that there are about six primary settings to be concerned with. But, since everyone pretty much uses the *same* settings, you can usually "set and forget." In fact, you might not have to set things at all on your particular system. Leave them as they are unless you're experiencing problems of some sort.

Notice in the figure "Communications" that you can set the following things: baud rate, data bits, stop bits, parity, flow control, connector, parity check, and carrier detect. We'll look at the first four settings here and examine the remainder in the next chapter.

Baud Rate and Bits of Every Sort

As noted previously in this book, the proper term for the speed of computer communications is "bits per second" or "bps." But let it go. Clearly, if the system you are calling cannot talk at 9600 "baud," you are not going to be able to communicate if you use that setting. So make it match with the system you're calling.

"Data bits" is a term that refers to the 1s and 0s computers use to communicate. Computers can only generate two signals. For convenience, we think of them as 1s and 0s. Alphanumeric characters are sent and received by computers as patterns of eight 1s and 0s. That's because everyone, everywhere, has agreed on the specific patterns that will be used.

This agreement is called the ASCII (pronounced "as-key") code set. The acronym stands for "American Standard Code for Information Interchange." The patterns of 1s and 0s assigned to each character were not chosen at random, of course. Each pattern is actually a number in the binary numbering system that computers use. But that need not concern us here. The important thing is that the pattern of 1s and 0s assigned to each character constitutes the **data bits** of a character.

> **data bits, start bits, stop bits,** *and* **parity bits**
> *All computer bits are the same—either 1s or 0s—but the meaning of a given bit is determined by where it falls in the communications stream and by what the receiving computer is expecting to see in the bit sequence you send it.*

"Well, of course," you say, "why wouldn't that be the case?"

Precisely. But what makes the term "data bits" at all significant is that there are other kinds of bits. Specifically, there are **stop bits**, **start bits**, and **parity bits**. They all look and sound alike, but they have different meanings to the receiving system.

Ten Bits Per Character Ten bits are required to send a single alphanumeric character, and they are sent in the following sequence: the start bit, seven data bits, one parity bit, and the stop bit. If the receiving computer expects eight data bits, there will be no parity bit.

The UART (Universal Asynchronous Receiver/Transmitter) chip in your comm port is responsible for re-orienting your computer's native eight-bits-at-a-time "parallel" formation into a one-bit-at-a-time "serial" formation. But it also adds the start and stop bits. Thus, the first bit out the door is the start bit. (Not that it's likely to matter to you, but the start bit is always a 0.)

The start bit says, in effect, "The bits behind me are the data. I'm just packing material, a 'framing bit,' you might say. And I'm feeling very depressed. But don't mind me. Just say 'Hi' to my brother, the stop bit, as you send us both into oblivion."

The receiving system reacts correctly to the start bit because it's *looking* for it. That's part of the standardization of things. The first bit received when a character is sent by a personal computer is always a start bit.

Data Bits and Stop Bits

Eight bits always follow the start bit. Those eight bits are followed by a stop bit (always a 1 bit) that signals the end of a character. One character's stop bit is followed by the start bit of the next character, and so on.

So what's all this stuff about seven or eight data bits? Why wouldn't there *always* be eight data bits? The answer is this: Using just seven bits, there are more than enough patterns available to symbolize every upper- and lowercase letter of the alphabet, all the digits from 0 through 9, plus most major punctuation marks. There are even patterns left over to be used as "control codes," as we will see later in this book.

In numerical terms, the binary numbers from 0000000 through 1111111 represent the decimal, human, numbers from 0 through 127. Everyone agrees on the characters each of these 128 numbers represents. That is the standard or basic ASCII code.

But computers have an eighth bit to work with. And because of the way the binary numbering system operates, this gives them the ability to represent an *additional* 128 code numbers (128 through 255, in decimal terms).

Trouble is, there is no agreement on what those extra "high" codes will stand for or what these "extended ASCII characters" will be.

Indeed, every computer manufacturer tends to treat the high codes differently. For example, the ASCII code number IBM-compatibles

Estimating Transmission Times

Since ten bits are required per character, to find the number of characters being sent per second, simply divide your speed by ten. For example, if you are connected at 2400 bits per second, you are sending and receiving 240 *characters* per second.

Once you know this, it is relatively easy to estimate how much time will be required to send or receive a given file, since a character is the same as a byte. Look at the size of the file and divide by the number of characters you will be sending per second.

For example, suppose you want to estimate the time required to send a 53K file at 9600 bps. Since a 53K file contains 53,000 bytes, you divide that number by 960, the number of characters or bytes sent per second. That gives you a quotient of 55 and a fraction—call it 56 seconds. So at 9600 bps, nearly one minute will be required to send or receive that 53K file.

assign to the British pound sign (ASCII 156) is used by Macintosh computers for an accented "u." For their part, Macs generate the symbol for *pi* with an ASCII 185, while *pi* in a DOS machine is an ASCII 227.

Now here is the payoff: Because everyone agrees on the basic seven-bit ASCII code, the lowest common denominator that lets you talk to *all* systems, regardless of make or model, is a setting of seven data bits. At this setting only standard ASCII text will be sent and received.

Parity Sense

Okay, so you're set for seven data bits. What happens to the eighth bit?

Since the eighth bit is always sent anyway, the powers that be have decided to put it to work as an error-checking mechanism. This is what parity sense is all about. This is an error-checking technique that depends on the two communicating systems adding up the 1s and 0s of the seven data bits. The sending computer uses the eighth bit to control the oddness or evenness of the sum.

For example, if parity is set to "even" and the bits of a character add up to an even number, the sending machine makes the eighth bit a 0, which leaves the total unaffected. Should the bits of a character add up to an odd number, the sender makes the eighth bit a 1 to make the total of all eight bits even.

The error checking, such as it is, occurs on the receiving end, where the receiving computer is adding up the seven data bits and the parity bit, too. If the sum comes out odd, and "even parity" is in effect, the receiving computer knows that something has happened to one of the bits in transmission—something like a crackle of noise has changed a 1 bit into a 0 or vice versa and thus thrown off the sum.

Whether the receiving system takes any action based on this discovery is another matter. Most systems don't do anything at all. In addition, parity checking is not really all that effective, since if *two* bits are changed by a crackle of electrical noise, the oddness or evenness of the unit might remain unaffected.

Parity sense is thus a rather poor means of error checking. But many years ago it was the only form of error checking available, and over the decades it has become an ingrained part of "the ways things are done."

Advanced Comm Program Settings

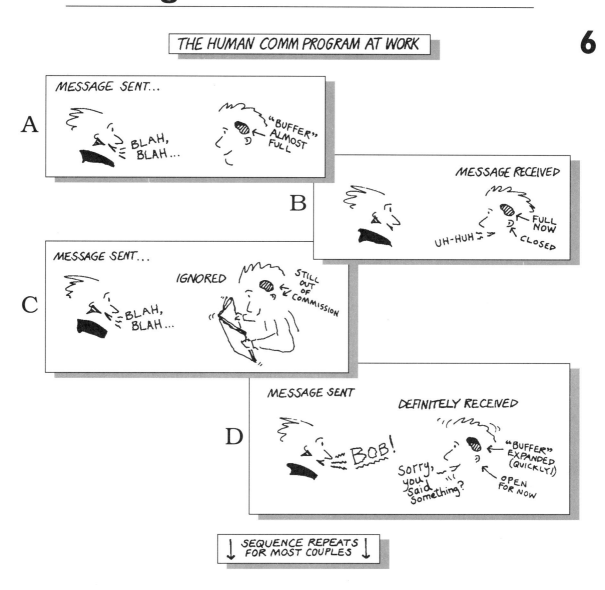

THE HUMAN COMM PROGRAM AT WORK

You really can't go far wrong if your comm program settings match those of the online service you are calling.

For most of us, that means either 7/E/1 or 8/N/1, as I said in Chapter 5. It is possible, however, to refine your comm program settings even further. If you experience any problems, you may have to look at the more advanced settings.

That's what you'll do here. As with Chapter 5, I will use the Windows Terminal program as my example. In fact, we can start by taking another look at the "Communications" screen, shown here in the figure "Communications." Notice the settings for flow control, connector, parity check, and carrier detect.

Flow Control

Let's look at flow control first.

All communications programs store incoming characters in an area of memory called a buffer. The characters are then displayed on the screen, stored in a disk file, or both. Sometimes you can tell your software how much memory to set aside as a buffer. But even so, there are times when that buffer can overflow—when characters come in faster than your system can deal with them.

In an electronic universe consisting of many different machines with different capabilities running at different speeds, this kind of problem comes up all the time. The most common solution is for the software on the slower system to send a special ASCII character to the transmitting machine when it notices its buffer start to overflow.

That special character tells the software on the remote machine to stop sending. Since "X" is often used as an abbreviation for "trans," as in "X-fer," this signal is called an "X-off." When the slower system is ready for more data, it sends out a different ASCII code called an "X-on" to tell the other system to resume the transfer. Since most systems today support this procedure, selecting "X-on/X-off" flow control is usually a good idea.

"Hardware" flow control, the next selection in the "Flow Control" box, can be used to accomplish the same thing, but only between your computer and your modem. If you are sending data to your modem faster than the modem can dump it to the phone line, the modem has to have a way to tell the computer to stop sending until it can catch up. Two signals, "Request to Send" and "Clear to Send," are used for this purpose. The signals use two of the wires in the cable that connects your computer to your modem.

The Other Stuff Referring again to the figure "Communications," the "Parity Check" checkbox tells the Windows Terminal program to actually do something if it detects a parity error. When this box is checked, the Terminal program will display a question mark in place of any character it believes was transmitted incorrectly.

The "Carrier Detect" checkbox lets you control how the Windows Terminal program determines that your modem has connected with another modem. Before your modem can communicate with another, it must receive and recognize a "carrier signal." That's what's taking place when you hear strange noises coming from the modem's speaker.

As soon as your modem detects the carrier signal, the noises cease, and the two

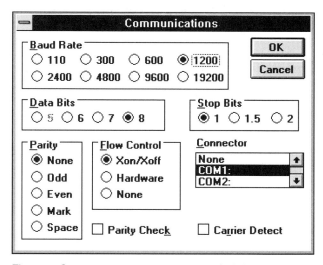

The main Communications settings screen in the Windows Terminal program.

modems lock on. Most modems also automatically notify your computer and your software that they have indeed acquired carrier by sending a signal on one of the wires in the cable that connects them to the computer. If you have a choice, opt to have your software look for a "Carrier Detect," or "CD," signal from the modem. (If you have an external modem, the CD light will glow when carrier has been acquired.)

Finally, under the "Connector" heading in the figure "Communications," you can tell the software which communications/serial port you are using for modem communications. IBM-compatible computers can use up to four communications ports. If you ever load a comm program and can't seem to talk to your modem at all, the chances are that your software is talking to a different port than the one used by your modem.

Terminal Type, Duplex, and Line Feeds

If you're following along using the Windows Terminal program, return to the main screen and click on "Settings" and then on "Terminal Emulation." That will produce a screen like the one shown in the figure "Terminal Emulation."

Terminal Emulation

The selections in the figure "Terminal Emulation" are "TTY (Generic)," "DEC VT-100 (ANSI)," and "DEC VT-52." The terminal type you want for 99 percent of your communications is TTY (Generic). With this set-

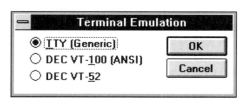

The Terminal Emulation screen of the Windows Terminal program.

ting, your computer looks to the outside world like a teletypewriter. Which is to say, it displays and sends text one line at a time.

The DEC VT settings, in contrast, make your computer look and behave like a Digital Equipment Corporation video terminal model. Here, information is presented a full screen at a time, instead of a line at a time.

That means you can move all over the display, changing and entering text, just as you can with a word processing program. It also means that the keys on your keyboard will suddenly operate differently.

Thus, unless you know for certain that your system must emulate a DEC VT terminal, opt for plain old generic "TTY."

Duplex: Seeing Double or Nothing at All

Next, return to the program's main screen and click on "Settings" and then on "Terminal Preferences." You will see a screen like the one shown in the figure "Terminal Preferences."

Only two items need concern us here. The first can be found in the "Terminal Modes" box. It is the "Local Echo" setting. In other comm programs, this setting may be called "half-duplex." The duplex setting determines where the characters that appear on your screen come from. When operating in "full-duplex" (FDX), the **host system**—the one you have called—echoes back the characters you send. (Which is why the really correct term is "echoplex," though no one uses it.)

That means that the "R" you just typed first went out of your computer and traveled to the host system, which echoed it back to your computer. Your computer then put it on the screen. The time required for that character to traverse the full loop was so short that it probably never occurred to you that the character didn't go directly from your keyboard to the screen. That's what full-duplex means.

> **host system**
> *The host system is always the system you have called, even if it is another computer just like your own. The terms "remote" and "local" are also used to describe this relationship. The remote system is the host system, and the local system is your own.*

If a host system does not echo characters—if it operates at half-duplex—then nothing will appear on the screen when you type if you are set for full-duplex. Among the leading online services, General Electric's GEnie is the only one that operates at half-duplex. If you want to see the letters you type appear on the screen when using such a service, you must turn on your comm program's "local echo." Should you ever see double characters like "tthhiiss," it is a sure sign that both you and the host system are echoing characters, so turn your own local echo off.

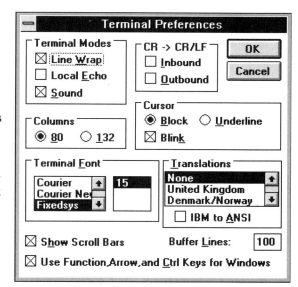

The Terminal Preferences screen of the Windows Terminal program.

Carriage Returns and Line Feeds

Computers must be told how to do absolutely everything. Each step has got to be spelled out for them. That's what the second item we need to consider in the figure "Terminal Preferences"—"CR" and "CR/LF"—is all about.

We take it for granted that when we hit the Enter or Return key, the cursor zips all the way to the left margin and the display scrolls up one line. But, as you can see, two separate steps are involved.

There's the "carriage return," or "CR," to make the cursor zip all the way to the left. And there's the "line feed," or "LF," to cause the display to scroll up one line. (The "carriage" referred to is the mechanism that carries the printhead of a teletypewriter or similar device, but with a computer, of course, what actually "returns" to the left is the cursor.)

Almost every system, yours included, puts a carriage return character at the end of each line it transmits. The question is: Who is responsible for adding the line feeds—you or the host system?

To make things even more interesting, there are two opportunities to add line feeds. You can have your software add them to the outbound text you're sending or to the inbound text coming into your machine.

This is actually less complicated than it appears. In almost every case, you shouldn't add line feeds at all. Mainframe host systems like to get text with carriage returns alone, and they will add line feeds to the text they send you. Should you ever see text on your screen that is double or triple spaced, however, it's a sure bet that your software is adding its own line feeds. Solve the problem by toggling off that feature.

To recap, then, here are the comm program settings you will use most of the time:

- TTY terminal emulation
- 2400 or 9600 bps or higher, depending on your modem and the host system's capabilities
- 7 data bits, even parity, and 1 stop bit (7/E/1); or 8 data bits, no parity, and 1 stop bit (8/N/1)
- Full-duplex (FDX, no local echo), except when using the GEnie online service
- No line feed (LF) on carriage return (CR), either for incoming or outgoing text
- X-on/X-off flow control enabled

Cool Control Codes

Like the X-on and X-off flow control signals mentioned in this chapter, the carriage return and the line feed are actually ASCII characters. More specifically, they are ASCII "device control codes."

The ASCII codes from 1 through 26, in fact, are called Control-A through Control-Z. That's why many computer keyboards have a key labelled "Control" or "Ctrl." When you hold down your Control key and strike a letter, you generate a control code.

If you are using a DOS-based computer, you can also hold down your Alt key and type in an ASCII code number on the keyboard's numeric keypad. If you are a Macintosh user, check out the Key Caps Desk Accessory instead. You may also be able to use the Option key. See your manual.

Either way, here are the control codes that really matter:

Control-C	(ASCII 3)	Acts as a "break" signal to interrupt a host system when it is sending you streams of text you do not want to see.
Control-G	(ASCII 7)	Generates a bell or "beep" on the receiving system.
Control-I	(ASCII 9)	The "tab" character. Saves transmission time since each tab replaces a specified number of spaces. Like those used to indent a paragraph or the items on a centered list. Most word processors can expand tab characters into however many spaces you wish.
Control-J	(ASCII 10)	Line feed.
Control-L	(ASCII 12)	Form feed. Causes the printer to start the next line at the top of the next blank page. If you've got a file containing a bunch of e-mail messages, use your word processor to add an ASCII 12 to the end of each message to get it to print out on its own, separate page. (In the DOS world, a form feed is symbolized by a circle on top of a cross, the old alchemist's symbol for "female.")
Control-M	(ASCII 13)	Carriage return.
Control-Q	(ASCII 17)	X-on.
Control-S	(ASCII 19)	X-off.
Control-Z	(ASCII 26)	Often used to mark the end of a file.

Save Those Settings!

Finally, once you've got your comm program set the way you want it, don't forget to *save* your settings—otherwise you will have to go through the setup process all over again the next time you run the program.

The Windows Terminal program has a rather awkward way of saving your settings. You must click on the File option and save your settings in a file ending with .TRM. To make your settings the defaults that will be loaded automatically, name your file STD.TRM. Other comm programs make saving settings much easier. The important thing, though, is to do it.

How to Use
Any Comm Program

LOOK FOR
THESE
FEATURES....

Beware of needless complexity. That's the most impor-
tant lesson when learning to use any general-purpose
comm program.

Communications programs are among the most straightforward
programs to write, since the basic functions any comm program must
perform are, well, so basic. After all, how much is there to sending and
receiving information using industry-standard modems and communications protocols?

Not much at all, actually. That's why, in a never-ending battle to
differentiate themselves from the competition, comm programs have
traditionally added more and more extra—and extra and extra—features
with each version.

That's both good and bad for you, the consumer and comm program user. Technically, more features give you more power. But, when
are you going to use all this extra power?

The Eight Basic Features

What good is it to own a sports car capable of delivering 130 miles per hour without breathing hard, with a built-in stereo surround-sound system and a television monitor to tell you your exact location thanks to a continuous connection with a geo-synchronous satellite?

Command scripts, or script files let you tell your program to automatically dial an online service, sign you on, check your mail, and so on.

Nice to think about, for sure. But where can you routinely drive at 130 miles per hour, after all? And do you really need all the extra gewgaws?

Probably not.

That's why I say that almost any comm program will do. As long as it gives you a handful of basic features. These are the features I believe to be essential, and once you know what they are, you can make short work of any comm program manual.

The features to home in on are the same ones discussed in Chapter 4, with a few additions:

1. Dialing directory or phonebook

Lets you record frequently called numbers and dial them by simply clicking on or otherwise selecting their entries on the dialing directory list.

2. Command scripts, or script files

Let you tell your program to automatically dial an online service, sign you on, check your mail, and so on. Beware, however: If the script is a plain text file, anyone who knows what to look for can easily raid your hard disk drive to discover your account numbers and passwords. Or they can simply copy your scripts to a floppy disk and use them with their copy of the program. That's why many programs let you "compile" the scripts you write into binary files. Binary files cannot be read to reveal passwords. Once you've done this, you can put your text scripts in a secure place.

3. Capture buffer

Opening a capture buffer tells your comm program to record your e-mail messages—and everything else that appears on the screen—in a disk file. If you are new to the online world, it wouldn't hurt to open a capture buffer each time you go online. That way you won't have to worry about missing anything. And you can always delete the capture file later.

4. Uploading and downloading

The power to transmit outgoing text (such as your responses to individual electronic mail messages or articles you want to contribute to a discussion forum) prepared at your leisure, offline, is called "uploading a text file" or "performing an ASCII file transfer."

You'll also want to be able to upload and download binary or "machine language" files. These might be program files (.COM, .EXE, etc.); graphics files; or files compressed with PKZIP, StuffIt, and similar programs. Or they might be files created by spreadsheet programs and word processing programs that contain special, non-text codes.

Zmodem is the best protocol to use when uploading and downloading binary files. Xmodem is the lowest common denominator, the protocol that every system supports.

Zmodem is the best protocol to use when uploading and downloading binary files. Xmodem is the lowest common denominator, the protocol that every system supports.

5. Scroll recall, or backscroll

It's essential to be able to put everything on hold for a moment and use your mouse or arrow keys to scroll *back* through text that has disappeared from your display screen.

6. Macros

Let you generate a multi-character command or even an entire string of commands by pressing a single key combination, such as Alt-F1 or Shift-F10.

7. Chat mode

"Chat" is the online term for real-time, multi-user conversations. CompuServe calls its chat feature the "CB Simulator," and that is an excellent image. Imagine scores of people holding conversations with each other via their keyboards. Each person's contribution appears on its own line, but the lines are all interleaved. That makes it difficult to prepare a message, since the words you type typically get broken up by incoming text.

Chat mode helps solve this problem. It divides your screen into two parts. In one part the incoming text of other users' chat is displayed. In the other part, you are free to compose your own comments. Your comments are not sent out into the communications stream until you hit your Enter key.

8. Host mode

Lets you turn your computer system into a basic bulletin board. Thus, if you're on the road with your notebook computer and you need a file on your desktop system, you can simply call your desktop system, log on, and order it to transmit the target file to you. Or you can leave mail for your friends, family, and associates on your desktop system.

You may find that your program offers online help that can be popped up at the click of a mouse or the touch of a key.

Mastering the Basic Features

The fastest way to master any communications program is to consult the manual to learn the commands or keystrokes needed to use these eight basic features. Alternatively, you may find that your program offers online help that can be popped up at the click of a mouse or the touch of a key.

In any case, unless you are experiencing problems, you can pretty much forget about everything except these eight features for the time being.

A Day in the Life: *Using* the Basic Features

To give you a better idea of how you will actually use these basic features, I thought it might be helpful to quickly step through "a day in the life" of an online communicator—namely, me.

At the Start of the Day

Like most people, I begin the day by checking my electronic mail. I've prepared scripts for each of the online services I check regularly. And, since I can load my comm program from the DOS prompt and tell it to start working through a script automatically, I typically key in `mci` at the DOS prompt to check MCI Mail or `cis` to check CompuServe Information Service.

Those commands load the comm program and the script. The script executes, dialing the correct number and logging me onto the target online service. There are almost always announcements and bulletins from the service to look at, and they always scroll off the screen. I use the scroll-recall feature to bring them back so I can give them a quick look.

If the system says I have mail waiting, I go to the mail section and open my capture buffer, telling my software to save all incoming text to the file MAIL.TXT. Then I look at my mail. Normally, I send a reply to each letter on the spot, so my reply is also captured to disk.

I then sign off, exit the program, and look at MAIL.TXT with my word processor. Many comm programs will let you "call" your favorite word processor or text editor with a single command, but I've never found that to be particularly convenient.

When I want to prepare a detailed response to an e-mail letter, I write it with my word processor, save it to disk as a plain ASCII file, sign back on to the target online service, and transmit the text file as an e-mail message.

Going Out for Software

Later in the day I may go online to hunt for software or information.

I have a number of excellent BBSs listed in my dialing directory, so I'll bring up that feature and select one. Since I don't access any single BBS often enough to make it worthwhile to prepare a script file for it, I use the dialing directory to dial, and then key in my name and password from the keyboard.

When I find a program or archive file I want, whether on a BBS or a consumer online service, I tell the BBS or the service that I want to download the file, and then I pick a transfer protocol and hit a key to start the process. Uploading works the same way, but in reverse.

Instant Mastery in Eight Steps

Forget everything else in your software manual. Search out the answers to the following eight questions, and you'll be communicating like a wizard instantly:

1. How do I record a phone number in the dialing directory or phone book?

2. What sample script files come with the comm program package, and how can I customize them by adding my own account number, password and local access phone number? Also, how can I run a script once it has been created? (A key tip: Make sure that you save any script you have customized with your word processor to your hard disk as a plain, pure, non-document ASCII text file.)

3. How do I open and close my text capture buffer?

4. How do I download and upload files, and what error-checking protocols does the program offer? Remember, Zmodem is best, but Xmodem is acceptable and widely supported.

5. How do I activate the program's scroll-recall, or backscroll, feature?

6. How do I record—and then issue—keyboard macros?

7. How do I get into and out of split-screen chat mode?

8. How do I activate host mode to let me call into my computer from another location?

As for macros, chat mode, and host mode, I personally rarely need them. If you're a halfway decent typist, it is much easier to key in `go mail` than to remember that you have macroed that command into the Alt-F8 key combination and must press those keys.

On the other hand, if you plan to do something often, like joining a forum on CompuServe, and if you know that the procedure requires you to key in your name every time, it can make good sense to record something like your name as a macro.

Split-screen chat mode is great, too, particularly if you have ever tried a chat feature without it. I wish I had more time to spend chatting, because chat is a fascinating online feature. If you really get into it, you will find a split-screen chat mode invaluable.

Finally, I've played with host mode, calling one of my computers from another down the hall. But my work is such that when I travel it is usually for pleasure, and then I make a point of leaving my notebook computer behind. It is easy to see, though, how a frequent traveler might want to set his or her desktop system to host mode to make it easy to call in and either leave or pick up messages or files from a distant location.

The Bottom Line

Think about any operating system or program you use frequently, whether it's DOS or Windows or System 7 or WordPerfect or Lotus 1-2-3. When you were first introduced to it, every feature appeared to have equal weight. You had no idea which features were really important and which you could safely ignore. You only gained that awareness over time.

It is my hope that this chapter has shortened your learning curve for any general-purpose comm program to about ten minutes. I promise you: No matter which computer or comm program you use, if you can figure out how to access the eight features cited here, you can become an instant communications master.

Take full advantage of the printed manuals, the on-disk text files, and any online help features a program may offer. Now that you know what you're looking for—the really important features—you can quickly slice through any form of documentation that comes with your comm program.

Online in an Instant!

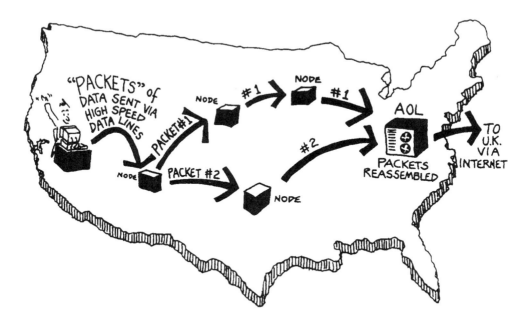

JOHN MODEMS A MESSAGE
VIA AMERICA ONLINE AND THE
INTERNET TO HIS COUSIN IN LONDON

Let's hear it now: Is everybody ready to go online?

Er, let me rephrase that: Is everybody ready to go online—and get some really neat stuff—for free? That's more like it!

If you're ready to go online for the first time, or even if you are an old hand, I'll show you some "secret" phone numbers, codes, and passwords to use to get some very valuable information. Don't worry. It's all perfectly legal. It's just that most newcomers to the field don't know about this stuff.

"Secret" Numbers and Free Connections

We're going to tap the in-house information systems offered by the leading **packet switching networks**. Packet switching networks are what make it possible for you to dial a *local* phone number and connect with CompuServe, Delphi, America Online, and thousands of other host systems without paying long-distance rates.

SprintNet, Tymnet, and Datapac are among the top providers of this kind of service. Each has an information feature you may use free of charge. When you make the connection, you will find a menu system that offers an ideal way to practice your online skills for free.

Later, you will want to use these resources for real, since their goal is to make it easy to find network access phone numbers for almost any location on earth— just the thing when you're planning a business trip and want to be able to log onto your favorite online system from many different locations.

---

packet switching network
A web of hundreds of computers and thousands of modems connected by high-speed (up to 56,000 bits per second, or 56 Kbps) data lines. Each location on the network is called a node. When you connect with a node, you tell it the address of your target system.

Then, like the counterman at a hardware store pulling lengths of rope off a spool and cutting them to a uniform size, the node computer cuts your computer's data stream into uniformly-sized packets of bits. It stamps each packet with the address of your target system and a packet sequence number, and sends it on its way.

Other node computers at various locations in the network receive the packets, check their address, and relay them to another node or to the host system itself. Thanks to the address and sequence number, however, the packets are received by the correct host in the correct order, regardless of the route each packet took to reach its destination.

Setting Your Comm Program

Set your comm program to 2400 baud, 7 databits, even parity, and 1 stop bit (7/E/1). Get into terminal mode, if you're not already there, and key in AT. Watch for an "Okay" on your screen from your modem. If you don't get this response, check your cable connections and, if you're working on an IBM-compatible machine, check the comm port your software is set to address (COM1 through COM4).

Next, open your capture buffer so you can save the incoming text to a file on disk.

Accessing SprintNet

Okay, here you go. Here are the steps to follow to tap SprintNet's free information system:

1. Key in `ATDT 1-800-546-1000`. You will hear your modem go "off hook" and dial the number. When your modem connects, the noise will go away, and you probably will see "Connect" or "2400/ARQ" or some other screen response from your modem. (If you do not have a Touch-Tone phone, use the command `ATDP` followed by the number above.)

2. After "Connect" or something similar appears, key in @. You should then see "Telenet" on the screen. (SprintNet used to be called Telenet.) You will be prompted for "Terminal=."

3. Respond to the "Terminal=" prompt by keying in `D1`. That's the terminal type for all personal computers, as far as SprintNet is concerned.

4. You will next see a prompt like this: YOUR AREA CODE AND LOCAL EXCHANGE (AAA,LLL)=. Your area code is obvious. Your

```
AT
OK
ATDT 1-800-546-1000
CONNECT 2400/ARQ

TELENET
800 12.60

TERMINAL=d1

YOUR AREA CODE AND LOCAL EXCHANGE (AAA,LLL)= 215,736

@mail

User name? phones
Password?

Welcome to Sprint's online directory of SprintNet local access
telephone numbers.

For customer service, call toll-free 1-800/877-5045.(option #5).
From overseas locations with non-WATS access, call 404/859-7700.
```

```
              US SPRINT'S ONLINE
    LOCAL ACCESS TELEPHONE NUMBERS DIRECTORY

    1. Domestic Asynchronous Dial Service
    2. International Asynchronous Dial Service
    3. Domestic X.25 Dial Service
    4. New Access Centers and Recent Changes
    5. Product and Service Information
    6. Exit the Phones Directory
```

A complete sign-on session for SprintNet.

local exchange number consists of the first three digits of your telephone number. So if your area code is 212 and your phone number is 757-1234, key in `212,757`.

5. The SprintNet "at" sign (@) network prompt will then appear. Key in `MAIL`. Then key in `PHONES` when prompted for a user name and `PHONES` again for your password. (The password "PHONES" will not show on your screen.)

6. You will then be welcomed to the system. Some bulletins will appear. And, finally, you will see a menu—which I will leave you to explore on your own.

The previous figure shows a complete sign-on session to guide you and to show you what to expect. You will want to use your own area code and phone exchange, however, when you access SprintNet yourself.

Getting International Information and Access Numbers

SprintNet also provides service in over 100 countries. For information on accessing this part of its service, key in MAIL at the "@" prompt as before. But this time key in INTL/ASSOCIATES at the "User Name?" prompt. Then key in INTL at the "Password?" prompt. As before, the password will not show up on your screen.

Accessing Tymnet

Tymnet offers the same kind of information that SprintNet does, but when using the Tymnet information system, you can also opt to download a file using a protocol. Here are the steps to follow:

1. If calling from North America, make a voice call to either 800-937-2862 or 800-336-0149 to get the number of your nearest Tymnet local access number. If you have trouble, or are calling from outside North America, call 215-666-1770, the Tymnet Technical Support number.

2. Key in ATDT followed by the number of your local Tymnet node, just as you did when dialing SprintNet.

3. When you see either garbage on your screen or "please type your terminal identifier," key in A.

4. This will lead to the "please log in:" prompt, at which point, key in information. And you're in!

The following figure shows the kind of thing you can expect to see on your screen.

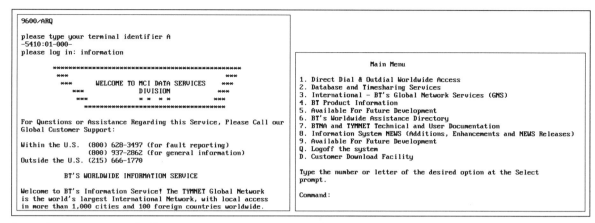

```
9600/ARQ

please type your terminal identifier A
-5410:01-000-
please log in: information

**************************************************
 ***                                          ***
 ***      WELCOME TO MCI DATA SERVICES        ***
  ***           DIVISION            ***
   ***           * * * *         ***
    *************************************
For Questions or Assistance Regarding this Service, Please Call our
Global Customer Support:

Within the U.S.  (800) 628-3497 (for fault reporting)
                 (800) 937-2862 (for general information)
Outside the U.S. (215) 666-1770

          BT'S WORLDWIDE INFORMATION SERVICE

Welcome to BT's Information Service! The TYMNET Global Network
is the world's largest International Network, with local access
in more than 1,000 cities and 100 foreign countries worldwide.
```

```
                        Main Menu

1. Direct Dial & Outdial Worldwide Access
2. Database and Timesharing Services
3. International - BT's Global Network Services (GNS)
4. BT Product Information
5. Available For Future Development
6. BT's Worldwide Assistance Directory
7. BTNA and TYMNET Technical and User Documentation
8. Information System NEWS (Additions, Enhancements and NEWS Releases)
9. Available For Future Development
Q. Logoff the system
D. Customer Download Facility

Type the number or letter of the desired option at the Select
prompt.

Command:
```

A complete sign-on session for Tymnet.

Datapac: For Canadians Only!

If you live in Canada, the Datapac packet switching network is likely to be your main gateway to the electronic universe. You will be pleased to know that Datapac offers a free online information system quite similar to that offered by SprintNet and Tymnet. Here's how to access it.

1. Call 800-267-6574 or 613-781-6436, the Datapac Customer Assistance Hotline, for your nearest Datapac access number. If you are already using a service like CompuServe, you may be able to get your nearest Datapac node number from that service. (Keying in `go phones` on CompuServe, for example, will take you to a feature that can be used to search for your nearest Datapac number.)

2. Once you have the number, see if you can set your comm software to "local echo" or "half duplex." The command may be as simple as Alt-E. But it's not crucial. If you can't enable your local echo, you will not be able to see what you type. If you can, you will. That's all there is to it. Now use the `ATDT` command discussed above to get your comm program and modem to dial your local Datapac number.

3. When the connection is made, watch for something like "2400" or "Connect" or a similar message from your modem indicating that the connection has been made.

4. At this point, hit your period key (.) three times. Then hit Enter if you are signing on at 2400 baud. (Use two periods for a 1200 baud connection; one period for 300 baud.) That will generate the "DATA-PAC:" prompt, followed by some numbers.

5. Now, carefully key in `92100086`. This will take you directly into the Datapac Information System. If you would like to use the French version of this system, key in `92100086,B` instead. You will then be welcomed to "Le Systeme d'Information Datapac (SID). Le SID vous informe, sans frais, sur les toutes dernieres nouvelles relatives au Datapac."

The following figure shows the kind of thing you can expect to see.

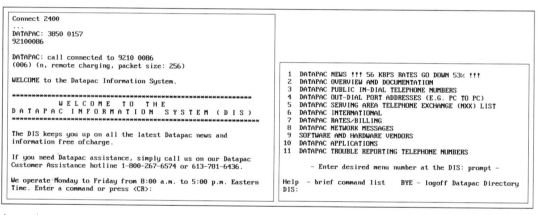

A complete sign-on session for Datapac.

DEAL Onward and Upward!

So what do you think? "Online in an Instant!" with all kinds of free—and useful—information. Pretty cool, huh? Today SprintNet, tomorrow the world!

Quick-Shot Troubleshooting

9

It is entirely possible that you will never encounter a situation that requires you to "shoot" the problem, as computer technicians say. But I'd like you to cruise through this chapter anyway, since it clues you in to a number of steps you can take to prevent *problems in the first place.*

Keep the Connection in Mind

It seems obvious, but the problems you may encounter will be related to one of three things: your own software, your own hardware, or the online service you're trying to call. The remedy depends on the specific problem, but you will find it very helpful to keep the entire connection in mind at all times.

Problems you may encounter will be related to one of three things: your own software, your own hardware, or the online service you're trying to call.

As you know from the previous chapters, any number of components are involved—connected—to make it possible for you to pick up your mail on America Online or your customized news clippings on CompuServe. And, sorry to say, any one of those components can go bad. It's not likely, but this is what I mean when I suggest keeping the connection in mind. Do not overlook any component.

A General Troubleshooting Procedure

Your first step in any computer troubleshooting procedure should be to *turn everything off*—computer, modem, printer, auxiliary speakers, even your desk lamp if you like. Then start again. Computers being what they are, it is entirely possible that this single step will eliminate whatever problem you may be having.

The problems you are most likely to encounter are a computer that cannot seem to talk to your modem or text appearing on your screen in a strange way.

Consider Your Hardware

As you know, you can test your computer-to-modem connection by loading your comm program, getting to terminal mode, and keying in AT. If you get an "Okay" or similar acknowledgment on your screen, you know the connection is good. If you don't see anything, then do the following:

- If you have never been able to successfully talk to your modem, check your cable connections, then skip ahead to the software troubleshooting section. (If you have an IBM-compatible machine, your comm program may be talking to the wrong comm port.)

- If your modem used to work, turn everything off again and check all of your cable and plug connections. Unplug every plug and plug it back in again, making sure that it is firmly and properly seated.
- If you have an internal modem, turn your computer off and open its case. Remove all external cables from your modem/comm port. Then gently rock the internal modem card out of its slot and examine the gold "fingers" on the card edge.

  Do not touch them with your own fingers. But if they are not shiny, consider using a simple pencil eraser to "buff them up." Then gently install the card again in the same slot, making sure that it is firmly seated.

  Leave your computer case open and turn the machine on so you can test the modem again. If everything works, turn the machine off and close its case.
- If you are certain that all of your hardware connections are solid and you still can't talk to your modem, then there are really only two possibilities. You either have a defective hardware component (a cable, plug, comm card, modem, or other piece of hardware), or something is amiss with your software setup.

  So check your software as advised below. And, if things still don't work, call your computer dealer or service person. Unless you're really into computer hardware, it is not going to be worth your while to locate and fix such a problem on your own.

The Software Side

It is entirely possible to have all of your hardware components and connections in perfect order and *still* not get a big "Okay" when you key in AT while in terminal mode. If so, then do the following:
- The very first thing to check, after double checking your hardware, is your speed setting. If your modem's top speed is 9600 bps, for example, and your comm program is set to talk at 14.4 Kbps, then you may not get any response when you key in AT.
- If your speed settings match your modem's capabilities, the next thing to check is the number of the comm port your software is set to talk to. By default, many comm programs come ready to

talk to COM1. But if you have a serial mouse and it is plugged into your COM1 port, you will definitely have a problem.

Macintosh users do not have to worry about this. But it can be a major headache for DOS and Windows users since their machines can use up to four comm/serial ports. The problem is that every piece of hardware and software usually arrives set for COM1.

If you think you might have a comm port conflict, see if you can figure out how to tell your communications software to talk to a different port. Change the setting and test things with an AT command. If you don't get "Okay," change the setting again and repeat the test.

If this fails, and you would really rather not get more deeply involved, call a computer guru friend or your dealer for help. You've fought the good fight and are entitled to do so.

Jumpers and DIP Switches If you are a tad more adventurous, you might consider consulting the manual that came with your internal modem, serial mouse, or computer. See if your internal modem arrived from the factory with its onboard **jumpers** set for COM1. Or check to see if the computer's built-in communications/serial port is set for COM1, which can be easily changed to COM2, COM3, or COM4.

If you can identify two components that are plugged into comm/serial ports set to the same comm port number, you are more than halfway there. You will almost certainly be able to solve the problem by making sure that each port has a unique address.

You may have to move a jumper or change a **DIP switch**, but you will have your manuals to guide you. Just be sure to make a written note of every setting you plan to change *before* you change it. That way, you can always get back to your starting point. Again, if you run into trouble, do not hesitate to call your friends, your dealer, or the manufacturer for help.

jumper
A jumper is a tiny piece of plastic with two metal-lined holes that is used to connect two upthrusting pins on a circuit board. The easiest way to remove and reposition a jumper is to use a pair of tweezers.

DIP switch
DIP is short for "dual in-line package," computer engineer talk for what most of us think of as a conventional rectangular chip with metal centipede-like "legs" on either side. "Switch" refers to the on/off switches added to a DIP. The switches are so small, you've got to use a ballpoint pen to manipulate them.

Truly Easy Software Troubleshooting

Almost any other problem you encounter is probably a software setting problem. Here's what to watch for:

- If you see double characters on your screen, set your software to full-duplex. But if nothing you type appears on the screen once you are connected to a remote system, set your software to half-duplex, or local echo.
- If you see too many blank lines between lines of text, change your software so that it does not add a line feed (LF) to each carriage return (CR) it receives from the host. If each line of text overwrites the text already on the screen, change your LF/CR setting so that you add a line feed to each incoming carriage return.
- If you see garbage characters on the screen when you sign onto a system, such as a lot of lowercase "x"s intermingled with strange characters, check both your parity and your speed settings. Make sure that both match those of the remote system.
- If your friends report that the messages you send them are missing characters, you may have to "throttle" back your text upload speed by introducing small delays between characters to give the remote system time to catch up. Check your comm program manual for more information.
- Finally, be particularly aware of any proprietary standards your modem may be able to use. If your modem can dial out but refuses to properly connect with the answering network or sys-

Block that Call Waiting Tone!

If you've got Call Waiting on your phone line and a call comes in while you are connected to a remote system, the Call Waiting signal will almost always break your modem connection.

There are two solutions. Get a separate phone line for your modem. Or get into terminal mode and key in ATDT 1170 immediately before having your modem dial a host system's number. In most areas of the country, this will turn off Call Waiting for the duration of that call. Verify this by checking the front of your phone book, or by calling the operator.

If you opt to use a Call Waiting line on a regular basis, consider making the turn-off code part of the dialing sequence for each number, like this: ATDT 1170, 555-1212. The comma (,) introduces a two-second pause in most modems. See your modem manual for details.

tem, check your modem's handshake and error control settings by keying in `ATB` and `ATM`, respectively. Either disable them or set them to CCITT standards (also now called ITU-TSS standards).

Get a Phone/Electrical Line Surge Protector!

I've had electronic components destroyed by lightning strikes on two occasions. Once it was an answering machine, and once it was a memory board. In both cases, the lightning-induced electrical surge got in through the phone wires.

Add to this the fact that electrical current in most locales is "dirty"—subject to variations, "spikes," and "surges"—and it is clear that the single most important step you can take to prevent *real* trouble ("real" as in "expensive to fix"), is to install a "surge protector" that will protect both your modem's phone line and your computer's electrical line.

Unfortunately, most surge protection devices on the market, including those built into power strips, are junk. And most do not protect your phone line. To get real surge protection, expect to spend about $100 and look for these specifications:

Resources

Surge Protectors
....

Americable
800-533-4418

American Power Conversion
800-800-4272

Best Power Technology
800-356-5794

EFI Electronics
800-877-1174

Exide Electronics
800-554-3448

Panamax
800-472-5555

Sutton Designs Inc.
800-326-8119

- A "first stage peak clamping voltage" of 200 volts, plus or minus 5 percent. This is the voltage at which the unit responds. The lower the figure, the better.
- A response time of five picoseconds. A picosecond is a trillionth of a second (1,000 times faster than a nanosecond, which is a billionth of a second). The faster the response, the better.
- Identical protection for *both* the electrical and the phone line. If you live in an area prone to frequent electrical brownouts, you should also consider a unit offering "voltage dropout" protection. Such units should automatically shut everything off if the power falls to 80 volts, plus or minus 5 percent.

Solving Connectivity Problems

Finally, there is the matter of plugs, sockets, and connectors. If you find that your plugs and sockets don't match—and if you and your favorite computer guru are absolutely sure of that fact—all is not lost. Incompatible plugs are always a nuisance, but there is almost always a way to make the connection.

One of the best sources of adapters to facilitate such connections is *Black Box Corporation*. Their catalogue is free. Their sales and technical support people are excellent: Just explain your problem, and they can either direct you to an off-the-shelf item or custom-build a cable that's the right length and that has the connectors you need.

Another excellent source for cables, adapters, and telephone and data communications equipment is *Inmac*, a mail-order company based in Irving, Texas. When you call, ask for the "Networking and Connectivity" Inmac catalogue. Both Inmac and Black Box offer free technical advice 24 hours a day.

Resources

Black Box Corporation
800-552-6816; 412-746-5500

Inmac
800-547-5444; 800-972-9233

On the Road:
Near and Abroad

10

The most important thing to know about communicating with your notebook, laptop, or other computer while on the road is that it is almost always a problem. The second most important thing to know is that the further you get from North American shores, the greater the problems and the greater the potential for problems.

Take Nothing for Granted!

In other words, if you are planning to go online while on the road, do not take anything for granted. Do not assume that you will be able to easily connect your computer to your hotel room phone jack. Do not assume that you can even bring your modem into a foreign country without a receipt showing where you bought it and what you paid.

It's ironic, but simply assuming that you will have problems is your best defense against them. That is the central message I want you to take from this chapter. I've got some solutions to suggest for the major problems. But nothing beats hands-on advice from someone who's actually been where you're going. So talk to your co-workers, associates, and friends. Tell them where you're headed, and ask for specific advice.

Domestic Problems

That said, let's look first at domestic travel and then at the mysteries of international phone systems and regulations. Domestically, you are likely to have four main problems:

- Gaining physical access to a phone line
- Using different online system access numbers
- Making modem adjustments
- Remembering required commands without a manual

Your Road Warrior Kit: Hot Wiring a Hotel Phone

It's hard to believe, in this day of "Road Warrior" executives, that there are still many hotels that don't make it easy for you to plug a modem into their phone systems. After all, business travelers are a hotel's bread and butter. If they can create suites with working fireplaces and efficiency kitchens, why can't they make sure that even the cheapest room has a standard RJ-11 phone jack?

Some do. But many don't.

Consequently, extraordinary measures are often called for. You could bring along your own acoustic coupler and try to communicate at 300 to 2400 bps using the phone handset, but that is rarely acceptable. That's why I have long recommended that travelers carry the following tools:

- An RJ-11 phone cable. Male on both ends. One end goes into your 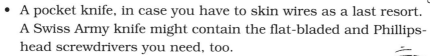 modem, the other, into an RJ-11 wall jack. ("RJ-11" is the term the phone company uses for the standard wall jacks we all know and love.)
- Small flat-bladed and Phillips-head screwdrivers.
- A pocket knife, in case you have to skin wires as a last resort. A Swiss Army knife might contain the flat-bladed and Phillips-head screwdrivers you need, too.
- Needle-nose pliers.
- A small flashlight to illuminate the dark corners where the phone jacks may be located.
- A Y connector that turns one phone jack into two. This lets you plug two telephone cords into the same phone jack.
- A telephone extension cord to let you place your computer wherever you want in the room.

- An electrical extension cord for the same reason.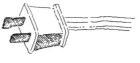
- A modular-to-spade-lug line. Which is to say, a standard RJ-11 or RJ-14 phone plug at one end, four color-coded wires at the other, ending in small alligator clips.

    This baby is the real business piece of hard-  ware, since it is likely to be responsible for your connection.

You may be able to find such cables ready-made at Radio Shack and similar stores. If not, you can almost always find a line cord with a modular plug on one end and loose colored wires terminating in spade lugs on the other.

Get two insulated alligator clips and attach them to the red and green wires. (You can ignore the yellow and black wires.) The modular plug is for your direct connect modem. The colored leads are for gaining access to the phone system.

Pre-Packaged Travel Kits

APS and TeleAdapt make travel kits. But Computer Products Plus, Inc., which first popularized the idea with its Road Warrior package, probably has the largest product line. There's a basic travel kit that includes cables, a screwdriver, and even a small flashlight.

And there's an international travel kit, including a 14.4 Kbps data/fax acoustic coupler that's designed to mate with any phone handset, international electrical and phone adapter plugs, and more (list price: $230), and everything in between.

Resources

Computer Products Plus, Inc.
800-274-4277

APS
800-233-7550

TeleAdapt
408-370-5105

Making the Connection

There are at least five points of telephone access in most hotel rooms: the mouthpiece, the transformer block inside the phone set, the wall jack, the phone wire junction box usually found along the baseboard, or the phone cable itself.

The first step is to make absolutely sure no RJ-11 jacks are available. Be sure to check for wall-mounted phones, many of which can be removed by sliding them upward on the wall. Most will have an RJ-11 jack behind them. (Hotel bathrooms often have wall-mounted phones.)

If there are no jacks you can use, start with the mouthpiece. Unscrew its cap, gently knock out the carbon microphone unit, and attach your alligator clips to the two contacts you will then see. It doesn't matter which clip goes where. If you can't get the mouthpiece off, remove the phone set housing and place the handset back on the hook. Then locate the transformer block with its maze of multi-colored wires. Attach your red and green clips to the red and green transformer wires.

If this isn't possible, see if you can find a telephone junction box along the baseboard of the room. Remove the wall plate and attach your red and green alligator clips to the red and green wires there.

A Last Resort If all else fails, gently scrape enough insulation off the phone cable to expose the red and green wires within and make your connection there. If you decide to do this, make your entry so the bare spots on the two wires can't touch each other. With a bit of luck, you may discover that someone else has previously done the same thing and you can use those contact points.

When dialing out through one of these hookups, leave the handset on the hook (unless you are connected through the mouthpiece) and proceed just as if you had a conventional connection.

The main thing to remember is that the red and green wires are almost always the only ones that count. Ignore the black and yellow wires in most cases.

The Other Problems

Gaining physical access to a phone line in your hotel room is the biggest challenge a Road Warrior faces domestically. The other problems can be solved without special equipment. All that's required is a bit of forethought—something that can be in short supply when you've been told at noon to be on a plane for Cleveland at 3 P.M.

The trick is to create a "cheat sheet" of key information. If you are going to be in Cleveland this evening, for example, what is the phone number you should dial to tap into your work group's local area network (LAN)? Or if you use CompuServe or AT&T Mail for all of your business correspondence, what are the phone numbers of the Cleveland nodes for those online services? And what about their customer service numbers, in case you have problems?

Semper Paratus

Every online service or system does things a bit differently. MCI Mail, for example, can be accessed from nearly anywhere using an 800 number. Or you can key in `help phones` while on the service for more information.

But if you need to use SprintNet, Tymnet, or DataPac, you will have to use the techniques revealed in Chapter 8, "Online in an Instant!" to generate a list of phone numbers local to a specific area. Or call the appropriate customer service desk using the numbers provided later in this chapter.

Many online services and systems also have a feature to let you search for access numbers by area code, speed, network, etc. So check the appropriate manual.

Take a Tipsheet Finally, there's the matter of remembering the commands needed to use various online services and systems. This is much less of a problem than in years past, thanks to service-specific software like the CompuServe Information Manager, Aladdin for GEnie, or the Prodigy and AOL front-end programs.

Many online services and systems also have a feature to let you search for access numbers by area code, speed, network, etc. So check the appropriate manual.

There's also the fact that most commercial services have a "Help" command that lets you instantly call up a list of appropriate commands.

Still, if there are commands that you think you may need, whether for a commercial service or your company's LAN, it would not hurt to jot them down before you go. While you're at it, jot down the number of your favorite in-house computer guru as well.

In short, "cheat sheets" are the answer to most of these problems. But the reality is that you won't really know what information you need to take with you until you've been on the road. So, as I said at the beginning, *expect* to have problems.

International Access: The Next Level

If you thought operating within the confines of Maine or California or Florida or Alaska was a challenge, just wait until you set foot, notebook, and modem outside these sunny shores.

"It is kind of a black art," says Mark Davis, an executive with American Express Travel-Related Services in New York. "No one seems to know the international phone systems that well."

Power Travel Tips

Pay attention to electrical power when planning a trip abroad. Get definitive confirmation that you will indeed be able to plug your computer into the electrical outlets at your destination. Remember, most of the world uses 220-volt alternating current (AC), but the U.S., Canada, and most of Central and South America run on 110-volt AC. Check your computer manual to see if your unit can adapt to different voltages.

Some countries operate on direct current (DC). In such cases, you will need a transformer "brick." This adds to your travel weight, but it is much safer for your machine than a lightweight "converter." Frequent travelers also advise *against* using the 110-volt outlet marked "Shaver" in your foreign hotel bathroom.

For more information on a specific country, you might want to contact Franzus Co. Inc., one of the leading manufacturers of adapter plugs for foreign travel. The company maintains an extensive database on international power requirements.

Resources

Franzus Co. Inc.
203-723-6664,
203-723-6666 (fax)

Or, listen to Jim Richey, Vice President of Marketing and Sales for Pharmacia Biosensor of Piscataway, New Jersey: "The phone systems are so different in the Far East and Europe that you have to carry an arsenal of different connections, including alligator clips and bare wire."

Your Best Bets!

I could give you all kinds of information about International Record Carriers (IRCs), NUI account numbers, Network User Addresses (NUAs), and DNICs. But that would bore you silly, and you would not pay attention to it anyway until the night before your plane leaves for Istanbul. And by that time, it would be too late.

So let me trot out the absolute 24-karat-gold solution to preparing for international travel with a communicating computer. To wit:

> Let someone else do all the work. Find someone else in your company who has already been there and already encountered (and solved) the problems. Take the person out to lunch if you have to, but let that individual be your guide as to what to take and what phone numbers to dial once you get to your hotel.

Use the Free Information Services If there is no such person, do not give up on this "Let George do it" approach. Instead, shift your focus to the leading packet switching networks. Both SprintNet and Tymnet (MCI Data Services) offer extensive online information and real, live human beings who can advise you before you head out to the great unknown.

Start with the "secret" access codes I gave you in Chapter 8, "Online in an Instant!" and tap those free information systems.You will find a wealth of information about communicating from a given foreign country, as well as the people to contact for more information in each case.

Resources

CompuServe Customer Service
800-848-8990

MCI Mail Customer Service
800-444-6245

SprintNet 24-hour International Assistance
800-827-4685

Tymnet/MCI Data Services International Assistance
800-937-2862

More Travel Tips and Good Advice

Save weight by leaving your portable printer at home and simply faxing yourself anything you want to print. You may be able to call the hotel fax machine directly from your room. Or, if your modem does only data, you can use the fax capability offered by MCI Mail, CompuServe, and most e-mail services instead.

Tape your business card to any piece of equipment you might accidentally leave behind. If you're a DOS user, consider putting your name and address and offer of reward in your AUTOEXEC.BAT file. (Use the ECHO command, followed by a line of text; and finish with the PAUSE command.) That way the information will appear whenever someone turns the machine on.

Battery life is a primary concern when on the road. So consider the following:

• Turn your CPU to slow.

• Set the display intensity to low. And set your software for LCD or monochrome instead of color or black-and-white.

• Turn off the printer and modem ports when not in use.

• Since some battery-powered modems preserve their batteries by drawing power from your computer when connected or turned on, disconnect them or turn them off.

• Minimize hard disk usage by installing a disk cache program like SmartDrive.

Who Ya Gonna Call?

A Roadmap to the Electronic Universe

11

Who are you going to call, now that you have your modem and communications software? There are lots of possibilities. Tens of thousands of them, in fact. But no one can blame you for asking, "I've heard of all these online services, but how and where does everything fit together?"

The answer is that they don't fit together. Every online service and every online database is fundamentally unique, and there are a lot of services and databases.

According to the authoritative *Gale Directory of Databases*, for example, in 1994 there were 822 online services offering a total of 5,300 databases. And, according to Jack Rickard, editor and publisher of *Boardwatch*

Resources

Gale Directory of Databases
Gale Research Inc.
800-877-GALE

Magazine, there were some 57,000 bulletin board systems in North America alone as of April 1994, and that number doubles every 18 months.

Resources

Boardwatch Magazine
800-933-6038 (voice)
subscriptions@boardwatch.com

Then, of course, there is the Internet, the world-spanning network that gives you access to thousands of university and other computer systems. At last count, the Internet was estimated to serve some 20 million users.

Five Basic Categories

It would be nice if everything would obligingly fit into neat categories. But all one can really do is draw some rough outlines based on the fact that practically everything you do online can be classified as being related to *communication* or *information* or *transactions*. Some online services are all one or the other, but some offer a mix of these activities. (The Internet is something else again.)

With this in mind, and with the caveat that the online world is in constant flux, most online services today can be placed under one of the following headings:

- Consumer online service
- Bulletin board system (BBS)
- Communications-only
- Information-only
- Transactions-only

Consumer Online Service

Consumer online services offer information, communication, and transaction services. With some notable exceptions, the information tends to be broad but shallow, rather on the order of *USA Today.* That's perfectly fine for most people, especially since real information tends to cost real money.

The transaction services—ordering Brooks Brothers shirts, Lands' End luggage, gourmet coffees, fine chocolates, and the like—are interesting, but you may find using a toll-free 800 number and a company's catalogue to be more convenient and more satisfying.

There are literally thousands of special interest groups on the consumer online services.

Where the consumer online services really shine, however, is in their communications services—specifically in their "Special Interest Groups," or SIGs. There are literally thousands of SIGs on the consumer online services, and each one of them serves as a gathering place for people who are interested in a particular topic or who need help using a certain product. Special Interest Groups are the single best reason for going online in the first place.

Bulletin Board System (BBS)

A bulletin board system is essentially someone's computer—running "host," or BBS, software—that's hooked up to a modem that has been set to automatically answer the phone. When you, the user, dial the BBS's number, the modem answers and the software prompts you for your name, location, password, and similar information.

BBSs differ widely in the features they offer. On most, you can post messages and questions, send and receive e-mail, upload and download files.

BBSs differ widely in the features they offer. But once you have successfully logged onto most systems, you can post messages and questions, send and receive private e-mail, upload and download files, and do just about anything else you can do on one of the leading consumer online services.

There are just two small hurdles to overcome. The first is finding up-to-date lists of BBS phone numbers. BBSs do tend to come and go. The second is getting connected to the board of your choice. The phone numbers for the best boards tend to be busy most of the time. But, as we will see in a later chapter, there are ways to effortlessly surmount both of these obstacles.

Communications-only

There are also online services that specialize in person-to-person or person-to-group communications. Your company may even use one of them. If so, then you know that you can not only send (and receive) e-mail, fax, telex, TWX, and cablegram messages worldwide, but you may also be able to order the service to print out a hard copy of your letter at a location near

With MCI Mail you can have the letter printed on a facsimile of your letterhead and signed by a facsimile of your signature!

your target address and drop that letter into the local mail. Or, you can order the letter to be printed out and delivered by hand. With MCI Mail, probably the best communications-only service, you can even have the letter printed on a facsimile of your letterhead and signed by a facsimile of your signature!

Information-only

I wish there were some other way to put this, but, frankly, an information-only service like Dialog or Nexis typically means high-octane information at high-octane prices.

We're not talking news headlines here or even the latest celebrity profile in *People*.

We're talking patent and trademark searches; the Library of Congress; decades worth of the full text of the *New York Times* or the *Wall Street Journal*; searches of every doctoral dissertation submitted to an accredited institution since 1861, the year when academic doctoral degrees were first granted in the United States.

> **An information-only service typically means high-octane information at high-octane prices.**

And these are but snowflakes on the tip of the iceberg when it comes to *real* information. I will take great pleasure in opening this door for you later in this book. But I take even greater pleasure in telling you that a huge amount of "real" information is available on the consumer online service everyone subscribes to—if you know where to look!

Transactions-only

Fidelity On-line Express (FOX), E*Trade, and Shoppers Advantage Online (formerly Comp-u-store Online) are examples of transactions-only services. FOX and E*Trade can be used to buy and sell stocks and securities. Shoppers Advantage Online offers a huge range of consumer goods at deeply discounted prices.

The transactions side of things in the electronic universe is probably the smallest of all. This is undoubtedly because the public's appetite for such services has been far less than anticipated. Several years ago, for example, the country's leading banks were falling all over themselves to offer online home-banking services. Today, almost all of those services are defunct.

Everything can change, but the key to success in this area appears to be finding a niche that makes sense, like securities trading by a discount broker. In the long run, however, like downtown specialty stores moving out to the mall, most transactions-only services will have to move to one or more of the consumer online services because that's where the people are.

Conclusion

Now that you have an overview of "who ya gonna call," the next step is to look at the various possibilities in greater detail. You need to know what a consumer online service is all about and how to pick the one that's right for you and your family. You need to get a capsule summary and characterization of each of the main consumer services to help you decide.

And you need to know about bulletin board systems, information-only services, and the other online establishments you can be expected to frequent. That is the kind of information you will find in the chapters that follow in this part of the book. Having laid the groundwork and presented a rough map, my next goal is to help you get hooked up with the service or services that are likely to be right for you.

The Essential Consumer Online Service: Subscriptions, Costs, and Features

12

The best way to begin your online adventure is with a subscription to one of the consumer online services like America Online, CompuServe, Delphi, GEnie, and Prodigy.

If you must keep expenses to the absolute minimum, you might instead use the tips presented in Chapter 20 to locate bulletin board systems in your area. Some BBSs charge membership fees, but most don't, so your chances of making a local call to get online are good.

What you find once you get there, however, is anyone's guess. While most BBSs are not difficult to use, it is not uncommon for first-time BBS users to feel lost and frustrated until they've had a little more online experience. Add to this the frustration of getting nothing but

Coupons and Free Time

The goal of this book—its prime directive—is to make it as easy as possible for you to tap in and begin using, enjoying, and profiting from the online world. That's why you'll find coupons for special discounts on modems, software, and subscriptions to online services at the back of this book.

I've tried to make it as inexpensive as possible for you to sample a wide range of online services. In almost every case, if you find that a particular service is not for you, you can simply cancel.

Also, be sure to check "The Online Cookbook" section at the back of this book for some really good suggestions on how to make the most of the free time a given service may grant you as part of your initial membership.

busy signals each time you call a popular BBS, and you can see why BBSs may not be the best introduction to the Information Superhighway for most people.

That's why I strongly suggest starting with one of the consumer online services. You won't get a busy signal, and you will find them quite easy to use. In many cases, you can do just about everything by pointing and clicking with your mouse.

Besides, you're eventually going to want to subscribe to one or more of these services anyway. That's because, like so many things, the online world tends to follow Pareto's Law (a.k.a. "the 80/20 rule"). There may be hundreds of services and thousands of databases, but a relatively small number account for the lion's share of usage.

The Essential Consumer Online Service

Every consumer online service is unique, and each has its own personality. But all such services have a number of points in common. That's what you'll explore here. You'll look at the various cost structures in a moment. But here are the features you can expect to find on every consumer online service:

1. Electronic mail

You can communicate with any other subscriber to the same service via e-mail. Usually, you can search for e-mail addresses by using a service directory. If you frequently correspond with the same person, you can add his or her name to your "address book" on the service. That way you can just key in `Tom` or `Judy` instead of an account number when addressing a letter.

You can also communicate with anyone who can send and receive mail via the Internet. (Contact the person by phone or some other way to learn his or her proper address.)

2. Real-time chat

CompuServe coined the term "CB Simulator" for this feature, and it remains the best shorthand description. Just imagine seeing interleaved citizens band (CB) radio conversations taking place on your screen. Fortunately, you can usually move to a less crowded "channel," and you can usually opt to make your conversations private. Most comm programs these days offer a "split screen" feature to make real-time online chat easier to use.

3. Special Interest Groups

You already know how I feel about SIGs: Whether for business, professional, or personal use, they are the very best reason for investing in a modem and going online in the first place.

CompuServe prefers the term "Forums." GEnie calls them "Round-Tables" or "RTs." Delphi calls them "SIGs," and other services call them "Clubs." No matter what you call them, they all have the same three basic features: a message board, a real-time conference area for chat, and file and software libraries.

Imagine being able to post a question or problem on a SIG's message board and have it read by literally tens of thousands of SIG members. Should you ask for help on hooking up your XYZ printer to your ABC computer, for example, it is a virtual certainty that some good soul will respond. The same goes for "Has anyone had any experience with the investment firm Dewey, Cheatum, and Howe?" Or "I've had a lousy zucchini crop in the past two years. What am I doing wrong?"

More than likely, a dozen people will have had the same problem and will reply to your query with a solution within 24 hours. This is one of the reasons I emphasize that it's *people* who really make an online service.

The real-time conference areas are used for chat among members. But their prime use is for guest "speakers." Imagine being able to chat with best-selling author Tom Clancy or with Apple inventor Steve Wozniak. Or with that ink-stained wretch Alfred Glossbrenner. All have appeared as guest speakers numerous times in different SIGs.

And talk about treasure troves, wait till you check out the SIG file libraries! In addition to transcripts of notable guest appearances in the conference areas, most libraries are positively stuffed with public-domain and shareware software, graphic images, game programs, and tons of other goodies that you can download and begin using immediately!

4. News, weather, and sports

Speaks for itself, actually. Most of this information comes directly off the Associated Press or some other newswire. For breaking stories and news roundups, I prefer CNN. But that doesn't mean that online news is useless.

The absolute best way to use online news features is to set up a personal "profile" containing the key words, company names, personal names, and so forth that are of interest to you. The result is an automatic electronic "clipping service" that puts matching stories in your mailbox. Now that's cool!

5. Interactive games

This is a big area destined to become truly huge in the years to come. Forget about playing blackjack or bridge against a computer. How about playing against three or four people located all over the globe? Right now! Tonight!

Or how about a space opera shoot-'em-up with teams of people located all over the country, most of whom you know only as "Reaper," "Bone-Crusher," "Star," or "Dipsy-Doodle?"

Feel like taking a Sopwith Camel out for a spin? Great! One command shows you the view over your left wing. Another command shows you the right-wing view. And, of course, there is the *Flight Simulator*-style instrument panel. But, as you fly with your joystick, you see this black dot approaching on your right. Could it be? As the dot gets closer you realize that it is indeed the fearsome Red Baron out for some easy pickings. You know that the Baron is actually Carl from Omaha, but you still want to see if you can best him. So you have at it on GEnie or Delphi in *Air Warrior*, one of the many interactive games available via the consumer online services.

6. Travel and shopping services

Travel services include airline schedules and fares, as well as text files that are little more than advertisements for specific cruises or vacation

packages. These things have long been a part of the online world, and I have yet to be impressed. Call your travel agent instead.

Online shopping services are nominally more convenient than TV shopping channels because you are in control. The best are those that let you specify what you're looking for in a product and then search a database for the best buy. The worst are the "mall"-type stores that offer only a limited selection of very ordinary merchandise at the full retail price. Why bother messing around online when you already get the store's catalogue and 24-hour, toll-free 800 number in the mail?

7. Reference and archival information

You gotta have an encyclopedia if you want to be a real consumer-oriented online service. The publication most have chosen is Grolier's *Academic American*—nice, but not rigorous. It's updated twice a year.

As for other "information," it can be anything from *Hollywood Hotline* and *Soap Opera Digest* to the full text of *Mac-World* and *PC Magazine*. As the commercial services add more and more "industrial-strength" information, it could also include the full text of *Progressive Grocer* or *McLean's*, as is the case with the ABI/Inform database on CompuServe's Knowledge Index feature.

How Do They Charge You?

Information-only services like Dialog, Dow Jones News/Retrieval, Nexis, and the like charge for their services in a bewildering number of ways. Things are different among the consumer online services.

After over a decade of experimentation, a basic pricing method for consumer online services has evolved. The industry began with a pure pay-as-you-go approach under which you were charged only for the time you remained connected to a service. The higher the speed of the connection, the higher the charge. But if you did not use the service at all, you were charged nothing.

Prodigy, the IBM-Sears service, changed all that by pricing itself like cable television. You pay a monthly subscription fee for access to a basic package of services, whether you use those services or not. At this writing, subscription fees for the major consumer online services range from $8.95 to $14.95 a month. And the access they offer for that price ranges from unlimited access to just four hours a month.

In every case, if you go beyond the number of hours included in the subscription—or if you opt to use services that are not part of the basic package—you are charged extra, usually on a "connect-time" basis. These fees range from $2.95 to $16 an hour, depending on the time of day and the speed of your connection.

"Front-End Programs" and Subscriptions

Most of the online services available today started out as ASCII-based services. Nothing fancy. Nothing pretty. Just plain text menus on a plain screen. Many are still that way today.

But, with the growing popularity of Windows- and Macintosh-like "graphical user interfaces" (GUIs) and the influx of new, inexperienced users, many consumer online services have taken steps to pretty themselves up by offering Windows- and Macintosh-style interfaces.

Two approaches are used: Either the service *requires* all subscribers to use its own special communications program, as is the case with Prodigy and America Online (AOL), or the service offers an optional "front-end" program that masks its native ASCII text screens behind a mouse-able graphical interface that lets you click on icons to issue commands.

The prime example of the latter is CompuServe and its CompuServe Information Manager (CIM) software (although nearly 20 other front-end programs for CompuServe exist, either as commercial products or as shareware).

The key point is that front-end software for a given service is often available as part of a subscription package or "membership kit." America Online, for example, offers *The Official America Online for Windows Membership Kit & Tour Guide* for $35. This is essentially a 382-page book, published by Ventana Press, that includes a floppy disk with the Windows version of the AOL access software. The kit comes with a coupon good for ten free hours of connect time, and the first month's membership fee is waived.

CompuServe has a similar deal (first month free and a $25 usage credit) for its CIM membership kits. These are available at computer stores and from mail-order firms. Current CompuServe members can download the latest version of CIM for $10 (key in `go cimsoft`).

The GEnie equivalent right now is the 600-page Osborne/McGraw-Hill *Glossbrenner's Master Guide to GEnie* by yours truly. This includes the latest version of Aladdin, GEnie's front-end program, plus a $12 usage credit coupon. (If you're already a GEnie subscriber, key in `order` when you're online; if not, see the "Glossbrenner's Choice" section at the back of this book.)

The point here is to be aware that there are usually several ways to subscribe to a consumer online service. You've got to use Prodigy's software, and you've got to use AOL's software. But with most other services, you can either use your favorite comm program or buy a graphical, mouse-driven front-end program. Such programs often come with usage credits that equal the cost of the package and thus make the software itself free.

How to Choose the *Right* Consumer Online Service

13

I'm going to assume that you agree with me. I'm going to assume that, now that you know what consumer online services are, you really do feel that they offer the best way to start life online.

Hence the question: Which one should I choose? And the other question: What points should I consider in making my choice?

This is not a life and death matter. Picking a service should not be agony. But the conundrum is real. In the old pay-as-you-go days, you could subscribe to lots of different services at little or no cost. Now, with everyone charging a monthly subscription fee, you've got to be more careful.

Most of us can no more afford to subscribe to every online service than we can afford to subscribe to every premium channel offered by our TV cable company. How many people do you know who can afford to pay $14.95 for Prodigy, $8.95 each for GEnie and CompuServe, $10 for Delphi, and $9.95 for America Online (AOL) each month? The grand total would be $52.80 per month. And that's just for the basic services. Anything you do beyond those services incurs additional fees.

Most people eventually make one online service their "home" service.

Simple common sense dictates that most people eventually make one online service their "home" service—the service they call every day, the place they know best, and the place where they expect to pick up most of their electronic mail. So how do you, Mr. and Mrs. John Q. Public from Anytown, U.S.A., decide which service to make *your* home? That's what I'll discuss in this chapter.

What are Your Needs?

We've all got different personal, professional, business, and family needs. And, while consumer online services can't satisfy all of them, they can be a big help much of the time.

Some moms and dads, for instance, use Prodigy as a babysitter. For a flat fee of $14.95 a month, the kids can play online—chatting with friends, doing research for homework assignments, and playing games—as long as they want. It may not rank with reading a book, but it's sure better than vegging out watching TV.

On the other hand, I've never heard of a businessperson using Prodigy for e-mail, competitive intelligence, or in-depth investment research. Nor are you likely to encounter on Prodigy or America Online the kind of high-tech gurus who can quickly answer your printer or software questions.

Real gurus, after all, don't mess with mice. That's why you are most likely to find them on more computer- and tech-oriented services like CompuServe or GEnie, where they operate from the command line.

Changing Needs Over Time

As I've said, it all depends on what you need. And your needs are likely to change over time. That's undoubtedly why some market-research firms report that the average length of time a subscriber stays with a consumer online service is about 18 months. And I know it is why many in the online industry who compete with Prodigy are pleased with that service's success.

Prodigy's parents, IBM and Sears, have spent huge amounts of money promoting the service in print and on TV. As a result, hundreds of thousands of people have been introduced to the online world. They have signed up—"You gotta get this thing!"—and enjoyed Prodigy. Then, once they have their "online legs," they've struck out for other pastures, landing in the laps of the other four major consumer services.

The Questions to Ask

Clearly, choosing an online service is not an irrevocable decision. You can always switch if you find that you are not happy or that your needs have changed.

As long as you approach things cautiously, you can usually get a very good feel for a service without spending much money. As with almost everything having to do with computers, your main investment is your time—in this case, the time you spend learning to use and explore a particular service.

In general, however, there are five criteria to consider when trying to decide to join or to stay with a consumer online service:

1. Which service do your friends and business associates use?
2. Do you have particularly well-defined needs?
3. What costs are involved?
4. What's the "user interface" like?
5. How do you feel about the features the service offers?

The order here is not accidental. Cost is third, for example, since cost should not be the main consideration. If you want the value online services offer, you have to expect to pay something for it. If money is your main concern, stick to the bulletin board systems (BBSs) in your local calling area.

Where are Your Friends and Business Associates?

Contrary to what most people think, the online world is not about information. It is about *people!*

As you may have noticed, this is a theme that runs throughout this book. Its truth is borne out by more than a decade's experience. Thus, the single most important criterion for choosing a consumer online service is: Who can I talk to?

It is likely that you have several friends, customers, suppliers, clients, or professional associates who are already online on one or more services. It's true that the Internet serves as a common link, making it possible to exchange mail among services. But it is so much simpler, and often cheaper, to exchange mail and files with someone who is on the same service you use.

Ask Your Friends!

Friends and associates of yours may be online, and you may not even know it. So ask! And when you find someone who is using one or more services, follow the time-honored tradition of personal computing and pick his or her brain: What do they like? What do they dislike? How much are they spending each month?

And so on. As with movies and books, word-of-mouth is enormously effective, provided, of course, that the mouth belongs to someone whose opinions and tastes you know and respect.

The other great advantage of going where your friends are is that they can serve as mentors and guides, introducing you to people and features on the service.

A Well-Defined Need?

Most people who are online today went online in the first place mainly to see what's there. They did not have a clearly defined need.

This is likely to be the case for years to come. After all, there are some 150 million DOS users worldwide, and tens of millions more Macintosh, Amiga, and other computer users. Nearly 30 million homes in the United States alone are equipped with at least one personal computer. And every one of these machines has the capability of going online.

Yet the total number of subscribers to consumer online services was estimated to be no more than 4 million worldwide in 1993. This estimate could be off by any number you care to name without altering the essential truth that only a tiny percentage of people who *could* be online actually *are* online.

So you yourself may not have a well-defined need. You may simply want to explore. There's nothing at all wrong with that.

Or a Need You Discover?

If you do need something in particular, that need should be a primary consideration. I've already noted that some parents use Prodigy as an interactive electronic babysitter.

I have a friend who's a senior citizen and whose main interest in life is monitoring (and constantly tinkering with!) his investments. For him, Dow Jones News/Retrieval is overkill, even assuming he would be willing to pay DJN/R rates. But he swears by the investment information available from CompuServe.

One of my brothers-in-law loves the Scuba RoundTable on GEnie. My computer repair person says he couldn't live without the updates, bug reports, and workarounds he finds on the Microsoft Knowledgebase feature on CompuServe. And so on.

None of these friends and relatives had any idea that they would discover such needs when they first signed on. But now, you can't keep them away from their computers and modems.

All You Have to Do is Ask! My point here is that millions of people have moved beyond the exploration stage. They have found that a given feature on a given service is their main reason for going online. If you have a clearly defined need to start with, you may be ahead of the game.

As I have been telling people for years, any topic you can name is almost certainly covered somewhere online. And any piece of information you can name is probably available via personal computer and modem. This is more true today than ever before.

All you have to do is ask. Ask customer service. Call them up and say, "What does your service offer on coin collecting? What about organic gardening? Is there a Special Interest Group for people who like Victorian novels?"

What are the Costs—*All* the Costs?

Profit maximization is what the pricing of consumer online services is all about: How many features do we have to include in the "basic" package covered by our monthly subscription fee to be competitive, and what other features are so desirable that we can charge extra for them?

For example, all services include electronic mail as part of their basic package. But after you send a certain number of messages each month, you may be charged for each additional message. You may get unlimited play on some standard human-versus-the-computer games, like *Adventure* or *Black Dragon.* But you will be charged extra for the time spent with the much more exciting interactive multi-player games. And so on.

In other words, when comparing costs, it is important to make sure that you really are comparing apples and apples. That's why you should look very closely at the *details* of the features offered as part of your basic monthly fee.

What's the User Interface Like?

With systems like Prodigy and AOL, you have no choice. You must use their graphical user interface (GUI) software. But CompuServe, Delphi, and GEnie offer a choice: You may find that a plain terminal program is perfectly fine when using the menus offered by these text-based services, or you may be more comfortable with one of the optional graphical front-end programs, available for free or for a nominal fee.

What About the Features the Service Offers?

I've made this the last consideration for three reasons: First, all consumer online services offer the same general features. Second, what matters most about a service is the *people* who are on it (not its features). And third, the mix of features on any given service is constantly changing.

Automated Online Sessions

Interestingly, whether it's a GUI or not, a service's interface may matter less than you think, thanks to shareware and commercial programs designed to fully automate an online session.

Such programs sign on to the service and pick up your mail. They then move to each of your favorite Special Interest Groups and pick up any personal messages that may have been posted to you, as well as all the latest public messages contributed to the discussions you happen to be following. Then the software signs off.

Now offline, with the connect-time meter no longer running, you can read your mail and messages and type in your replies. The software will then sign on again and transmit your replies and comments to the proper e-mail address or SIG message board.

In short, unless you want to engage in a real-time chat, you never have to spend time online running up charges, trying to remember a command, composing an e-mail message, or deciding whether you want to download a certain file. There is really no need, most of the time, to interact with the service at all.

Most commercial front-end programs also have these abilities. But, if you want to save on software as well as on connect time, the shareware programs to get are TAPCIS for CompuServe, Aladdin for GEnie, and D-Lite for Delphi. These programs can be downloaded from the services themselves. The DOS and Windows versions are also available from Glossbrenner's Choice.

Still, features are an important consideration, particularly if you are looking for something special. That's why one of the techniques you'll find in "The Online Cookbook" section at the back of this book is how to get an index or overview of each service.

Now What?

The consumer online service profiles in the chapters that follow are designed to give you the flavor of each system. If you've got the time, take advantage of the free offers at the end of this book to try them all.

And keep your eyes peeled for the *new* services scheduled to appear. Ziff-Davis, AT&T, Microsoft, and Apple Computer have all announced plans to start up consumer online services. The more the merrier!

A Quick Cost Comparison

Service	Startup Cost	Monthly Fee	Includes
America Online	None	$9.95	5 hours free; $2.95 for each additional hour.
CompuServe	None	$8.95	Unlimited basic services; about 60 e-mail messages sent; $4.80 to $9.60 per hour for non-basic services.
Delphi	None	$10.00	4 hours free; $4.00 for each additional hour; surcharge of $9.00 per hour for access via Tymnet or SprintNet during weekday business hours.
	None	$20.00	20 hours free; $1.80 for each additional hour; surcharge of $9.00 per hour for access via Tymnet or SprintNet during weekday business hours. (A one-time fee of $19.00 applies to this plan.)
	None	$3.00	Full Internet access for $3.00 more per month.
GEnie	None	$8.95	4 hours free; $3.00 each additional hour; surcharge of $9.50 per hour for prime-time access; surcharge of $6.00 per hour for 9600-bps access.
Prodigy	$29.95	$14.95	Unlimited access to Core features; 2 hours of Plus features; 30 e-mail messages sent.

America Online

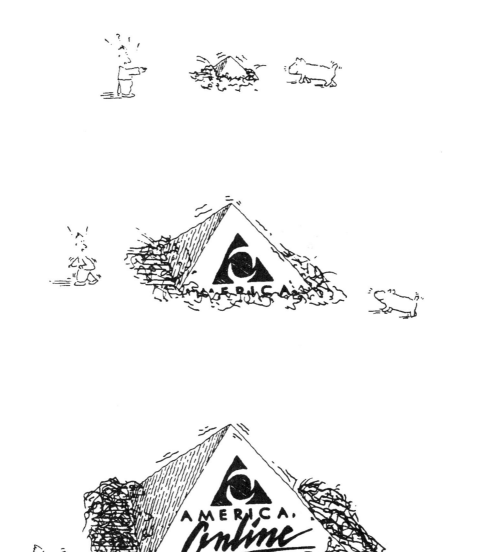

14

If happiness is a warm puppy, then America Online is the personification of online joy. America Online, or "AOL," is so dedicated to pleasing its users that even *hard-bitten command line veterans will quickly be won over. So much thought has gone into the design of the service and those thoughts have been so superbly executed that it is simply impossible not to like AOL. It may not be the service you ultimately stay with, but it is the service the vast majority of readers should start with.*

Not a Flash in the Pan

AOL probably gets more press than any of its competitors. That's because, right now, it is the only "pure play" for those interested in investing in the Information Superhighway. All the other online services are either private concerns or part of a larger public company.

Yet AOL did not just spring onto the scene. Its roots go back at least to 1985, and still further back when you consider the fact that the original company was founded by Bill von Meister (one of the visionaries who created a wonderful, now defunct service called The Source). Before it became America Online, the firm was known as Quantum Computer Services, purveyor of Q-Link, AppleLink, and PC Link. These were online services, respectively, for Commodore, Apple, and IBM-compatible computer users.

My point is that AOL has a long corporate history and that the people who run the service obviously paid close attention during the 1980s. They learned what the marketplace had to teach, and they designed a service from the ground up that was graphical, affordable, and exceptionally well thought-out and easy to use.

An Outstanding Installation

For example, I have never seen such an easy installation procedure. Basically, you load the software and tell it your account name and password and where you live. Then you sit back and watch as the program dials a toll-free number, talks to a distant computer, and automatically configures itself.

The next time you click on the AOL icon in Windows or on your Mac, or key in `aol` at the DOS prompt, the software will load and be all set to dial the SprintNet number nearest to your location. It will know your account number, so all you need to enter is your password.

The entire process is remarkable because it works, of course. But what's even more remarkable to an online veteran is that this procedure even exists in the first place. The AOL installation process represents a great deal of forethought, planning,

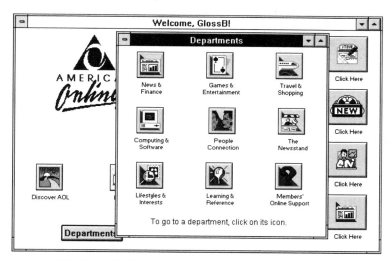

America Online's graphical interface.

programming, and testing. The company is clearly committed to making it as easy as possible for even the biggest "techno-klutz" to get online. Sadly, this is not something one can yet say about the other consumer online services.

Pros and Cons

This is a personal opinion. But, putting myself in the shoes of a first-time online communicator (and probably a relatively new computer user as well), I believe that America Online has the best user interface of the leading online services. It's clean, it's mouse-driven, and it's easy-to-use. And, unlike Prodigy, AOL does not fill the bottom of every screen with distracting, annoying advertisements.

My one complaint about the interface is that AOL tends to use the same icons over and over again. And the meaning of a given icon is not necessarily consistent across various features. Still, as with most icons, it's not the picture but the image that's important.

More specifically, it's what you associate with a given image in a given feature that matters—just as a monkey comes to learn that pressing a button with a triangle in a circle yields banana chips, while pressing a button with a circle in a triangle produces a mild electric shock.

Outstanding Features

Although AOL does offer news and business and investment information, these areas are not really its strong points when compared to other online alternatives. At least right now, the depth just isn't there.

The best thing about AOL is that it makes it easy and fun to communicate with other people. Its e-mail has always been good. And, as you read this, the service will almost certainly offer *full* Internet access. In addition, America Online's Special Interest Groups are a joy to use. In fact, AOL may offer the best implementation of the SIG concept in the business. The interactive chat feature is also exceptionally well done.

As a brand-new user, what you may like best about AOL is its interface and ease of use. I admire that too, but as an online veteran, what appeals to me most is the spirit of innovation that seems to suffuse the service. I like the fact that I can use AOL to search the classified ads in the *Chicago Tribune*. If nothing else, it helps me get a better idea of what my low-mileage 1981 Toyota hatchback is worth.

I also like the fact that at least some portion of the articles that appear in *Time* or the *Atlantic Monthly* are available for reading, magazine-style, online. And there is a whole section devoted to cartoons from the editorial pages of the nation's newspapers. These features aren't fantastic, but they are certainly interesting.

And the Center Stage Game Show concept, through which hundreds of AOL users can attend and participate in online events, is neat. So is KidsNet, "the only computerized clearinghouse devoted exclusively to children's audio, video, radio, and television programming." Charter members include the Arts & Entertainment network, Bravo, The Discovery Channel, The Disney Channel, Nickelodeon, and many others.

Resources

America Online
800-827-6364

SeniorNet and AOL

SeniorNet, "computer networking for the over-55 set," is also available exclusively via America Online. For the record, SeniorNet was a well-established service when it made the decision to move to AOL in the fall of 1991. For $9.95 a month, you can get unlimited evening and week-end use of SeniorNet, plus one hour of regular AOL online time.

I'm about a decade short of qualifying as a senior, but I've checked SeniorNet out and recommend it highly. It is an absolutely wonderful way for seniors to exchange information—whether it's a topic like the old raisins-soaked-in-vodka trick as a relief for arthritis or a serious debate on health care reform.

Indeed, if you are new to the field, you would be amazed at the number of seniors who are deeply involved in personal computing. They are well represented at the user group meetings I address, and hardly a week goes by that I don't hear from a senior who has read one of my computer books (borrowed from the library, of course).

Resources

SeniorNet
International Community of
Computer-Using Seniors
415-750-5045 (modem)

If you're over 55, SeniorNet is definitely worth your time. Or if you have a parent or grandparent who is amenable to personal computing, get them into this! I promise you, they will *love* it.

Conclusion

In my opinion, *everyone* should try America Online. Grizzled online veterans should try it if only to get a good look at the future. And new users should try it because it is such a pretty service, so friendly, and so people-oriented.

This is not the place to look for industrial-strength information. Nor should you expect AOL to offer the most extensive collection of down-loadable software. It would also be surprising if AOL attracted very many hardware and software gurus whose expertise you could tap via an online SIG.

It is crucial to point out, however, that AOL does offer information, software, and computer expertise. It's just that the breadth and depth aren't there—at least not right now and not when compared to what's available on a service like CompuServe.

But, by golly, AOL does have substance and innovative features, and it is a lot of fun to use. And it does an exceptional job of making it easy for you to get in touch with other people.

It is true that AOL has experienced growing pains in the past. In July 1993, for example, it had 350,000 subscribers. By August 1994, that number had grown to over 1 million.

America Online's Rates

You can get the AOL software and spend ten hours online with the service for free, using the coupon at the back of this book. If you don't wish to continue after that, you can simply cancel your subscription.

If you do wish to continue, the cost is $9.95 per month. That includes five hours of connect time. After that, the cost is $2.95 per hour. The price is the same whether you go online at 2400 bps or 9600 bps.

Inevitably, there was a lag between adding subscribers and adding the computer capacity needed to handle them. As a result, during peak usage periods, it was not uncommon to connect with AOL, only to be told that the system was too busy to take you at the moment. Or, if you did happen to get on, you might find that the delay between the time you clicked on an icon and when the system responded was unacceptably long.

As AOL continues to grow, there are no guarantees that similar delays won't occur in the future. So far at least, AOL has done a pretty good job of bringing new computers online to serve its new subscribers. In my experience, the "bad periods" last for about two weeks, and then the system is fine for the next six weeks or so. As the service's growth rate slows to a more moderate pace, I have no doubt that such problems will be eliminated completely.

Bottom line: Use the coupon at the back of this book to try America Online. You have absolutely nothing to lose, and you may discover, as I have, that you genuinely like the service.

CompuServe

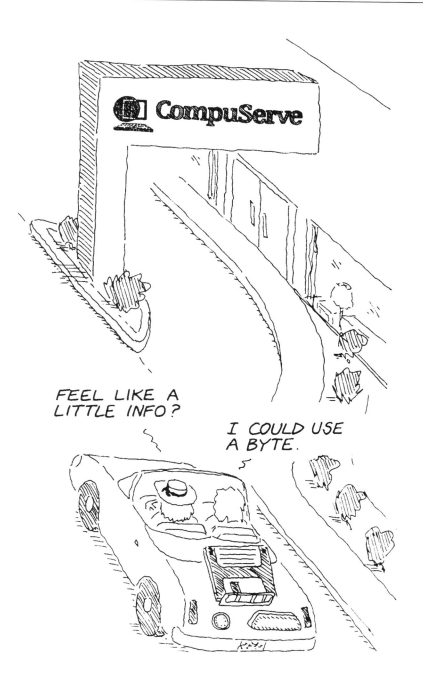

15

The range and depth of features available on the Compu-Serve Information Service (CIS) is simply incredible. It is clearly the service to choose if you are primarily interested in business and professional information, computer hardware and software support from companies and from fellow subscribers, and investment information. But the service's entertainment and hobby-oriented features are no slouches, either.

CompuServe, in truth, does it all. And it does it remarkably well. The main criticism you'll hear about CompuServe is that it's a bit more expensive than its competitors, a characteristic that has long caused some wags to refer to it as "CI$." Of course that was *before* the 40 percent price cut CompuServe implemented in February 1994. At $8.95 a month for unlimited access to a nice package of basic services, and a cost of $4.80 to $9.60 an hour for using non-basic services, Compu-Serve's pricing is very much in line with the other consumer online services.

When Mainframes were King

Long a subsidiary of H&R Block, CompuServe is the oldest consumer service. The company began in 1972, a time when mainframe computers ruled the world. "Big iron" like that was so expensive that only the largest companies could afford to lease such a machine. So companies like CompuServe would purchase a mainframe computer and sell its processing power piecemeal to banks, life insurance companies, financial institutions, and anyone else who needed it.

The technique was called "time-sharing," and the business was called "remote data processing" or "RDP." Customers would ship their data—say, a bank's daily transactions—to the mainframe shop over the telephone. The RDP site would process the data and ship it back to the customer.

Trouble was, demand for mainframe services dropped dramatically come 6 P.M. or so during the week, and it was virtually nil over the weekend. But you can't just switch off a mainframe. It continues to run and to cost money, even if no one is using it.

Let the People Play!

In 1979, Jeffrey M. Wilkins who, with his father, had founded Compu-Serve nearly a decade earlier, introduced a solution. Why not make the mainframes available to the growing ranks of computer hobbyists at night and on the weekends for $5 an hour? Subscription kits to the new "MicroNET," as it was called, were sold for $29.95 through Radio Shack stores. This made sense because Tandy's TRS-80 computers were among the leading machines of the day, and users could buy a Radio Shack acoustic coupler at the same time.

As one of those early subscribers, I can testify that things were done on the cheap. The documentation consisted of z-fold printouts from mainframe printers in desperate need of a new ribbon. But this parsi-monious, go-slow approach paid off in the end. In a time when other companies were losing scores of millions of dollars on ambitious online ventures, CompuServe was quietly puttering along, adding a feature now and then and constantly adding subscribers.

Reaching Critical Mass

At some point, the service reached a critical mass. Now, with over 2.2 million subscribers, each of whom pays a monthly fee, CompuServe can do pretty much anything it wants. The company has used its power well.

Its documentation and marketing materials were upgraded long ago. In recent years, it has concentrated on adding what I call "indus-trial-strength" information to the service. As a result, today you will find databases on CompuServe that used to be available only through Dialog and similar services.

CompuServe invented the online Special Interest Group (SIG) concept and has applied it quite skillfully. Undoubtedly because of its origins as a service for computer hobbyists, CompuServe has always had a large and robust core of SIGs devoted to every aspect of personal computing. This makes CompuServe the best place to seek answers to your hardware and software questions.

The company has also effectively marketed the SIG concept to leading software and hardware vendors, almost all of whom have been scrambling to find some way to minimize the dents that customer service costs put in their bottom lines. That's why you'll find over 400 SIGs or SIG libraries on CompuServe devoted to supporting various products.

The CompuServe Interface

It may be, however, that the greatest test of CompuServe's power is yet to come. Like GEnie and Delphi, CompuServe is a text-based service. You can sign on using any old communications program and navigate using menu options or commands.

The CompuServe Information Manager for Windows.

If you prefer a graphical environment, however, you can use a front-end program—like the CompuServe Navigator for Macs or the CompuServe Information Manager (CIM) for DOS or for Windows—which the company virtually gives away for free. Third-party front-ends are also available.

Unfortunately, while CIM and the others look good on the surface and while they may appear to be identical to the interfaces offered by America Online and Prodigy, it is impossible to hide the underlying text-based system completely. Probably nothing short of a complete system redesign could do that.

The CompuServeCD

CompuServe is aware of these problems, of course. And it has come up with a very interesting CD-ROM–based solution. Introduced in the spring of 1994, the CompuServeCD is "a multimedia extension" of the service that "combines CompuServe's online services with CD-ROM–based information, sound, graphics, and video in an interplay that makes the best use of each medium's strong points."

I tried the charter issue, and it's clear that you could easily spend hours watching music videos from the likes of Jimmy Buffett and Willie Nelson or playing with the demo of the Kodak photo-to-digital converter and the free GIF image viewer. It was neat to hear the

The opening page for the pilot issue of the CompuServeCD.

sysop of the Fine Arts Forum discuss his Forum's purpose and goals.

The CompuServeCD has lots of other features as well, including free updates to CompuServe Information Manager for Windows and CompuServe Navigator. It also has updated IBM File Finder and Graphics File Finder lists—so you can search for files offline. At any given screen, actually connecting with CompuServe is as easy as clicking on a button.

In short, this is an impressive product that puts a tremendous amount of information, images, sound, and software at your fingertips cheaply. The CompuServeCD is published every other month. The cost is $7.95 per issue, but you may find that a $5 CompuServe usage credit is included, bringing your total cost to $2.95, plus shipping and handling.

The only caveat concerns the hardware you will need. You must have a 25 MHz 386 or faster system, a SoundBlaster or compatible sound card, four megabytes of RAM, Windows 3.1, and a double-speed CD-ROM drive. But if you've got the equipment, the CompuServeCD offers about the cheapest way imaginable to sample "multimedia" on your PC.

Remarkable and Unremarkable Features

CompuServe is definitely *not* the place to go if you're interested in graphical games. Things could change, but at the moment, the games on the service appear to have been frozen in the mid-1980s. Many are multi-player and interactive, but they are mainly text-based with no genuine graphics.

CompuServe created the concept of the Electronic Mall and never passes up a chance to promote it. But most "mall" stores offer only selected items, and some offer only information on how to order the store's free catalogue.

As noted, the service's SIGs are broad and deep. Its electronic mail features are second only to MCI Mail, and its financial and investment features give Dow Jones News/Retrieval a run for their money. But what's really remarkable are the information databases on the service. These are not the kinds of things you would expect to find on a consumer online service. Here is just a small sample:

1. PhoneFile
Nothing less than a "White Pages" for the entire country. Key in a phone number and get the address, or key in a name and location and get the phone number and address.

2. *Thomas Register* Online
The famous 25-volume "who's who" and "who makes what" reference work known as the *Thomas Register of American Manufacturers*.

3. Citibank's Global Report

Updated around the clock from sources all over the world, this feature integrates and organizes financial data and news for quick retrieval.

4. IQuest

Menu-guided searching of more than 800 industrial-strength databases offered by systems like NewsNet and Dialog/Data Star.

5. Knowledge Index

After-hours, menu-driven access to over 100 Dialog databases. A truly incredible resource.

6. Computer Database Plus

The full text and fact-packed abstracts of over 100 computer- and technology-related magazines, dating from yesterday back to 1988.

Resources

CompuServe Information Service
800-848-8199

CompuServe's Rates

CompuServe offers two main types of subscriptions. The Standard Pricing Plan costs $8.95 per month and includes unlimited use of a package of basic services. Time spent using non-basic services is billed at $4.80 per hour for 2400 bps access or $9.60 per hour for 9600 and 14,400 bps access.

The Alternative Pricing Plan costs $2.50 per month. Under this option, you are charged a connect-time rate of $12.80 per hour (for 2400 bps access) or $22.80 per hour (for 9600 and 14,400 bps access) for just about everything except services explicitly marked "free."

The best deal of all, however, is what CompuServe terms its "Executive Service Option." In return for agreeing to spend a minimum of $10 on the service each month, you get all the benefits of the Standard Pricing Plan, plus discounts and access to a range of business and investment features not otherwise available. Plus, you get to set up an automatic electronic clipping search profile to monitor the newswire for items of interest to you.

Best of all, perhaps, your $8.95 monthly Standard Pricing Plan fee counts toward the $10 minimum, meaning you get all these benefits for just a buck more a month. (Key in `go rates` once you're on the service for the latest rate summary.)

Conclusion

If you stay in the online world, sooner or later you will want to subscribe to CompuServe. America Online and Prodigy are bound to add more and more features, but it is hard to imagine that they will ever match what CompuServe offers to business people, professionals, and serious computer users. In fact, I'm not sure they would want to, since AOL and Prodigy seem to be going after an entirely different market.

If you must have a graphical interface, try CIM or the CompuServe Navigator. But, as you will see in "The Online Cookbook" section at the back of this book, you can operate much faster (and more economically) using a plain terminal program, and all you need is a small handful of commands.

Delphi

16

A product of Delphi Internet Services Corporation, Delphi is a service for the adventurous. In some respects, it always has been. It was founded in 1983 by Wes Kussmaul using the profits of a particularly successful *investment. Then, in September 1993, it was bought by Rupert Murdoch's The News Corporation, which also owns TV Guide, HarperCollins Publishers, the Fox television network, and lots of newspapers and other publications worldwide.*

Delphi has always been small, fast-moving, and flexible—a service characterized by a sense of fun and surprise and "we'll try anything once." At this writing, it still is. But changes are certainly afoot.

The Worst Interface in the Business

On the one hand, like many longtime online communicators, I have always had a special love for Delphi. On the other hand, the service has what is arguably the worst user interface in the business. (Actually, it's a toss-up between Delphi and GEnie for this dubious honor.)

Let me explain. In the past, you never knew what wonderful surprise was going to greet you when you signed on. It might be a "collaborative novel" for which members were invited to contribute chapters to a never-ending story. It might be the excruciatingly funny musings of the late Bob Fried's "Articles of Lasting Strangeness." Or it might be a reference feature called "The Dictionary of Cultural Literacy," apparently based on the book of the same name.

That sense of delight is still there today. But it may not be tomorrow. "Delight" is not a word normally associated with the products and services offered by huge corporations. But even if the innovativeness remains, you've got to be diligent in learning to use the service.

Delphi's electronic mail system is strictly "bytehead." Its menu system doesn't even number the menu items. To select an item, you must type in its name or "abbreviate it to uniqueness."

It is probably not fair to call it "user-unfriendliness." After all, it was state-of-the-art a decade ago. But little has changed since. Apparently, some kind of graphical front-end program has long been in the works. With luck, it will be available as you read this. For now, though, I stand by the statement that Delphi is for the adventurous (and for those communicators with a little online experience). It is definitely not the place for a brand new user to start life online.

Full Internet Access!

On the other hand, Delphi has made a *tremendous* splash by offering full access to the Internet for $3 per month. Given Delphi's rate structure, this means that you can get four hours of access to Delphi and to the Internet for $13 a month, with a charge of $4 per hour after that. Or you can get 20 hours of Delphi and Internet access for $23 a month, with a charge of $1.80 per hour after that. Access during weekday business hours carries a $9 per hour surcharge if you use Tymnet or SprintNet.

This fact is significant because, at this writing, Delphi is the only service offering access to *all* Internet features. This is just a temporary advantage, but Rupert Murdoch has made the most of it. It is wonderful to open the *Wall Street Journal* or *Business Week* or nearly any other leading publication these days and see an ad for Delphi. The little black sheep has suddenly made good!

The number of ways to tap into the Internet grow with each passing day. But Delphi makes things quick, clean, convenient, and cheap. Plus, it has an Internet SIG staffed with people who are dedicated to helping you. You can ask questions, download help files and files of "FAQs" (Frequently Asked Questions, pronounced "facts"), and basically feel that you are being supported as you step out into the great electronic unknown.

But the interface still stinks. It is workable, but it is acceptable only if you are an experienced computer user. And I say this as a fan of text-based online interfaces and a basher of the current mindless obsession with graphics. (Show anybody ten icons and ten equivalent words, and they will click on the text without hesitation. Half the time you can't tell what an icon means. And they call that "ease of use." Pagh!)

Resources

Delphi Internet Services, Inc.
800-695-4005

Custom Forums: A Delphi Exclusive

One of the smartest things Delphi ever did was to lure John Gibney away from CompuServe. Gibney designed and programmed that company's famous SIGs, and he soon performed the same service for Delphi, improving on things by adding features like member polling and voting.

Another really smart move was to put Bob Adams in charge of a unique variation on the Special Interest Group theme: Custom Forums. For an initial fee of $29.95 and a monthly maintenance fee of $5, anyone can create a Forum on Delphi.

Examples include Forums called:

- The Mommy Track
- NASCAR Fans' Forum
- Divorce Support Board
- Textile Arts Forum
- The ARABNET Forum
- Single Parents Network
- Online Naturist Club
- In Full View—The Gay Forum
- Inventors & Inventions

- Codependency Support Group
- Statuesque And Rubenesque
- Flush Limbaugh
- Bridge Players' Forum
- Dittoheads Unlimited
- Animal Rights And Vegetarian Living
- Irish Roots
- Scotland Online
- Men Against Circumcision

There is simply no better example than this of the kind of creativity and innovation Delphi is famous for. No other service offers a feature that is even close to this.

Should your own hard work and creativity attract people to your Forum, Delphi will reward you. The greater the number of hours of usage you attract, the greater the rewards until, finally, you will be asked to make your Forum a regular Delphi SIG, which Delphi will *pay* you to operate.

Features that Make Delphi Special

No press release has been issued at this point, but after spending hours on the service recently, it is clear to me that the master plan is to integrate Delphi and the Internet. When you use a Delphi menu, one of the choices will often be some related Internet-based feature.

It is already happening on the service. When you access the Delphi News-Weather-Sports menu, for example, you see selections like those in the following figure.

Notice the option "Seasonal & Weather Gopher." If you are not an Internet user, you will scratch your head at the term "Gopher." But as Internet users know, a "Gopher" is a menu system that makes it easy to go get the information you want on the Net. Thus, when you make this selection, you will be taken to a menu system offering "The Most Comprehensive Weather Gopher WorldWide!"

Which is to say, you will be given a menu with items that include earthquake information, marine coastal advisories, recre-

```
NEWS-WEATHER-SPORTS Menu:

Business News               Seasonal & Weather Gopher
Entertainment News          Sports News
Financial & Commodity News  UPI News Service
Human Interest Stories      Views on News
International News          Weather
National News              HELP
Product Information        EXIT
```

The Delphi News-Weather-Sports menu.

ational forecasts, satellite weather images, ski resort reports, and international forecasts, among other items. All such items come from the Internet. Delphi's genius has been to integrate Internet information features with the information features it has been offering for more than a decade.

This is a really neat idea. To my knowledge, no one else has yet done it. And it certainly bodes well for Delphi's future. When you see it, you think, "This is exactly how the Internet treasure houses should be used: not as a free-standing network, but as integral parts of a service that—unlike the networks the Internet links—has been designed for the consumer."

Conclusion

Somehow I think that Mr. Murdoch will succeed in replacing Delphi's archaic, bytehead interface with something quite friendly indeed. And it is a foregone conclusion that The News Corporation's print publications, like

Delphi's Rates

All Delphi members have two membership options: the 10/4 Plan and the 20/20 Advantage Plan.

The 10/4 Plan costs $10 per month. It includes the first four hours of use each month. Additional use is $4 per hour (actually billed as 6.6 cents per minute). There is no initial fee.

The 20/20 Advantage Plan costs $20 per month. It includes the first 20 hours of use each month. Additional use is $1.80 per hour. There is a one-time enrollment fee of $19.

Full access to the Internet costs an additional $3 per month, regardless of the membership option you choose.

There is a surcharge of $9 per hour if you access Delphi via Tymnet or SprintNet during weekday business hours.

TV Guide, will find their way onto Delphi in electronic editions. Personally, I would love to see an online feature that let me prepare a list of my favorite shows, complete with VCR Plus code numbers.

Now more than ever, Delphi is clearly the service to watch. I urge you to take advantage of the special Delphi offer at the back of this book. But, unless you're chomping to get full Internet access right away and are willing to put up with Delphi's interface (it can be done easily enough, with a little patience), I suggest you save it till last. If you're the adventurous sort, you've got a real treat in store.

GEnie

17

GEnie is the General Electric Network for Information Exchange, a name cooked up by industry veteran Bill Louden one weekend shortly after General Electric hired

him away from CompuServe and commissioned him to
create a consumer-oriented online service.

"GEnie" is probably the best name of all for such a service, since it conveys the sense of wonderment, magic, and power you feel when you go online. The symbol of a magic lamp followed naturally, as did the name of GEnie's front-end program, Aladdin.

Like CompuServe, GEnie was designed, as Stewart Alsop once put it in his *PC Letter*, "to sop up excess capacity" at its parent company. The parent in this case is General Electric Information Services (GEIS), a world-spanning communications network and database provider to business and industry. That's why GEnie was originally available only after regular business hours, when demand for GEIS resources typically drops off dramatically.

The opening screen of GEnie for Windows.

For a while, GEnie and CompuServe competed more or less head-to-head, rather like Burger King and McDonald's. Both services have their own strengths, weaknesses, and unique features, but they essentially offer the same thing. As with most products and services, however, market positioning in the online field tends to ebb and flow. In recent times, GEnie has fallen far behind its competitors.

The Two Best Reasons to Subscribe

As the author of the Osborne/McGraw-Hill book, *Glossbrenner's Master Guide to GEnie*, it is especially painful to have to say this, but there are really only two good reasons to subscribe to GEnie. First, if there is a particular feature you want in an online service, there is a good chance that GEnie offers it for less. Second, if you are interested in graphical, multi-player games, no one else comes close to GEnie.

Online For Less?

At this writing, GEnie offers about 125 Special Interest Groups, called "RoundTables," or "RTs," on the service. CompuServe offers more than 600. The difference is that on CompuServe, depending on the speed of your connection, you usually have to pay $4.80 or $9.60 an hour to use a SIG since most are not part of the basic $8.95-per-month CompuServe subscription package.

GEnie's Rates

A subscription to GEnie costs $8.95 per month and includes four hours of connect time at 2400 bps between the hours of 6 P.M. and 8 A.M. After that, the rate is $3 per hour for most GEnie features.

A surcharge of $9.50 an hour is levied for prime-time access (8 A.M. to 6 P.M.), and a surcharge of $6 an hour is levied for signing on at 9600 bps.

Thus, if you have not used up your four hours for the month, and you sign on at 9600 bps in the evening, you will be billed at the rate of $6 per hour, because of the surcharge. After you have used up your four-hour allotment, you will be billed at $9 an hour ($3+$6 per hour) for connecting in the evening at 9600 bps.

GEnie Premium Services carry charges in addition to the applicable hourly rate. Premium Services include features like:

- Charles Schwab Brokerage Services
- Dow Jones News/Retrieval
- GE Mail to Fax
- The Official Airline Guide, Electronic Edition
- Travel Service
- QuikNews Clipping Service
- Investment ANALY$T

Be sure to key in `rates` from any menu prompt on GEnie to be taken to the feature that will give you the exact costs of GEnie Premium Services. In situations where GEnie is merely providing a "gateway" to connect you to services like Charles Schwab, Dow Jones News/Retrieval, or Dialog, you may discover that you are better off opening your own subscription to such services.

On GEnie, in contrast, you pay $8.95 per month and get four hours of non-prime-time, 2400-bps usage of most features, *including* GEnie RoundTables and interactive games. This means that if GEnie happens to offer a SIG or other feature that you're particularly interested in using, doing so on GEnie is likely to be cheaper than on CompuServe.

Connect time spent on GEnie beyond four hours is billed at $3 an hour, assuming it's non-prime-time usage and at a speed of 2400 bits per second. It's important to emphasize those two assumptions, since surcharges apply if you access the system during normal business hours or if you sign on at 9600 bps. The surcharge for using GEnie in prime time (between 8 A.M. and 6 P.M.) is $9.50 an hour. The surcharge for signing on at 9600 bps at any time of day is $6 an hour.

Thus, in the absolute worst case, if you had already used your four hours for the month and were to sign on to GEnie during prime time at 9600 bps, you would be charged $3 per hour, plus a $9.50-per-hour prime-time surcharge and a $6-per-hour 9600-bps surcharge. That totals a whopping $18.50 per hour.

This compares to a rate of $9.60 per hour on CompuServe, any time of day, at 9600 or 14,400 bits per second, when using a SIG or other feature not included in CompuServe's basic package.

Like you, my eyes tend to glaze over when comparing the rates charged by online services. The bottom line with GEnie, then, is simply this: If GEnie happens to offer a feature you love, and if you are willing to limit yourself to using it only during the evening at 2400 bps, then you can save money. If these conditions do not apply, you will undoubtedly be happier looking somewhere else.

The Tragedy of GEnie

The most charitable way to characterize GEnie is that it is currently in a rest period. Someone inclined to be more critical might suggest that a few years ago the service's corporate parent decided that GEnie should revert to its role of sopping up unused computer and network capacity and that any revenues the service contributed should be viewed as pure gravy.

I don't know. All I can say is that GEnie is manifestly dead in the water. Unlike CompuServe, GEnie's corporate parent has never made the commitment to developing a superb online service. That's a tragedy since, if it wanted to, General Electric could make GEnie the online service to end all online services. And it could do so without raising a sweat, since GE's pockets are so deep.

This could still happen. Certainly GEnie has the *potential* to be one incredible service. On the other hand, it also has the potential to collapse completely. One day, some bureaucrat at corporate headquarters could decide that the million dollars or so GEnie contributes each year just isn't worth the paperwork and could order the service shut down entirely.

Resources

GEnie
800-638-9636

Playing the Games Card!

GEnie and Delphi may currently be the leading contenders for the Worst Online Interface Award. On both services, the electronic mail feature is medieval and, while they were fine in their day, the Special Interest Groups are a challenge to use, to say the least.

Fortunately, both services make (or soon will make) front-end software available to shield users from their interfaces. In GEnie's case, the hot new programs are GEnie for Windows and GEnie for Macintosh. The DOS, Amiga, and Atari versions of Aladdin have long helped GEnie users maximize efficiency and minimize expenses.

All of which leads to perhaps the most important reason for subscribing to GEnie—its collection of highly graphical, interactive, multiplayer games. Most of these games require you to download special software that essentially replaces the GEnie interface with a graphical environment.

You will find much more information on this aspect of GEnie in Chapter 38. For now, the sidebar "Games on GEnie," will give you a quick overview of GEnie's games.

Conclusion

I wish I could say otherwise, but unless you are a real game enthusiast, GEnie as it exists today is of limited appeal. On the surface, it is cheaper than its competitors—provided you are willing to limit yourself to tapping the service in the evenings and at a rate of 2400 bps. And

Games on GEnie

Not all of the many games you can play on GEnie fit into the graphical, multi-player category. But many do, and frankly, no one does games better than GEnie. Here's a quick summary:

- *Adventure 550* (text)
- *Air Warrior* by Kesmai
- *Black Dragon* by Bob Maples
- *Castle Quest* by Bob Maples
- *CyberStrike* by Simutronics
- *Dor Sageth* by Runge and Thonssen
- *Dragon's Gate* by AUSI
- *Federation II*
- *Galaxy I* by Mark Jacobs
- *GemStone III: The Shadow World*
- *Hundred Years War*
- *NTN Trivia* (Countdown, etc.)

- *Nightside Trivia*
- *Orb Wars*
- *Original Adventure* (text)
- *QBI*
- *RSCARDS Backgammon*
- *RSCARDS Blackjack*
- *RSCARDS Bridge*
- *RSCARDS Checkers*
- *RSCARDS Poker*
- *ShowBiz Quiz*
- *Stellar Emperor* by Kesmai
- *Stellar Warrior* by Kesmai

provided that GEnie happens to offer one or more features you really want to use.

If you look closely, though, you will discover that GEnie is not that *much* cheaper, especially when you consider the premiums it charges you for business-hour and 9600-bps access. And you will discover that the array of features GEnie offers is more limited than any other consumer online service.

My fondest hope is that someday, someone at General Electric will wake up to the incredible possibilities the GEnie service offers. If GEnie's parent would only make the commitment to developing a superb online service, there is no telling how far GEnie might go!

Prodigy

18

One of the definitions given for the word "prodigy" in Webster's is "a highly talented child." The degree of talent may be open for discussion, but the name is certainly apt for this online service. Prodigy is the child of two corporate parents, IBM and Sears. A third parent, CBS, was also present at the creation in 1984. But, after *investing an initial $20 million and being informed that it would have to invest an additional $80 million to help bring the infant to maturity, CBS dropped out.*

An Electronic Magazine

I emphasize Prodigy's parentage because it speaks volumes about what the service is designed to do—namely, to sell things. The original concept was that CBS would provide the entertainment and information expertise, Sears would provide the merchandising input, and IBM would provide the computer hardware and software know-how.

This is the key to understanding—and appreciating—Prodigy. It is an electronic medium that is being used to sell things. There is absolutely nothing wrong with that approach. After all, to a radio or television executive, it's the programming that is the necessary evil—necessary to attract an audience—not the commercials that make the profits and pay the bills. Magazines and newspapers operate the same way, using news, features, pictures, and information to attract an audience for their ads.

Indeed, "electronic magazine" is really a good descriptive term for Prodigy. It has everything you would expect to see in your favorite magazine, including an ad on every page. All of it is presented in a graphical, mouse-driven format at a cost of $14.95 per month for unlimited usage of most features.

You Gotta *Try* This Thing!

Its sales-oriented approach makes Prodigy unique. All online services offer things for sale, but no one else puts an ad on every screen. And certainly no one else tracks your usage of the service to get a handle on your interests and then makes sure you are shown ads that match those interests.

America Online offers an integrated graphical interface, and other services offer graphical front-end programs. But no one except Prodigy gives you all that plus unlimited access to so many features at a cost of

$14.95 per month. In addition, like each online service, Prodigy has unique, innovative features available nowhere else.

For these reasons alone, I can wholeheartedly endorse the company's slogan, "You gotta get this thing!" After you've got it, only you can decide whether you want to stay with it or not. But Prodigy is so unique and so well-executed that, if you're truly interested in the online world, you've got to at least give it a try.

Prodigy is so unique and so well-executed that, if you're truly interested in the online world, you've got to at least give it a try.

Two quick tips: You will probably be happier with Prodigy's looks if you "jump" to "change display" and opt for "bold." Also, to capture information to a disk, click on T for tools and change your printer options to print to a file instead of to a printer. Then just "print" the information you want to save on disk.

Changing Through the Years

It is certainly true that the online field did not develop the way anyone back in 1984 thought it would. Like all of us, Prodigy has had to adjust. Among other things it had to learn the same lessons Knight-Ridder, Times-Mirror, AT&T, and so many others had to learn before it. The primary lesson is that regardless of what they may say in focus-group discussions, what people most want from an online service is not access to news and information. They have enough of that already. What people really want when they go online is access to other people.

To management's surprise, e-mail proved to be Prodigy's most popular feature. At one point, the volume of mail so clogged the service that Prodigy imposed a 30-message-per-month limit on its basic subscription package. (You can send more, but after message number 30, each costs extra.)

Then there were the censorship controversies. As a "family" service, Prodigy was worried about having anything deemed offensive appear on the service's bulletin boards. Steps were taken to censor postings, something many users saw as tantamount to censoring the U.S. Mail. Things appear to be more relaxed now, but the episode illustrates how different Prodigy is from a conventional consumer online service.

Prodigy's *Real* Competitors

Clearly, Prodigy's management should have known better than to censor postings. On the other hand, if corporate performance is any guide, competence has been in short supply at IBM and Sears in recent years. If Prodigy's owners had not been so intent on selling things, they might have taken the time to find out what online services are all about.

Fortunately, the powers that be at Prodigy appear to have learned some valuable lessons. Accordingly, they are offering a far better, more attractive, and more interesting service now. But it would be a mistake to ever assume that the service's users count for anything more than a TV network's viewers. With Prodigy, as with a television network, it is the *advertisers* who are the real clients. Users and viewers are simply the customers.

That seems like a harsh assessment, particularly when compared with the approaches taken by the four other consumer online services. But that's very much the point. Prodigy is *not* like the other online services. It is something else again. Its real competitors are not CompuServe and America Online, but the three main TV networks and Fox as well as CNN and everything else you can get on cable.

Prodigy's "Highlights" screen.

The Prodigy Approach

Once you allow Prodigy's similarity to a television network to inform your expectations, everything else falls into place, and Prodigy doesn't look bad at all.

For example, as with television, and in stark contrast to all other online services, almost everything on Prodigy is filtered through some kind of editorial process. Thus, as *PC Magazine* (March 15, 1994) says, "The news is timely, but the information is first edited in the service's newsroom before being posted. This makes Prodigy's news service more of an electronic newspaper than a news bureau."

Exactly! A newspaper. A magazine. But not a traditional online service.

Similarly, I had great hopes for a feature called "Philadelphia Guide—Members Rate the Best and Worst." I assumed there would be some good tips and leads and some entertaining criticism of places I happen to know in the area. Unfortunately, only nine restaurants were listed on the menu, and this for a city that everyone acknowledges has gone through an incredible "restaurant renaissance" in the past five years.

As for critical comments, the sharpest was on the order of "I love Geno's cheese steaks, just across from Pat's, which is overrated." Nearly everything else consisted of positive comments excerpted from user letters. Indeed, the strongest "worst" comment was on the order of "It's expensive, but worth it."

Once again, it is necessary to remind yourself that Prodigy is an electronic magazine. How many times have you ever seen *Travel and Leisure* or *Condé Nast Traveler* flay the living hide off a truly awful restaurant, resort, hotel, or anything else? Ain't gonna happen, my friend. Not in print. And certainly not on Prodigy. Nearly *everything* is filtered.

Resources

Prodigy
800-776-3449

Capacity to Spare

Prodigy's native interface is second only to that of America Online. No accident there. AOL was designed at a time when it had become clear that the Macintosh and Windows approach to graphical interfaces would take over the world. AOL opted for GeoWorks, a Windows-like interface that requires far less memory and resources than Windows itself.

Prodigy was designed a bit earlier, at a time when NAPLPS (North American Presentation Level Protocol Syntax) graphics offered the only efficient way for an online service to cause graphics to be displayed on the screen.

Actual, bit-mapped graphic images take too long to transmit, even at 9600 bps. The NAPLPS system solves this problem by storing basic graphic shapes on your disk. Thus, to display an ad for, say, the latest Chevy Blazer, Prodigy has to send only a few short commands to your computer.

I'm simplifying greatly, but the NAPLPS approach lets Prodigy quickly send a few bytes that say, in effect, "Display frames 134, 207, and 738 in screen location 12," instead of sending each and every bit needed to paint that area of the screen.

My experience is that most Prodigy screens appear quite quickly. It is only a few needlessly elaborate screens found in a few features that require an unacceptable amount of time, even at 9600 bps, to appear. The ads are annoying as they flicker into place, but, like TV commercials, you can visually tune them out most of the time.

Prodigy appears to have capacity to spare. Regardless of the time of day or night, I have always been able to get online. I have always found the service to be responsive. And if it doesn't snap you from screen to screen quite as quickly as you might wish, who cares? It's not costing you anything.

You are far more likely to become impatient with the lack of powerful "search" features. Prodigy lets you move from anywhere to anywhere on the service by keying in a "jump word," or keyword. But once you get there, you usually have to page through the feature to get to the information you want. Thus, you must page through *Consumer Reports* to get to the write-up on air conditioners, instead of being able to search for that particular article.

Also in the capacity department, I have tested Prodigy's customer service, and found it to be excellent. Whenever I have called, I waited less than three minutes for a representative to come on the line. And the person was always quite pleasant and knowledgeable.

Outstanding Features

Prodigy is among the last bastions of online banking, a feature that was thought to hold great promise several years ago. Prodigy's home banking and bill paying is done through the popular nationwide MAC

Prodigy's Rates

There is an initial sign-up fee of $29.95. This includes your Prodigy Membership Kit and all necessary software.

Membership Plan	Monthly Fee	Core & Plus Hours Per Month	E-Mail Messages	Additional Hours
Value Plan	$14.95	Flat-rate Core; 2 hours Plus	30 per month free	$3.60 per hour thereafter $.25 each
Alternate Plan	$7.95	2 hours Core & Plus combined	$.25 each	$3.60 per hour
Alternate Plan 2	$19.95	8 hours Core & Plus combined	$.25 each	$3.60 per hour
Alternate Plan BB	$29.95	25 hours Core & Plus combined	$.25 each	$3.60 per hour

No charge for 9600-bps service in all plans for most features.

Core features include hundreds of news, sports, weather, information, and entertainment features. Plus features include most bulletin boards, stock quotes, company news, and Eaasy Sabre (the computerized reservation system from American Airlines).

system, which gives the concept at least a fighting chance of finally fulfilling its promise.

Prodigy offers all kinds of newspaper columns and reviews: Leonard Maltin on movies, Dick Schapp on sports, Digby Diehl on books, and so on. There are also Prodigy exclusives, like Larry Magid on personal computers.

One of the neatest Prodigy offerings is "Total Television," a feature that is like an electronic version of *TV Guide.* You can get program listings based on network, day, or time of day. Or you can opt to get a listing of just the movies that will be on this week.

The entertainment area of Prodigy also includes an entry called "Guests" that presents a schedule of which celebrities, authors, etc., will be appearing on the service and where. A single recent listing included Joan Lunden from *Good Morning America*, Brent Spiner from *Star Trek: The Next Generation*, and Gene Simmons from the rock group Kiss. You can use Prodigy bulletin boards to ask guests questions and to read their replies.

Conclusion

I confess there was a time when I did not think Prodigy would make it. I once felt that way about the Apple Macintosh, too. There is simply no telling what will happen in this business. My sense is that not only is Prodigy quite secure now, but it is actively positioning itself for the digital future of multimedia and interactive television.

We may be seeing as through a glass darkly, but Prodigy definitely offers a glimpse of one portion of our digital future. And for that reason alone, not to mention some of its truly neat features, Prodigy is worth a look.

The Joy of
Bulletin Board Systems

19

IO-KEY NIGHT ON THE BALLROOM BBS

For sheer fun, enjoyment, and adventure—not to mention low- to no-cost connections—you simply can't beat dial-up bulletin board systems (BBSs). Everyone needs the power and scope offered by a consumer online service, but you'll really be missing out if you never "work the boards."

In the Beginning ...

The personal computer bulletin board was invented by Chicagoans Ward Christensen and Randy Suess. Their accomplishment became official on February 16, 1978, when they brought up CBBS #1 (Computer Bulletin Board System Number 1) to serve members of CACHE, the Chicago Area Computer Hobbyist Exchange.

The idea was to create a system that would emulate a cork-and-thumbtack bulletin board. Message postings were public for all to see: "John, please bring your Altair to the meeting next Tuesday." "Will the person who picked up my Trash 80 manual please return it to the chairman at the next SIG meeting?" "Does anyone know where I can get CP/M programs on 8-inch disks for a CPT 6500 word processor?" And so on.

All of this was taking place on a North Star Horizon running CP/M, the operating system that once rivaled DOS. The computer had a "huge" 5MB hard disk drive and an auto-answer modem. Unbeknownst to many CACHE members, the CBBS software included a secret file-upload and download area. The reason was simple: Ward Christensen was the group's assistant software librarian at the time, and he wanted to make it easier to send and receive the public-domain programs members would write.

To that end, he invented and implemented on CBBS #1 the Xmodem, or "Christensen," protocol for error-free transfer of binary programs and files.

And the Innovations Just Keep on Keeping On

The Xmodem file transfer protocol has since become the *de facto* standard in the online world. It is not the fastest or the best protocol, but it is the one every online system, large or small, supports.

I have told you all this, however, to illustrate another point entirely. And that is the fact that, from the birth of the first board, the BBS concept and BBS software have been continually evolving. It started as a cork-and-thumbtack analog. Shortly thereafter, a file-transfer capability was added.

```
T H E   P I N E   P L A N K   M E S S A G E   S Y S T E M

----- C O M M U N I C A T I O N S ----- --- UTILITIES --- -- ELSEWHERE --
 PERSONAL MAIL        SYSTEM COMMANDS
 E)nter a Message     A)nswer Questions  H)elp             D)oors Subsystem
 K)ill a Message      B)ulletins         J)oin Conferences F)iles Subsystem
 P)ersonal Mail Found C)omment           V)iew Conferences G)oodbye
 R)ead Messages       I)nitial Welcome   X)pert on/off     Q)uit to other
 S)can Messages       O)perator Page     ?)List Functions    Subsystems
 T)opic of Msgs Shown W)ho else is on                      U)tilities Subsystem

MAIN command <?,A,B,C,D,E,F,H,I,J,K,O,P,Q,R,S,T,U,V,W,X>
57 min left
```

Most BBSs still offer only plain text menus.

Today, over 15 years later, BBSs have added so many features and become so sophisticated that you can easily think you are using a consumer online service. In fact, I've been on any number of boards that make the typical online service look sick by comparison.

If you are using the right comm program and call the right board, you will be dazzled with graphics, animation, and even sound. You will be able to mouse all over the screen, clicking on sculpted, 3-D buttons as you would with Windows or with the Macintosh. You will be able to view graphics files as they are transmitted to your computer. And you will almost certainly be able to connect at 14.4 Kbps whenever you call. (CompuServe, in contrast, currently offers 14.4 Kbps connections in just ten cities.)

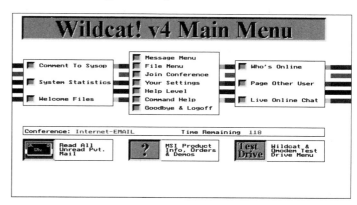

But many have begun to offer attractive Windows- or Mac-style screens with 3-D buttons you can click on with your mouse.

Features, Features, Features

Don't get me wrong. There are literally tens of thousands of boards in the United States alone, and only a small percentage of them are equipped to dazzle you this way, at least at this writing. But even the boards that do not put on a sound and light show for every caller can be impressive—all the more so when you realize how little is needed in the way of hardware and software to set up a board.

The "Bulletins" menu of the Wildcat! BBS package is truly classy. But your comm software must support RIP graphics (explained in Chapter 22) to be able to view it.

No BBS is easy to *operate*, of course. But physically, most consist of nothing more than a personal computer, a modem, and a BBS software package. And the software may be available as a free public-domain program or a try-before-you-buy shareware package. In short, almost anybody can set up a bulletin board.

Yet even an average board can easily emulate the look, feel, and features of your favorite consumer online service. For example, any number of boards offer international and transcontinental electronic mail, full-fledged Internet connections (often delivered via a satellite dish plugged into the board), newswires, real-time chat, multi-player games, and huge CD-ROM–based file collections.

A Matter of Scale The only thing that prevents BBSs from putting a real dent in the commercial online industry is the matter of scale. Consider: A single-line bulletin board system that is available 24 hours a day can handle 17,520 calls a year, assuming each call lasts half an hour.

That's a lot of calls, to be sure. But that number doesn't even register when compared with the number of calls services like America

Online, Prodigy, and CompuServe get every year. Prodigy alone has over 40,000 modems ready to receive calls from its millions of users.

In contrast, at this writing, the biggest BBS in the world, Exec-PC, can accommodate a maximum of about 300 simultaneous callers. By BBS standards, that is simply incredible, particularly when you know that Exec-PC began as a very modest single-line system.

Businesses and Labors of Love

Though few people run an operation even half the size of a commercial enterprise like Exec-PC, many do charge a subscription fee of some sort. The fee might be a token amount, on the order of $10 a year, to help the "sysop" (short for "system operator" and pronounced "sis-op") pay for equipment wear and tear. Or it might be in the range of $30 to $75 in cases where a board is being run as a profit-making business. Boards with fees like that typically offer lots of phone lines and a wide range of services, including extensive CD-ROM–based file collections and access to the Internet.

It is important to emphasize, however, that most bulletin boards do not charge fees of any kind. Most are operated as a labor of love.

I've interviewed many a sysop over the years, and without exception, they all remember that first call that came into their boards.

It's like listening to a parent describe the birth of a first child. Long-time sysops, like inveterate fishermen, never lose the fascination with someone or some thing hitting their lines. That's a good thing, since running a truly outstanding board is a lot of work, requiring a lot of dedication.

It is this dedication—and the independence it implies—that makes bulletin board systems so fascinating and so different from consumer online services. After all, every online service is a profit-making enterprise whose content is ultimately in the hands of a corporation.

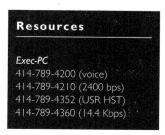

Resources

Exec-PC
414-789-4200 (voice)
414-789-4210 (2400 bps)
414-789-4352 (USR HST)
414-789-4360 (14.4 Kbps)

A bulletin board, more often than not, is the sole property of the sysop who spent the time and money needed to set it up. It can be anything the sysop wants it to be and can carry any information that does not violate the law.

A Personal Publishing House

It follows that whatever the sysop says, goes. If a sysop wants to limit the board's discussion areas to ancient Roman coins or the cultivation of orchids, he can easily do so.

If another sysop wants to make X-rated images and files available for download, she can also do so. But most smart sysops insist on receiving a written notice from you attesting to the fact that you are over 21 before giving you access to the X-rated area of the board.

I don't want to hit this too hard, but the simple fact is that each bulletin board amounts to nothing less than a personal publishing house and radio/TV station—an electronic medium, in effect, that carries *whatever* the sysop wants. This fact alone makes bulletin board systems among the most remarkable developments of the entire online revolution.

I'm not sure it's a good idea for a complete computer novice to start with bulletin boards, because they can be quirky. Treat BBSs as the deep end of a swimming pool. You can splash around, but you will never really be comfortable until you've learned to swim. Let your chosen online service teach you the basic strokes first. Then, and only then, take the plunge.

Treat BBSs as the deep end of a swimming pool. You can splash around, but you will never really be comfortable until you've learned to swim. Let your chosen online service teach you the basic strokes first. Then, and only then, take the plunge.

If you follow this advice, you will have such a wonderful BBS experience that you may never want to leave this corner of the electronic universe. You will see each BBS as a new book to be taken off the shelf, and you will know how to quickly scan the book to determine whether or not you want to spend more time with it.

Tens of Thousands of Boards to Call

There are a lot of boards to choose from. To find out how many, I asked my longtime friend, Jack Rickard. Jack is the self-styled "Editor Rotundus"—and founder—of the highly successful *Boardwatch Magazine* and founder of the annual ONE BBSCON trade show and conference. Jack tells me that there are currently some 57,000 BBSs in North America alone and that that number *doubles* every 18 months.

He didn't say anything about the attrition rate. But it's an important consideration since, historically, BBSs have come and gone like mayfly hatches on a trout stream. Many sysops find that running a board is

BBS Conferences on the Internet

If you have an Internet connection via Delphi or some other system, you might check out the following newsgroups. This list is excerpted from the comprehensive list maintained by David C. Lawrence at UUNET Technologies, Inc., in Falls Church, Virginia. See "The Online Cookbook" section at the back of this book for hands-on instructions on how to tap into these groups:

Newsgroup	Description
alt.bbs	Computer BBS systems and software.
alt.bbs.ads	Ads for various computer BBSs.
alt.bbs.allsysop	Sysop concerns about all networks and technologies.
alt.bbs.first-class	The FirstClass Mac GUI BBS.
alt.bbs.gigo-gateway	Garbage in, garbage out—alt.* in a nutshell.
alt.bbs.internet	BBSs that are hooked up to the Internet.
alt.bbs.lists	Postings of regional BBS lists.
alt.bbs.majorbbs	The MajorBBS by Galacticomm, Inc.
alt.bbs.metal	The METAL Telecommunications Environment.
alt.bbs.pcboard	Technical support for the PCBoard BBS.
alt.bbs.pcbuucp	The commercial PCBoard gateway.
alt.bbs.unixbbs	UnixBBS, from Nervous XTC.
alt.bbs.wildcat	Wildcat! BBS from Mustang Software, Inc.
comp.bbs.misc	All aspects of computer BBSs.
comp.bbs.tbbs	The Bread Board System bulletin board software.
comp.bbs.waffle	The Waffle BBS and Usenet system on all platforms.

simply too much work. But even if 10 to 20 percent of those boards folded tomorrow, there would still be tens of thousands left as well as thousands of new sysops setting up boards to take their place.

The topics covered are as varied as the human imagination. For example, a board may carry propaganda from the extreme right or the extreme left of the political spectrum. Or it may offer an online salon where writers, artists, and musicians intermingle, sharing their ideas and their works. Or it may be a focal point for community needs.

It may be a place for Jewish or Christian singles to meet or, at the other extreme, a place for swinging couples of all sexual persuasions to make dates for physical encounters. And there is almost certainly a board someplace dedicated to just about any hobby you can name.

Where to Get the Best BBS Phone Numbers

20

A large percentage of the boards available today have been around for years. They are veritable institutions in the BBS community. But bulletin boards in general tend to come and go, with the average board lasting perhaps 18 months to two years.

Sysops move. They change jobs. They have children. Or they simply decide that they no longer want to spend the time required to keep the board going. That's why it's important to make sure you're using a current list of BBS phone numbers. Otherwise, you might dial the "Sex-is-Us" BBS at one o'clock some morning and hear a sleepy, grandmotherly voice through your modem's speaker saying "Hello. Hello? Is anybody there?"

I did that once. It was years ago, before everyone—even grandmothers—had answering machines. And I'm ashamed to say that I took the coward's way out, which was to key in "ATH" to tell my modem to hang up right away. I felt just awful. And ever since, I've taken great care when keying in a BBS number or when using a list of BBS numbers.

The Need for Fresh Phone Numbers

Using a fresh list of BBS numbers is even more important these days than in the past, at least for those of us who live in the more densely populated parts of the country. On both coasts, AT&T seems to add a new area code every three months. And it is now routine for the phone company to run cables into newly constructed houses with the capacity to carry up to five separate phone lines.

The chances are greater than ever that the phone number of the defunct board will quickly be assigned to someone else.

The demand for phone numbers, in short, is huge, and it is increasing. All of which means that when a sysop takes a board down and has its phone line disconnected, the chances are greater than ever that the phone number of the defunct board will quickly be assigned to someone else.

That's why it's more important than ever to make sure you are using a current list of BBS numbers before setting out to "work the boards." Later, after you have found one or more boards you like, you probably won't be so interested in checking out other BBSs. After all, there are only so many hours in the day and so many dollars in your bank account to pay long distance charges.

Electronic and Printed BBS Lists

You won't be surprised to learn that lists of BBS phone numbers can be found both in printed form and as computer files. Both formats are valuable, but the electronic format is the most useful.

Generally, when magazines present BBS lists, they give you a paragraph or more of information, like this sample from *Computer Shopper:*

Michigan * 810

Berkley 541-2325. Redline Express BBS; sysop Charlie Marracco. 1 line—486; 430Mb running TBBS 5.02 with U.S. Robotics at up to 14400 bps. Established 05/93; no fee. Shareware and adult files. Running 2 CD-ROMs online and WME message exchange.

Clinton Twp. 286-0145. The Serial Port; sysop Stu Jackson. 9 lines—486; 7000Mb running TBBS 2.2M with ZyXel at up to 19200 bps. Established 08/83; $30 biannually. Large database of PD and adult files. Ham radio areas with online call lookup. Home satellite sections, more.

Flint 235-0158. The Carnival BBS; sysops Silvia and Mickey Rat. 1 line—Atari 8-Bit; 85Mb running Pro BBS 4.0B with Supra at up to 2400 bps. Established 04/89; no fee. Supporting IBM, Commodore, Amiga, Mac, Apple, and Atari. Featuring 30 message bases and online games.

The information itself is submitted by the sysop—and who better to give you a sense of the board and what you will find there? Equally important, to remain on the *Computer Shopper* list, the sysop must send in a card every three months acknowledging that the board is still in operation.

Few print publications give you as much information about individual BBSs as *Computer Shopper*. Most of the others follow the same format used in electronic BBS lists, devoting only a single line to each board, like this:

Phone	State	City	Sysop	Name, Features
519-555-0069	ON	Guelph	B. & R. Spencer	RGB Computing
519-555-5663	ON	Corunna	David Empey	Mandate Systems
601-555-0539	MS	Hattiesburg	Craig Brown	Citadel
601-555-0589	MS	Hattiesburg	Chuck Hosey	PrometheusDesgn

Electronic Versions of Computer Shopper

To get the *Computer Shopper* list in electronic form, tap the Ziff-Davis Computer Library Plus on CompuServe by keying in `go compdb` on CompuServe. Specify *Computer Shopper* as the publication you want to search. Narrow the results by publication date ("September 1995," for example). Then narrow the results once again by "keyword," specifying "bulletin boards" as your keyword.

Bulletin boards get so much coverage in *Computer Shopper*, including a regular column called "Treading the Boards," that you need to narrow the search this way to avoid getting a list of hundreds of articles. This technique will produce a list of about two items:

Computer Database Plus   Article Selection Menu

1. Treading the boards. (AEGIS AIDS-information, Wizard's Gate wide-ranging and Animation Station Amiga bulletin board systems) (Column), Computer Shopper, April 1994 v14 n4 p612(2). Reference # A15048831   Text: Yes (2033 words) Abstract: Yes

2. Bulletin boards. Computer Shopper, April 1994 v14 n4 p617(28). Reference # A15048889   Text: Yes (40704 words) Abstract: No

In this case, it is the second article that you want. The *Computer Shopper* BBS lists are always titled "Bulletin boards." Open your comm program's capture buffer and make your selection. At the next prompt that appears, hit `s` to get the article to "scroll" continuously. The cost for using Computer Database Plus and obtaining the article will total about $3.

Note that in early 1994, *Computer Shopper* began publishing only half of the main list in each issue, since the number of boards has grown so much. To get the complete listing, you will need the lists published in two consecutive months.

You can save some money if you can find a library in your area that subscribes to Ziff-Davis's Computer Select CD-ROM product, since each monthly CD-ROM includes the full text of 12 month's worth of *Computer Shopper* and about 150 other magazines.

The great advantage of getting these lists on your own disk is that you can then use your word processor software to *search* for "jobs" or "adult" or "Internet" or any other keyword of interest. This makes it very easy to identify the boards that specialize in a given subject area and saves you hours of pouring through thousands of BBS descriptions.

This is not much to go on. But electronic BBS lists do have two significant advantages. First, they are often more current than printed lists. Magazines typically go to press two to three months before they appear in your mailbox or on a newsstand. Some electronic lists, in contrast, come out every month or even every two weeks.

Second, and most important of all, if you have a list in electronic form, you can almost certainly find a way to put it into your comm program's phonebook or dialing directory—automatically—without having to key in a single phone number.

Electronic Lists: The Two Best Sources

The two best online sources of BBS lists are bulletin board systems themselves and communications- or BBS-oriented Special Interest Groups on the major consumer online services.

Boardwatch Magazine, for example, publishes its famous "List of BBS List Keepers" in each issue. This list consists of nearly 100 BBSs worldwide that specialize in compiling and maintaining lists of bulletin boards—by area code, by topical category, or whatever. Sample list categories include: "Ham and Amateur Radio," "Medical Issues," "Conservation and Nature," and "The North America Nudist List."

You don't need this list of list keepers to find a board with a list you can use, however. Nearly every BBS going has one or more lists of bulletin board numbers to offer. All you have to do is check its "Files" section and search on the terms "BBS list" or "list."

Tapping Online SIG Libraries for Numbers

Better still is the option of searching the files maintained in various Special Interest Group libraries on the main consumer online services. And the best service to search, in my opinion, is CompuServe. No other service has as many users who are actively interested in computers and computer communications. Thus, CompuServe subscribers typically upload lots of BBS lists.

There is also the fact that, at this writing, no other service makes it so easy to find SIG files, thanks to CompuServe's various "File Finder" features.

For example, if you are a Macintosh user, you need only sign on to CompuServe and key in `go macff` to get to the "Macintosh File

Finder." Opt to search on "Keyword," and key in "BBS" as one of your keywords and "list" as a second. No need for a third.

The system will search the libraries of most Macintosh-oriented SIGs and come back with a list of all files whose descriptions match your specified keywords. When I did it recently, the "MacFF" feature found 25 files. Here are just two of the file descriptions:

Forum Name: MACCOMM   Library: BBS Systems   (9)
Accesses: 1444   Size: 26240
File: FCBBS.SIT   Submitted: [70511,2065]   05-Apr-94

Here's the latest FirstClass BBS list, with over 600 operational public access BBSs worldwide. FirstClass is a fully GUI based e-mail and BBS system for Mac and Windows, and has a VT-100 mode for other users and machines. There are over 4000 systems running FirstClass world-wide; the systems on this list have opened their modems to the public for anyone to access. Maury Markowitz SoftArc Inc.

Dearchive with STUFEX.SEA

Forum Name: MACCOMM   Library: BBS Systems   (9)
Accesses: 1552   Size: 129089
File: THELIS.TXT   Submitted: [72517,666]   07-Mar-94

The BBS List is a monthly (generally!) updated list of nearly 1000 bul-letin boards system worldwide.

Don't be concerned about how you actually get these files. The needed techniques are covered in Chapter 40. But here's a hint: Key in go maccomm to get to the Forum; join the Forum so you will be permit-ted to download files; select Library 9 (BBS Systems), and key in dow fcbbs.sit or dow thelis.txt at the library prompt. Notice that you will need to "unstuff" (decompress) the first file with STUFEX.SEA or a similar program before you can use it.

If all of this is mysterious to you, don't give it a second thought for now. All will be explained in Part 7 of this book. The only other thing to add at this point is that the same kind of magic works for IBM users who key in go ibmff on CompuServe. Use the same keywords and the same techniques to download desired files. The only difference is that IBM users are likely to need to "unZIP" a file instead of "unstuffing" it.

One caveat applies to everyone: Pay attention to the *dates* the files of BBS lists were submitted and to any information in the descriptive paragraph about updates and the like. System operators on both BBSs and consumer services tend to avoid the time-consuming task of weeding out old files.

Automatically Importing BBS Phone Numbers

There aren't enough hours in a lifetime to sample each of the tens of thousands of bulletin boards that are out there. Yet, clearly, it is important for most of us to try a large number of boards before deciding to make one or more our bulletin board "home."

But no one wants to spend tons of time keying in BBS phone numbers. That's why the *best* way to prepare to "work the boards" is to instantly import whole bunches of BBS phone numbers into the dialing directory or phonebook of your communications software program.

Remember, once a phone number has been entered in a comm program dialing directory, you never need key it in again. You can merely mouse to the entry and click or otherwise select the number. If the line is busy the first time the comm program calls, the program will wait a moment and dial it again. And, if you tell your software to dial an entire *list* of numbers, it will diligently keep dialing until it gets an answer. When you're finished with that call, it will remove the number from the list and keep on dialing the other numbers until you tell it to stop!

So, how do you instantly import BBS phone numbers into your comm program's dialing directory or phonebook? Believe it or not, it's a lot easier than you think.

First, you need a file of BBS phone numbers on your disk. The file must be arranged so that each BBS listing occupies a single line. As long as the phone number and name of each board always begin at the same columns, you can easily import the entire list using the right public-domain or shareware program.

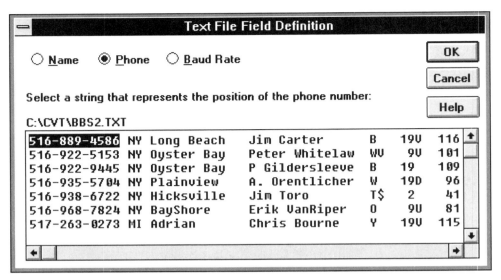

Teaching CVTT where to look for a BBS phone number.

The figure "Text File Field Definition," for example, shows Peter Pauly's Windows-based CVTT program. All you need do with CVTT is use your mouse to highlight the phone number and then the board's name, and CVTT will produce a dialing directory file in ProComm, Pro-Comm Plus 1.0, Telix, or text format.

This may seem limiting, but ProComm and Telix are so popular that most competing programs include the option of converting ProComm or Telix directories. There is thus a good chance that your favorite comm program will be able to convert the dialing directories created by CVTT. And, of course, there is always Mark Ellis's DIRCOPY program for converting among Telix, Qmodem, ProComm, ProComm Plus, Bitcom, and ASCII formats. (Both CVTT and DIRCOPY are in the "Glossbrenner's Choice" section at the back of this book.)

With lots of good, fresh numbers to choose from, I'll now show you what's really involved in "working the boards."

"Working the Boards"

21

Are you ready to rock 'n' roll? Are you ready to "work the boards?" Good!

I'm going to assume that you've got a list of at least four or five BBS numbers. If you haven't, you'll find a few suggestions later in this chapter. I'm also going to assume that you have put the numbers into the dialing directory or phonebook of your communications program since this will save you a great deal of time.

There is simply no point in keying in `ATDT` followed by the BBS number in your comm program's terminal screen. The modem will dial, but the BBS number might be busy. Then you'll have to key in the number again. And possibly again. Take my advice: Use the dialing directory or phonebook feature of your comm program instead. That's what it's there for.

Initial Settings and Sign-On

Your goal is to get onto a board as quickly and with as little hassle as possible. Therefore, set your communications parameters for 9600 bps (or your modem's highest speed), 8 data bits, no parity, and 1 stop bit (8/N/1). Set your comm program's terminal type or emulation to "ANSI," if that option is available. There are two reasons for these settings.

First, any sysop worth his or her salt has by now converted to 9600 bps modems. At this writing, they may not have made the leap to 14.4 Kbps or 28.8 Kbps, but if 2400 bps is still their top speed, they are not likely to be worth your bother.

Second, while many boards can detect and deal with settings of both 7/E/1 and 8/N/1, you will usually have more options if you set your system for 8/N/1. Specifically, you may be able to opt to use a given board's graphical interface instead of being limited to plain text.

"ANSI" terminal emulation is available in many DOS and Mac programs. This feature allows the BBS to do some interesting things with color, text, and block graphics characters. (For a complete explanation of ANSI and details on making the most of the DOS ANSI.SYS driver, please see the Random House books *DOS 5* or *DOS 6* by Alfred Glossbrenner.)

Paper in the Printer?

Before you begin working the boards in earnest, make sure that your printer is "online" and loaded with plenty of paper. This can save you a lot of time.

I advise keeping your capture buffer open at all times. This is a good safety measure, since even if you miss something as it scrolls off the screen, you will have a copy on disk.

It can be a nuisance to comb through a huge capture file, however, so it's good to be prepared to print on the spot any screen of interest. That way you will know you've printed a copy of the information you want and can simply delete the capture file later without looking at it.

Logging On

Now you're ready to dial a board. Use your comm program's dialing directory, as I advised, to dial a single number or to mark several numbers for your program to dial in turn. When you get a connection, your comm program may alert you with a beep. That's your signal to open your capture buffer. I suggest naming each capture buffer file after the board you are using.

```
┌■■■■■■■■■■■>>»            Exec-PC BBS            «<<■■■■■■■■■■■─┐
│                  The Business Knowledge Exchange                │
│                      ASP Approved BBS                           │
└─── 288 PHONE LINES - LARGEST AND MOST POPULAR BBS IN THE WORLD ──┘
              The largest LAN-and-microcomputer-based BBS in the World!
                       8.8 Million callers since 1982
            100+ uploads per day! 658,888 files in compressed files
                      500,888+ active messages online
                        4,588+ callers per day!
        Home of Hyperscan(tm), searches through 28,888 files in 2 seconds!

     Via: Global Access,CompuServe,V.fast,V.32bis,HST,MNP,CompuCom,V-series
                     Fidonet Address: 1:154/288

  ■■>> IMPORTANT NOTE:  YOUR COMMUNICATIONS PARAMETERS MUST BE SET TO 8,N,1 <<■■

  Your are logged in as ALFRED GLOSSBRENNER
  If this is incorrect, please hang up at this time.

  Press any key to continue ->
```

The Exec-PC greeting screen.

You will next see a greeting screen announcing the board's name, focus, sysop, or whatever. If there is no response after about ten seconds, hit your Enter key once or twice.

A Few Questions for Our Files After the greeting screen, a prompt for your first name and last name will almost certainly appear. The BBS software will look at your name and check to see if you have been on before. If this is your first time, you may be asked to key in your city and state, and possibly your birthdate. You will almost certainly then be asked to select a password.

Key in the password of your choice, and the board will ask you to key it in again for confirmation. The characters probably will not show on your screen. You'll see asterisks instead. From then on, you will be a member of the board and simply be prompted for your name and password each time you call. What happens next depends on the BBS software and the desires of the sysop.

Macro Keys

If you frequently sign on to new boards, you will find yourself keying in your name and address a lot. Some boards even ask your date of birth and home and business phone numbers. You can save yourself a lot of time and bother if you simply assign these various pieces of information to a "macro," or key combination, in your comm program. That way, keying in, say, Alt-3 will transmit your street address, while keying in Alt-4 will transmit your city and state.

The *Boardwatch* "Top Ten" Starter List

Each year, *Boardwatch Magazine* asks BBS users to vote for their favorite boards. The results are then tabulated to produce the "Top 100 BBSs" in the country. The fact that sysops are free to vigorously campaign and even offer prizes for user votes does not seem to matter. But you should probably view the list a bit more skeptically than you would a Gallup Poll.

Nonetheless, no one seriously contests the fact that the top-rated boards deserve to be top-rated, though connoisseurs may quibble about the exact rankings. Certainly you will have a good experience sampling any of the top ten of the top 100.

The Top Ten Boards from *Boardwatch Magazine*'s "Top 100 BBSs" List

[From the September, 1994 issue of *Boardwatch*. Total votes cast: 26,015.]

Rank	Name	Phone	Place	Sysop
1.	Software Creations	508-368-7139	Clinton, MA	Dan Linton
	Primary source for Apogee and other entertainment software.			
2.	Exec-PC	414-789-4360	New Berlin, WI	Bob Mahoney
	World's largest BBS, 35 Gig., Full Internet Access, and more.			
3.	GLIB	703-578-4542	Arlington, VA	Jon Larimore
	Information serving the gay, lesbian, and bisexual communities.			
4.	Monterey Gaming System	408-655-5555	Monterey, CA	David Janakes
	Custom interactive gaming and multi-user conferences.			
5.	Blue Ridge Express	804-790-1675	Richmond, VA	Webb Blackman
	Large files base with 3 Gigibytes and CD-ROMs.			
6.	Deep Cove BBS	604-536-5885	White Rock, BC	Wayne Duval
	News, publications, Internet e-mail, shareware, games.			
7.	AlphaOne Online	708-827-3619	Park Ridge, IL	Gloria La Hay
	Adults only, matchmaking, personals, shareware.			
8.	America's Suggestion Box	516-471-8625	Ronkonkoma, NY	Joe Jerszynski
	13 Gigs of Shareware, Internet e-mail, USENET newsgroups.			
9.	Lifestyle Online	516-689-5390	East Setauket, NY	Marc Kraft
	Chat system, adult lifestyles, personals, e-mail.			
10.	Prodigy Genealogy	800-775-7714	Prodigy ID: UXJF71A	Mark Rivas Sachs
	Information and help of searching for people.			

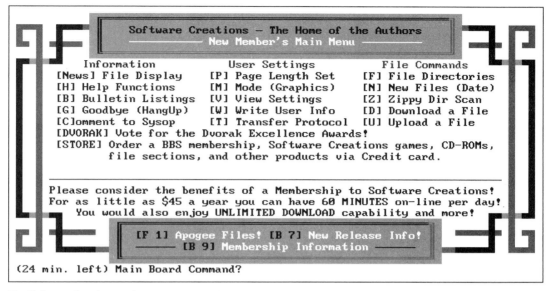

```
┌─────────────────────────────────────────────────────────────────┐
│      Software Creations - The Home of the Authors                 │
│ ──────────────── New Member's Main Menu ────────────              │
│                                                                   │
│    Information          User Settings         File Commands       │
│ [News] File Display   [P] Page Length Set   [F] File Directories  │
│ [H] Help Functions    [M] Mode (Graphics)   [N] New Files (Date)  │
│ [B] Bulletin Listings [V] View Settings     [Z] Zippy Dir Scan    │
│ [G] Goodbye (HangUp)  [W] Write User Info    [D] Download a File   │
│ [C]omment to Sysop    [T] Transfer Protocol  [U] Upload a File     │
│ [DVORAK] Vote for the Dvorak Excellence Awards!                   │
│ [STORE] Order a BBS membership, Software Creations games, CD-ROMs, │
│         file sections, and other products via Credit card.        │
│ ───────────────────────────────────────────────────────────────── │
│ Please consider the benefits of a Membership to Software Creations!│
│ For as little as $45 a year you can have 60 MINUTES on-line per day!│
│    You would also enjoy UNLIMITED DOWNLOAD capability and more!    │
│                                                                   │
│     [F 1] Apogee Files! [B 7] New Release Info!                   │
│ ──────────────── [B 9] Membership Information ────────────        │
│                                                                   │
│ (24 min. left) Main Board Command?                                │
└─────────────────────────────────────────────────────────────────┘
```

The Software Creations main menu.

If the board charges a fee, you will be informed as part of your first sign-on. Fees vary from a low of $10 a year to $75 or more a year. But some boards give anybody access to certain sections for free. They want to give you a sample of what the board has to offer.

Naturally, what you get for any subscription fee will also vary. I realize that there is nothing like love at first sight. But if you are new to this game, I advise against subscribing to any board the first time you sign on. Wait until you've played the field a little and have a better idea of what other boards are offering for the same amount of money.

I should reiterate here that the vast majority of bulletin boards do *not* charge fees of any kind, so the question may not even come up.

Online Explorations

Sysop policies vary, but once you have logged onto a board, you will probably be allotted a certain number of minutes to explore. A half hour to an hour is typical. And it is not difficult to understand why such limits are imposed. Most sysops are interested in getting as many calls as they can. That is how many find satisfaction in a largely thankless pursuit.

Most know all too well how a few "takers" can hog their boards, downloading file after file and never uploading or contributing anything, while preventing others from getting on.

Don't let these limits inhibit you. Take your time and get to know a board. If your time expires before you are finished, you can always come back tomorrow. And there are plenty of other boards to play with.

As you explore, you will find that boards offer file areas, conferences, real-time chat among people who are currently online, games, private e-mail, FidoNet mail, "doors," and some form of access to the Internet. You will also discover that any number of boards have a similar feel, set of menus, and command structure. That's because many BBSs run the same BBS software.

As you work the boards more and more, you will come to recognize this software and be able to bring your former experiences with it to bear. But generally, you will find that you can expect certain basic features on any BBS and you will quickly learn to use them.

Boardwatch Online!

Boardwatch publishes lists of the BBSs in a given area code in every issue, as well as the "List of List Keepers" BBSs and the annual "Top 100 List." All are presented in the one-line-per-BBS format that is perfect for importing into a comm program phonebook or dialing directory—if you can get them in electronic form.

Well, you can! To get anything in *Boardwatch* in electronic form, dial the *Boardwatch* BBS. You will have to subscribe to the print version of the magazine ($36) to gain full access to the electronic version. But you can do so via the bulletin board or by calling *Boardwatch*'s voice line.

Alternatively, you will also find issues of *Boardwatch* via the "doors/magazines" offerings of Exec-PC. Once you subscribe to Exec-PC, you will be able to dial in via your local CompuServe number and thus avoid long-distance charges.

Resources

Boardwatch
800-933-6038 (voice)
303-973-4222 (BBS)

Exec-PC
414-789-4210 (BBS)

How to Evaluate a BBS

Experienced users can make up their minds about a BBS in about two minutes. They know just what to look for to determine whether the board is worth exploring and whether it is worth frequenting on a regular basis.

It's not difficult to do. But here are some things you may want to consider:

1. Has the sysop made the board "caller friendly"?

You can't really blame a sysop for insisting that you identify yourself the very first time you sign on. This tends to discourage the uploading of stolen credit card numbers, pirated software, and other illegal activities for which the sysop may be held liable. But the next time you call, you should be able to get to the main menu quickly, without being forced to sit through screens of boring information, like the number of callers, the number of uploads, and so on.

2. Is the system conveniently organized?

Ideally, message areas and libraries will be organized into logical categories. This makes it easier to find files and messages on the topics of greatest interest to you—much better than having everything lumped into one big area.

3. Are the messages and files fresh?

Look at the first and last messages uploaded to the board. They will be the ones with the lowest and the highest number. That will give you a sense of how active and popular the board is. If the most recent messages are several months old, it's a sure sign that the board is either so new that it has not yet gained a following or that it is dead. Either way, it is probably not the place to look for lively discussions or the most current shareware programs and files.

4. Is the sysop truly committed or just playing around?

In addition to support for 9600 bps and faster modems, a board should be available round the clock, except for announced periods of maintenance. It should support the Zmodem file transfer protocol, and most of the files in its libraries should be compressed into archives.

As I explain in Chapter 41, archive files end in .ZIP, .ZOO, .LHA, .LZH, .ARC, or .ARJ in the DOS world. Mac archives typically end in .SIT. Either way, archived files can be downloaded in as little as half the time required for their uncompressed versions.

5. Do you like the way the board "feels"?

Finally, ask yourself if you are having fun using the board. Does the sysop's personality show through, and if so, is he or she a likable sort? From the messages you read, do you think you like the kind of users the board attracts? In short, does the place just "feel" right?

In the end, everything depends on what you want from a BBS. You may want to find and download files; you may want to ask questions, discuss current events, and play games; or you may simply want to have a friendly, inexpensive place to "hang" online. One thing is certain: Whatever you want, there is a bulletin board out there somewhere that can provide it. That's part of the joy of "working the boards!"

RIP, ZIP, Fido, and BBS Culture

22

Bulletin board culture is a doctoral thesis waiting to be written. Indeed, with our universities minting so many Ph.D.s each year, most with little prospect of gainful employment, one or more dissertations on the BBS world has almost certainly already been committed to paper.

The culture—the customs, the codes of behavior, the "way we do things here"—is broad, deep, and constantly changing. There is far more to it than can be covered in any single chapter. Ultimately, your best bet is to simply take the plunge. As you do so, however, you will find that the pointers presented in this chapter can help you rocket up the learning curve.

ANSI Graphics

You will often be asked when you sign on to a board if you want to use ANSI graphics. "ANSI" stands for the American National Standards Institute. There are many accepted ANSI standards. But in this case, the standard involved concerns the handling of the screen and the keyboard.

When intelligently implemented, ANSI graphics can make a board's menus and everything else easier to read and understand.

When you set your comm program's terminal emulation to "ANSI," the program will respond to ANSI "escape codes" sent to it by the BBS. These codes, each of which begins with the ASCII escape character (ASCII 27) and a left bracket ([), control the foreground and background colors used to display a character. They can make a character or series of characters blink on and off. And, when used with the box-drawing and block graphics characters of the IBM extended ASCII code set, they can produce some very pleasing effects. (Many Mac comm programs can emulate ANSI graphics of this sort.)

When intelligently implemented, ANSI graphics can make a board's menus and everything else easier to read and understand. The only downside is that at speeds lower than 9600 bps, enabling ANSI graphics can noticeably slow things down. This is definitely something you should try, however, if you have a color screen.

ANSI Music

Like the managers at consumer online services, serious BBS sysops are constantly striving to make their boards more attractive and feature-filled. Recently, some boards have gone beyond ANSI graphics to offer "ANSI music" as well. Since there is no ANSI standard for music, the term is a misnomer, but it does convey the concept.

ANSI music is a variation of the escape sequence technique. Bulletin boards that offer ANSI music transmit sequences of text characters to control what notes are played, how long each note lasts, and so on. The tunes are played through your computer's speaker, and they may be used to herald the appearance of a menu or the end of a download, or in connection with some game.

To experience ANSI music you must use a DOS comm program like Qmodem Pro or GT Powercomm, both of which specifically support this feature. (I know of no Macintosh equivalents.) You will also need to find a board that offers ANSI music. The best way to find such a board is to get a list of BBSs on disk and search for the word ANSI with your word processor. Shareware programs are available to help you create ANSI music or to convert music files created by the Pianoman program into ANSI music files.

BBS "Doors"

In BBSspeak a "door" is any option that lets you temporarily leave the main BBS program to run some piece of software available on the host system. Depending on how it is implemented, a BBS door could let you control the BBS computer as if it were your own.

In practice, most BBSs offer a door option to let you play games, read magazines, or answer quizzes and questionnaires. From the sysop's point of view, using BBS software with "doors" makes it possible to offer callers even more than the standard message exchange and file library areas found on all BBSs.

Download/Upload Ratios

Let's face it: There are many people out there—and we all know one or two—who are simply *takers*. They never offer anything of their own. They never think about anyone but themselves. And they will bleed you dry if you let them.

Bulletin boards are particularly vulnerable to the takers of the world. Yet most sysops are generous souls. They are happy to have someone sign on and take the files they have to offer. But, like most of us, they resent being taken advantage of. That's why some sysops have "download/upload ratios." The idea is that for X number of kilobytes you upload to the board, you can download Y number of kilobytes of files. If you don't contribute something, you can't download anything.

This sounds like a great idea. Unfortunately, if a caller wants a given file on a given board, there is nothing to stop him from uploading any old piece of trash to satisfy the board's download/upload ratio. There is also the fact that for every board that imposes such a ratio, there is at least one that does not, so callers can simply go elsewhere.

Consequently, while you can sympathize with the sysops, it seems likely that the days of download/upload ratios are numbered.

Exit Gracefully

You should never, ever, simply hang up the phone when using a BBS. Doing so breaks the connection on your end, but it leaves the line busy on the BBS end. The BBS won't hang up until it "times out" due to lack of activity on your former connection. That delays the time when the line is free for some other caller.

The proper way to leave a BBS is to do so from a menu. The command is normally g for "good-bye." If you are offered a chance to leave the sysop a private note, and if you have enjoyed the board, by all means take a moment to key in a few lines of appreciation.

FidoNet, EchoMail, RIME, and OneNet

In November of 1983 a wizard programmer named Tom Jennings hit upon a way for a caller in, say, Asbury Park, New Jersey, to send a message to someone in, say, Bakersfield, California, for free. Or if not completely for free, for a very small charge.

That was the time when Mr. Jennings brought up FIDO #1, a BBS named for his dog. The concept was simple. Find a bunch of sysops across the country who want to participate in FidoNet, and assign each one of them a node number. Then equip each system with the necessary FidoNet software.

That software makes it possible for someone in Asbury Park to dial a local number to connect with a nearby FidoNet board. The caller can then address a message to some friend in Bakersfield whom he knows regularly calls a FidoNet board based in that California town.

In the wee hours of that same night, the Asbury Park BBS will begin exchanging messages with other FidoNet boards. This is called "mail time" in BBSspeak. The Asbury Park board may dial the Bakersfield board directly and exchange messages. Or it may dial a board in

Chicago and transmit its California-bound messages to it for forwarding during the next "mail time."

One way or another, the New Jersey message will make its way to California, and neither sender nor receiver will have to pay for a long-distance phone call. The various FidoNet sysops may pay the freight along the way, and they may pass costs along to their users. There is no way of saying for certain. That's why I like Bernard Aboba's comment in his wonderful Addison-Wesley book, *The Online User's Encyclopedia:*

> FidoNet is the world's largest BBS network, with over 22,000 public nodes worldwide and possibly as many private nodes. It's anarchic, feisty, and totally out of control, but I like it anyway. (After all, I'm from Berkeley.)

Other, similar networks and BBS software packages exist. Generally anything with a dog-related name—McWoof, Collie, etc.—is probably a Fido clone or compatible. And FidoNet itself has expanded beyond simple message exchanges into full-fledged discussion groups and the exchange of their messages and message threads (collections of messages). This is called "EchoMail" because your comments are echoed (transmitted) throughout the FidoNet system.

RIME is the name for a similar network of BBSs running PostLink software. OneNet is a network of BBSs running FirstClass software, a popular Macintosh BBS package.

Even as a longtime admirer of FidoNet and its clones, however, one cannot avoid the question of the future of such networks in light of the wide availability of the Internet. Why fiddle with Fido when you can be sending and receiving messages and files and participating in discussion groups on the Internet for free or for as little as $1.80 or less an *hour*? I may be missing something, but these days, FidoNet and its clones hardly seem worth the hassle.

Message and Mail Etiquette

Every BBS has a unique personality created by the combination of the sysop and the people who visit the board on a regular basis. You will sense this personality as you begin to read the messages posted on the board. It's like entering a room of strangers and overhearing their conversations.

You are certain to be welcomed, for almost every such "community" enjoys a new voice, a new point of view. But you will be even more welcome if you follow a few simple customs.

First, don't post messages in all capital letters. This is seen as SHOUTING and will earn you no friends. If you want to emphasize a word, as with italics, frame it with two asterisks, like *this*.

If you disagree with something someone has said, do so politely. Personal attacks, snide remarks, name-calling, and other forms of verbal bullying are called "flaming" and are generally considered in bad taste.

Be considerate of the sysop and of your fellow board members at all times. That means reading your private mail and messages promptly and deleting them ("killing them") when you're done. They can then be removed to free up the sysop's disk space.

Be mindful of message threads—the various collections of messages that constitute the discussion of some issue. Remember that public messages are intended to be read by everyone. So don't delete one of your messages if it is part of a discussion thread.

When you are replying to a specific message, do not assume that all your readers are familiar with that message. Assume instead that they are just joining the conversation and need to be told, briefly, what point or points you are responding to.

Finally, *participate!* Your fellow board members genuinely want to hear from you. What do you think? How do you feel about an issue? What's of interest to you? Don't be shy. Be as polite and considerate as you would when entering a room full of people you hope will eventually become your friends, and you cannot go wrong.

Quick (.QWK) and Reply (.REP) Packets

With his DOS QMail reader program, Mark "Sparky" Herring has done for bulletin boards what TAPCIS and Aladdin do for CompuServe and GEnie. The concept is simple.

You call a board that supports the QMail approach and access a "door" program to create a list of the conferences you wish to follow. From then on, you can access the "door" and the BBS software will *automatically* pack up all of the messages in those conferences that you have not read and send them to you as a single large compressed file, known as an archive, or .QWK, file.

When you've finished downloading the file, you sign off the system, decompress the archive (.QWK) file, and read the messages with a QMail-compatible mail-reading program. You respond to any messages of interest, and the QMail program packs them up into a new archive file (.REP) of replies. Transmit this file to the BBS, and the BBS software will automatically post your replies to the correct conferences.

The commercial comm program Qmodem Pro supports the QMail approach with its Offline Xpress mail-reading module. QMail-supporting shareware packages are also available.

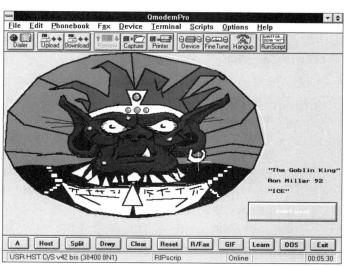

Resources

RIPscrip, RIPdraw, and RIPpaint
TeleGrafix Communications, Inc.
714-379-2131 (voice)
714-379-2133 (BBS)

Qmodem Pro and Qmodem Pro for Windows
Mustang Software, Inc.
805-873-2500 (voice)
805-873-2400 (BBS)

NovaLink Professional for Mac
ResNova Software, Inc.
714-840-6082 (voice)
714-840-8641 (BBS)

RIPscrip Graphics

The Remote Imaging Protocol (RIP) script language created by Tele-Grafix Communications, Inc., has become enormously popular among DOS and Macintosh BBS users since its introduction in mid-1993. The concept is quite similar to ANSI graphics, but the results are spectacular.

You will need a comm program, like Qmodem Pro or NovaTerm, that supports RIP graphics. Set its terminal type to "RIP emulation." Then call a BBS that you know supports RIP graphics. The BBS software will transmit special escape codes to your program telling it how to paint the screen.

Everything depends on

The Goblin King—drawn by animated RIPscrip before your very eyes.

the implementation, but you can expect to see sculpted buttons and drawings that are as crisp and as inviting as anything America Online or Prodigy puts up. And it's all done by transmitting nothing but standard (as opposed to extended) ASCII characters. RIPscrips can even do animation and music.

FirstClass and TeleFinder Graphics

RIPscrip isn't the only game in town when it comes to high-quality BBS graphics. There are also the graphics techniques developed by SoftArc for its FirstClass program and by Spider Island Software for its TeleFinder suite.

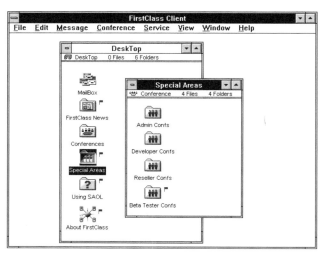

Here's what your Windows screen will look like when you contact a FirstClass BBS using FirstClass client software.

Both products began in the Macintosh world, and both follow what's called the client/server model. This is just a fancy way of saying that if you want to be able to use a FirstClass or TeleFinder BBS, you've got to dial in using the FirstClass or TeleFinder communications program. The BBS software is thus the "server," while the program callers use is the "client" software.

Not surprisingly, SoftArc and Spider Island encourage the free distribution of their client programs. They make their money by selling the server software to BBS sysops. According to a recent issue of *MacUser*, there are over 1,000 FirstClass BBS sites in existence and about 3,000 TeleFinder locations. Presumably those numbers will have grown by the time you read this.

The Windows client programs for both FirstClass and TeleFinder are available from the "Glossbrenner's Choice" section at the

Resources

SoftArc
905-415-7000 (voice)
905-415-7070 (FirstClass BBS)

Spider Island Software
714-669-9260 (voice)
714-730-5785 (BBS; use "guest" for logon name and password)

back of this book. If you're a Mac user, contact your local user group or check the file libraries of your favorite consumer online service. The figure "FirstClass Client" gives you an idea of what to expect when using FirstClass client software to tap a FirstClass BBS.

.ZIP, .ARC, .LZH, .SIT, and Other Archives

They sound intimidating, but compressed, or archived, files aren't hard to deal with, once you have the needed decompressing/dearchiving program. In fact, you will find it enormously convenient to work with compressed files since they will save you a lot of time and money.

Compressed files can often be downloaded in half the time, and they let you get an entire package—a program, its documentation, and all its support modules—in a single file. There's no need to download each component separately as you had to do years ago.

Generally, any board or other library that offers compressed files also offers the program you need to decompress them. In the DOS world, look for PKUNZIP, ARC-E, and LHA or LHARC. In the Macintosh world, look for StuffIt. (You'll find more on compressed files and archives in Chapter 41.)

Viruses

Technically, a virus is but one of an entire rogues' gallery of destructive programs. But the term has come to be applied to any piece of software designed to slip past your notice and do unexpected things.

It might be something as harmless as lying hidden on your disk until a predetermined date and then popping up some kind of message ("Workers of the World Unite," "Happy Earth Day," or some such silliness). Or it could be a program that erases your hard disk drive or surreptitiously nibbles away at your files.

The people who run the SIGs on the various consumer online services are required by contract to check each and every program for viruses before making it available for you to download. A conscientious sysop will do the same with the programs uploaded to his or her board.

But not all sysops are conscientious. Therefore, unless the sysop specifically says that all programs have been checked for viruses, it is only prudent to assume the worst. DOS 6.x comes with an anti-virus utility that can both check a program for a virus and prevent a virus from writing to your disk. Shareware programs like John McAfee's SCAN and CLEAN are also available. Three popular Mac anti-virus programs are Disinfectant, Virex, and SAM.

There is no need to be paranoid. But there is every reason to be cautious. And, fortunately, the tools now exist to deal effectively with most virus threats. Just be sure to use them!

Your Own BBS: For Fun and Profit

23

So you wanna be a sysop?

Well, pilgrim, you've come to the right chapter! This is not a book about how to make a million dollars offering things to online callers. But, it is worth noting that there is money to be made operating a BBS, and anyone can make it.

Suppose it costs you $1,000 to set up a single-line BBS. Suppose your customers are willing to pay you $4 an hour to use this BBS. That means you will need 250 paid hours to break even and pay off your initial $1,000 investment.

Now, suppose that you get 12 hours of paid caller time per day. At that rate, you will break even at 21 days. Let's round that upward and call it a month. Basically, you have recouped your investment in a single month. Everything you make after that will be gross profit.

A profit of $1,000 a month or $12,000 a year? For a single-line bulletin board? Suppose you were to add a second board, would the profits be doubled?

It could happen.

But, to attract enough callers willing to pay $4 an hour, you've got to offer something truly special. And you've got to advertise, which costs money. Nor would it hurt if you could accept Visa or MasterCard for your subscriptions, which costs you maybe 5 percent of the total amount charged.

Virgin Territory

Operating a BBS is not easy. And operating one for profit is not exactly easy money. Certainly not as easy as some may make it sound. But if you've got a concept and are knowledgeable, it can be done.

Remember, the hardware and software are cheap—so cheap that they almost do not matter. What's important is the advertising and promotion you do to get your board known and the time you spend to make it the best board it can possibly be.

There may be some 60,000 boards out there right now, and the number is certainly growing. But there are literally hundreds of millions of computer users worldwide. Clearly, it's still virgin territory, with opportunities aplenty.

The single best source of guidance and advice I've found is the book and software package, *How to Successfully Run a BBS for Profit* by S. Carol Allen and Cary C. Harwin. Chapters include "Surveying the Marketplace,"

Resources

How to Successfully Run a BBS for Profit
InfoLink
800-776-3818

The Business BBS

You may not want to run a BBS as a business. But you may have a business that could benefit from operating a BBS—by providing customers with information on your product, by accepting orders, by providing technical support, or whatever.

Clearly there is a need for what might be termed "third-party BBS services." And one of the companies I've found that does a truly outstanding job in this area is The Business BBS, which offers graphics, fax, databases, search engines, RIPscrips, photographic images, and much more. It's definitely worth looking into.

You may also want to look for *Bulletin Board Systems for Business* written by Lamont Wood and Dana Blankenhorn and published by John Wiley and Sons. And *Creating Successful Bulletin Board Systems* by Alan D. Bryant from Addison Wesley.

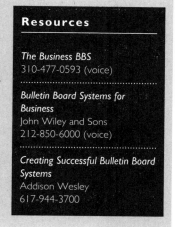

Resources

The Business BBS
310-477-0593 (voice)

Bulletin Board Systems for Business
John Wiley and Sons
212-850-6000 (voice)

Creating Successful Bulletin Board Systems
Addison Wesley
617-944-3700

"Choosing the Theme of Your BBS," "Pricing for Profits," "Getting the Word Out," and "Owning a Gold Mine."

The cost is $49.95, plus $5 shipping and handling. The book includes coupons worth over $1,000 off BBS products and services, including $10 off a subscription to *Boardwatch Magazine*, and carries a 90-day money-back guarantee.

Just for the Fun of It

If you're a DOS user and you want to get your feet wet and see what it's like to be the sysop of your own board, you can do so quickly and easily with the shareware version of Wildcat! from Mustang Software, publishers of Qmodem and the commercial version of Wildcat! BBS software.

The shareware version is full-featured and full-powered. In fact, it used to be the latest commercial version. The on-disk manual is over 500K long. And you can have your Wildcat! board up and running in less than ten minutes, most of which will be taken up by the automated installation program as it copies and decompresses files.

BBS Software for Macintosh Users

If you're a Macintosh user interested in setting up your own BBS, you have a number of choices. Unfortunately, at this writing, none of them are shareware. That could change, but the trend does seem to be in the other direction: packages that used to be shareware are now going commercial.

In any event, the leading Macintosh BBS programs include:

- FirstClass from SoftArc
- TeleFinder from Spider Island Software
- Second Sight from FreeSoft
- Hermes from Computer Classifieds

The cost of packages like these ranges from about $100 to about $500 to $1,000 or more. It all depends on the software producer and on the number of simultaneous users you want to be able to handle.

Before making a decision, I suggest you use your favorite comm program to explore BBSs that use each of these programs. Leave messages for the sysops asking them how they like the software and soliciting their advice. You may even want to arrange to chat with these folks on the phone. It's also a good idea to contact the manufacturers of these programs to request price lists and additional information.

Resources

Hermes
Computer Classifieds
206-643-2316

Second Sight
FreeSoft
412-846-2700

FirstClass
SoftArc
905-415-7000

TeleFinder
Spider Island Software
714-669-9260

The American BBS Association

If you decide to continue as a sysop, you will undoubtedly want to explore all the software, CD-ROM, "doors," and other options. You will also want to contact other sysops to find out how they do things. And you will have other concerns as well. Thus you may want to look into the American BBS Association. I've spoken with Rocky Rawlins, the association's founder, and with John Kay, its current president. They're good people who, in addition to being sysops themselves, are dedicated to helping other sysops and giving the entire BBS community a "voice."

Resources

The American BBS Association
Westlake Information Systems
2603 North Main Street
Dayton, Ohio 45405
513-225-3087 (voice)
513-461-6967 (BBS)

For Your Personal Use

If you don't want to put up a board but would like to be able to access your computer remotely, such as calling up your office system from home or while you are on the road to upload or download files and run programs, Wildcat! will work just fine for DOS users.

But you may prefer an even less elaborate program. Many Macintosh and DOS comm programs include a "host mode" or a "mini-BBS" feature, so be sure to check your comm program's manual. Such features let you call into your computer from a remote location. You can even opt to have your computer demand a password of any caller.

For a bit more power, but still keeping it simple, you may want to consider the DOS shareware program Megahost from Don Mankin. This shareware program gives you all the features you need for a multi-user BBS, but it is so tightly coded that you could run it from a floppy disk if you had to do so!

The Internet:
The Network of Networks

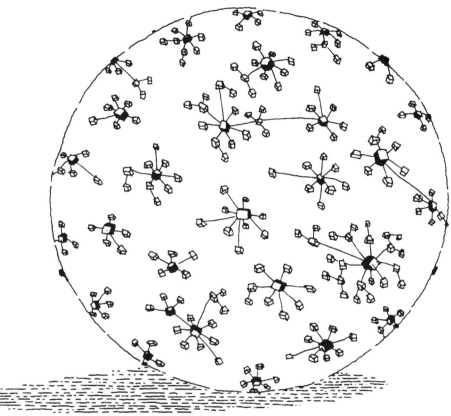

JUST THINK OF THE INTERNET AS THE GLOBAL NETWORK THAT LINKS THOUSANDS OF THESE OTHER NETWORKS TOGETHER. ANY QUESTIONS?

YEAH, ARE INTERNET MESSAGES SECURE? ALSO, WHO PAYS THE PHONE BILL? HEY, WHO'S THE SYSOP ANYWAY? AND WHAT IF I FLAME BORIS YELTSIN AND START WORLD WAR III, COULD I BE SUED? AND WHAT ABOUT....

According to a Louis Harris and Associates poll, as of April 4, 1994, only 33 percent of American adults had seen, heard, or read something about the "Information Superhighway." What the poll did not say was that those of us who have heard of it are sick to death of the metaphor. Consequently, there will be no cute references to potholes, on-ramps, or rest stops in this chapter.

Still, regardless of the form such an electronic highway eventually takes, its design will certainly be heavily influenced by what today is known as "the Internet." The Internet really is the "network of networks" in two senses. First, it really is a network that links together other networks. Second, as a result, its size and scope make it unquestionably the ultimate online network—a network to top all other networks.

If CompuServe, Prodigy, America Online, and the rest can be thought of as the Great Lakes, the Internet is the Atlantic Ocean. At this writing, for example, CompuServe reports 2.2 million users worldwide. The Internet, in contrast, has over 20 million users. As Peter Lewis pointed out in a *New York Times* column (April 5, 1994), that is roughly equivalent to the populations of New York City and Paris combined. And the number of Internet users is reportedly growing at a rate of 10 to 15 percent per month!

What's the Buzz?

For those of us who routinely stroll through the forests and fields of conventional information—magazines, newspapers, CNN, and National Public Radio—the Internet amounts to a commotion we hear off in the distance. It is persistent. It is there nearly every time we enter the park. It is ultimately irresistible. Eventually, seemingly on their own, our footsteps carry us in the direction of the noise.

What's the buzz? Tell me what's happening. Do I *need* to know about this? Do I *want* to know about this?

You will find the answers in this chapter. But, since you will also find "The Online Cookbook" section at the back of this book, you can probably guess the general answers to these questions.

Internet Essence

If you would understand the Internet, keep the "network of networks" image firmly in mind. Do not think of the Internet as you think of CompuServe or GEnie or AOL. It may be referred to as a single entity—*the* Internet—but it is actually anything but that.

If you've read the profiles of the five leading online services earlier in this book, you know that each of them is different. Each has different features, different files, different ways of doing things. Now imagine a single networking system that linked them all.

To tap into this imaginary system, you would dial a single phone number of a nearby host. Once logged onto your host system, you could move effortlessly from CompuServe to Prodigy to GEnie to Delphi to America Online and back. That's basically what the Internet is like. Except, instead of just five separate systems, the Internet links *thousands* of systems, and through them, *millions* of computers.

Only recently, with the end of the Cold War, has Internet access become widely and commercially available.

What we now call the Internet was born in 1969 as the ARPANET, the Advanced Research Projects Agency Network. The idea was to link together the computers at the Defense Department, research universities, and defense contractors. Although longtime members of the online community knew about ARPANET (and DARPANET, as it was later called), access was restricted. Only recently, with the end of the Cold War, has Internet access become widely and commercially available.

Physically, the Internet consists of the high-speed (56 Kbps to 45 Mbps) phone lines that connect the various computer systems and the networking software that facilitates those connections. The computer systems that are part of the network can range in size from Defense

Department supercomputers to university mainframes to a local area network (LAN) at a Fortune 1000 company to a single Macintosh or DOS machine sitting in the basement of an abandoned warehouse in South Bend, Indiana—or New Delhi, India, since the Internet is worldwide.

Anything Goes!

Think about this for just a minute: millions of computers, tens of millions of users, all over the world—the concept simply boggles the mind. If the Internet has 20 million users and only 1 percent of them upload a file or contribute a comment to an ongoing discussion group on any given day, that's 200,000 new files, comments, or pieces of information *each day!*

Is it any wonder that the answer to the question "What kinds of things can I find on the Internet?" is "Anything and everything you can possibly imagine!"?

There are computer graphics files of exquisite beauty and there are files of X-rated images. There is pornography. There is the world's greatest literature—Dante and Dickens keyboarded by volunteers, ready for you to download. There is sound, music, and video. In short, the computers connected to the Internet offer everything from the silly to the sublime, in just about any format you can imagine from plain text to graphics to music to computer software.

"You have to have a frontier mentality. If an orderly universe is important to you, you're not going to enjoy the Internet."

Network Control? Not! Absolutely anything goes. That's because no one owns or controls the network. There are customs. There is most definitely a network culture. There are associations and societies. But, ultimately, the only standards and rules are those that apply to hardware and software connections, not to content.

As John Makulowich, an Internet trainer, said in *Business Week* (March 28, 1994), "You have to have a frontier mentality. If an orderly universe is important to you, you're not going to enjoy the Internet."

That may be a slight overstatement. But it is a point to bear in mind. Certainly the Internet is constantly changing. I've looked for any number of files and newsgroups referenced in recently published books about the Internet only to find that they have disappeared. As on Prodigy, GEnie, and CompuServe, files come and files go. The only constant is constant change.

What Adventures You'll Have!

Years ago, I had the privilege of doing some consulting for Bell Labs. Over lunch, my client told me that she had had to fire her assistant for spending all her time reading Usenet newsgroup postings. "Oh, I said," having only a slight idea of what she was talking about, "I guess that can be a problem. Could you pass the salt?"

Now that I've been on the Internet myself and seen what newsgroups are all about, I really do understand. Newsgroups are simply fascinating. I can see how easily you might get hooked. Call it "infoaddiction" or anything you like, just so long as it's covered under health care reform, since it is a very real problem.

As you read this, people all over the world are expressing their most learned opinions and most lurid fantasies by posting messages to one of the 10,000 or more newsgroups on the Net. Others are uploading or downloading files, while still others are sending or receiving electronic mail. Some are engaged in real-time chat and still more people are playing online games. With apologies to Paul Simon, "It's all Happening on the Internet." (See Chapter 35 for more on newsgroups.)

What Should I Do?

Just for a moment, let me adopt the role of an uncle or elder brother. Through my books and articles published over the past 12 years I have probably put more people online than any other single individual. You should know that I really want you to try the Internet. I will give you all the tools and information you need to do so.

But I will also give you this piece of seasoned advice: The Internet really is the wild and woolly frontier. It is not DOS-based. It is not Macintosh-based. If anything, it is based on UNIX, a powerful operating system of obscure commands that has never been a commercial success. If the DOS command line gives you the willies—if you have never used CompuServe, GEnie, or Delphi without a graphical user interface—you're in *big* trouble if you plan to access the Internet.

Things are getting better. On America Online, for example, you can point and click your way through most Internet features. Still, if you want to use the Internet today, you will probably have to learn certain key commands—all of which you will find in "The Online Cookbook" section at the back of this book.

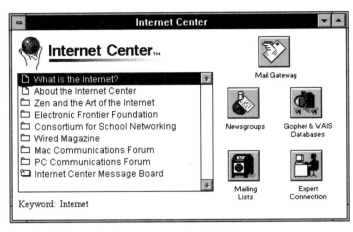

America Online makes Internet access "graphical."

Cost, of course, is another consideration. In many ways, the Internet is "your tax dollars at work," since it is still subsidized by the federal government. If you work for a company, a university, or a government agency with an Internet connection, you can probably arrange to gain access for free. If that is not your situation, there are other ways to plug in at a reasonable hourly charge.

My point is simply this: The Internet is wonderful. It is everything you have heard about and more. But it is *not* the place for brand-new computer owners or brand-new online communicators to test their wings. Learn to sail on a lake before you test your mettle against the ocean.

Start with AOL or Prodigy—or CompuServe, GEnie, or Delphi. Think of it as learning to ride a bicycle with training wheels. Get a *feel* for the online world. Get comfortable with your communications software.

Then you'll be ready to venture into the Internet. Every now and then, the waves will slap you back—as they slap *me* back when I make some misstep, like forgetting that on the Internet upper and lower case *matters* when keying in file names and directories! But you will have built up the experience and the confidence to see it through.

As an added benefit, you will find that there is a tremendous amount of helpful Internet-related information on the main consumer online services. Every one of them has a telecommunications or Internet Special Interest Group that you can use to ask questions or to obtain helpful files about the Internet.

Internet Access

This leads quite naturally to the next point: how to get Internet access. If you cannot gain access through your employer, the best option at this writing is to get an account on Delphi.

Right now, the other consumer online services offer Internet electronic mail and possibly one or two other features. But as you read this, the situation may have changed. You may find that AOL and CompuServe offer *full* Internet access. The particular service doesn't really matter, assuming their prices are roughly equivalent.

The fact is that unless you want to pay hundreds of dollars or more a month to become an Internet site yourself—not to mention putting up with hardware and software nightmares—the quickest and easiest way to gain full access to the Internet is by subscribing to Delphi, or to one of the other online services, once they make full Internet access available.

Respecting Your Elders

It is impossible to overemphasize the importance of "network culture" when discussing the Internet. The culture—"the way we do things here"—has been developing for more than 20 years. No one can keep you off the Net, but a given group can sure as heck "shun" you, ignoring your comments and contributions and transforming you into a "nonperson."

So watch yourself. Longtime Internet users see the network as *their* territory. You are welcome—even encouraged—to participate. But do so respectfully, as if you were a new senator or congressman who wouldn't dream of making a maiden speech on the floor until you had been around awhile.

It doesn't matter how smart you are. You are *not* their equal, not until you have paid your dues and earned your place in their online society. In short, you can take the people out of the drawing room and put them online, but you cannot take the drawing room out of people. Politeness, courtesy, and respect for those more experienced than yourself count as much on the Internet as they did in any nineteenth-century novel.

The Components of the Internet

Now let's get to the details. What, exactly, can you *do* on the Internet?

The answer is relatively simple: You can do anything on the Internet that you can do on any of the online services. That means searching for and downloading files, be they programs or text. It means participating in discussions, as you might do on a SIG message board. It means engaging in CB radio-style real-time chat or playing real-time games. Of course, it also means sending and receiving electronic mail.

Though not completely accurate, it is not too far off the mark to say the Internet is like CompuServe taken to a much higher power. On both systems, there are nooks and crannies galore, and hardly a day goes by without the announcement of some new feature or variation. But, in the end, the Internet boils down to about six major functions: electronic mail, newsgroups, mailing lists, files, real-time chat, and "Telnet" access to a remote computer.

Overlaid on top of these core functions are utility programs, like Gopher, Archie, Veronica, and the World Wide Web (WWW), that are designed to help you *locate* information and *use* the core features.

The Six Main Functions

Let's look now at the basic outlines of the six main Internet functions. I will save the utilities like Gopher and Archie for "The Online Cookbook" section at the back of this book.

1. Internet e-mail

Everyone with an account on any system connected to the Internet automatically has an Internet e-mail address. Subscribers to Compu-

Serve, GEnie, MCI Mail, AOL, and many other services can exchange mail with friends on different systems or on Internet-connected systems. All that is required is the correct Internet address, like Alfred@Delphi.com, my address on Delphi. "The Online Cookbook" section at the back of this book shows you the address format required by each service.

2. Usenet newsgroups

These are essentially ongoing conferences devoted to a specific topic. There are no membership requirements. Anyone who can read a newsgroup's messages is free to add comments to a given message thread. (In fact, though it is not advisable for new users, anyone can start a newsgroup on any topic.)

The main drawback is that at any given time, a newsgroup will be able to show you only a limited number of messages. Previous messages will have "scrolled off" the board, unless some user has taken the time to collect previous messages into an archive file somewhere.

3. Mailing lists

Mailing lists are similar to newsgroups, but they are far less interactive. The items uploaded to a list are more likely to be articles and longer pieces rather than the short comments that typify newsgroups. Also, while you must key in a command or two to read the latest newsgroup messages, the material sent to mailing list members automatically arrives in their electronic mailboxes.

4. Files

The uploading, downloading, and transfer of files is probably closer to the heart of the Internet than any other function. The files in question could be anything from a piece of music to a graphical image to the full text of a Supreme Court decision. The main Internet technique for locating and downloading files is called "FTP" (File Transfer Protocol).

Basically, you "FTP" to some system, use the DIR command to see what's there, and then use the GET command to tell the Internet to transfer the file to your computer (or to your "workspace" if you are accessing the Internet through Delphi).

5. IRC or Internet Relay Chat

This is the Internet version of the real-time chat features offered by each of the main online services. Like those real-time chat features, IRC resembles text-based CB radio conversations. And the content is just about as meaningful.

6. Telnet

This function allows you to access certain areas of a remote computer system as if you were actually sitting at the keyboard of one of its consoles. Accessing library card catalogues and Campus Wide Information Systems (CWIS) are good examples of the use of this feature.

Conclusion

You now know more about the Internet and the Information Superhighway (as it exists today) than 90 percent of the American people. By all means, see "The Online Cookbook" section at the back of this book for hands-on instructions on tapping Internet resources. But please start with one of the online services. Get your feet wet in the Great Lakes before striding out into the ocean!

Other Online Services

25

*As of 1994, there were over 822 online services avail-
able to anyone with a computer, a modem, and a telephone. (A fat bank account wouldn't hurt, either, since
some such services are quite expensive, indeed.) Or, to
put it another way, "There are a million stories in the
Naked City . . ."*

A book of this sort can't possibly do justice—let alone even mention—them all. The services cited here, however, are worthy of your
consideration, for at least two reasons. First, while I would not recommend them to everyone, they are broad-based enough to be of interest
to large numbers of online users. Second, while they are reasonably
inclusive, they also tend to be highly focused.

Thus, if you are dissatisfied with the depth of investment information offered on, say, AOL, and are willing to pay the freight, you will
definitely find what you need on Dow Jones. And if you want to know
more about industrial-strength online information, you will definitely
want to send for information from Dialog, BRS, and the like.

BIX: The *BYTE* Information Exchange

Never has an online service been more aptly named. Although it was
created by McGraw-Hill in November 1985, it is now owned by Rupert
Murdoch's The News Corporation, the same company that owns Delphi
Internet Services (as well as *TV Guide,* HarperCollins Publishers, the
Fox television network, and many other properties).

It has been said that on CompuServe you will find the computer
gurus and masters of various leading software packages, but on
BIX you will find the programmer who *created* those packages. In
short, you'll find exactly the type of person who regularly reads *BYTE*
magazine.

BIX is organized into conferences that are a lot like the standard SIG model. You will find a few conferences devoted to topics like parenting, automobiles, hobbies, and "On and About New England." But most conferences focus on topics like UNIX on the Amiga; digital music; any operating system ever created; animation; LANs; protocols; Sun workstations; the Micro Channel Developer's Association; and any programming language you'd care to name, from Ada to COBOL to Smalltalk.

Resources

BIX
800-695-4775 (voice)
bix@genvid.com (e-mail)

BRS: Bibliographic Retrieval System

BRS is one of the original major-league online information services. Unfortunately, either through lack of vision or lack of luck, it has never really fulfilled its potential. Things appeared to be looking up for the service in December 1988, when the late Robert Maxwell's Pergamon organization bought both BRS and Orbit. But with Mr. Maxwell's death, the service was thrown into a limbo from which it is only now emerging.

Things are almost certain to shake out since BRS offers such an excellent collection of databases—particularly if you are a medical doctor or health care professional. Among other things, you will find the full text of such books as *The Merck Manual*, *MacBryd's Signs and Symptoms*, and *Holland and Brew's Manual of Obstetrics.* The full text of most leading medical journals also can be found here, from *Age and Aging* to *Plastic and Reconstructive Surgery.* Education, social science, oncology, AIDS, and pharmacology— there are multiple databases in each of these areas, plus *Books in Print*, the *Readers' Guide to Periodical Literature*, the *Wilson Art Index*, and much more.

Resources

BRS
CD Plus Technologies
800-950-2035

If BRS is of interest to you, be sure to ask about the BRS Colleague service for medical professionals and BRS AfterDark, a lower-cost, off-hours service that gives you access to many BRS databases.

Dialog: The World's Premier Electronic Information Service

Dialog was created, and for many years led, by Dr. Roger K. Summit as part of an in-house research project at the Lockheed Missiles and Space Company in 1963. The research resulted in the world's first interactive information retrieval system, which was put to good use in 1969, when it was applied to more than half a million documents generated by the space program. Lockheed called the system RECON (Remote Console Information Retrieval Service) and the command language used to run it, "Dialog."

Since that time, Dialog has grown to become the world's leading electronic information service. It was acquired by newspaper giant Knight-Ridder in 1988, which has continued Roger Summit's original goal of providing effective access "to civilization's recorded knowledge."

I urge you to do two things if you are seriously interested in major-league information. First, call Dialog and request a database catalogue and information packet.

> **Resources**
>
> *Dialog Information Services, Inc.*
> 800-334-2564

Second, if you are a CompuServe subscriber, some evening after 6 P.M. your local time, key in `go ki` to reach Dialog's Knowledge Index system. "KI" gives you menu-driven access to over 125 of Dialog's nearly 500 databases for a very low after-hours price. (GEnie subscribers can reach Dialog itself by simply keying in `dialog`, but I urge you *not* to do so until you have received the Dialog information packet.)

If you like what you see, do a third thing. See my book *How to Look It Up Online* for easy, hands-on instructions designed to let anyone effectively search Dialog (and many other major-league services).

DJN/R: Dow Jones News/Retrieval

I *love* Dow Jones News/Retrieval. The service became available to the personal computer-using public in 1980, and for awhile, it was positioned to compete directly with CompuServe and The Source as an online service for the home, offering something of interest to the entire family.

It has changed marketing direction many times since. But it has also grown tremendously and added lots of features that are simply mouthwatering to those of us who are information addicts. Despite all that, some 14 years after it began, DJN/R has yet to enter the 1990s. Its text-based user interface is just about the worst of any large online service. Even the menus it does offer are substandard.

And its new, March 1994 pricing policy of charging $1.50 ($2 in Canada) for every 1,000 characters displayed couldn't be more retrograde. One thousand characters, including spaces and carriage returns, is only about 150 words, or just about the text found in the three paragraphs ending here.

Resources

Dow Jones News/Retrieval
609-520-4000

Information to Die For

Forget the fact that DJN/R's financial information is the best in the business. Indeed, leave all the investment stuff aside. DJN/R *still* offers tons of things that the average online user or small-business owner would love to have, starting with the ability to search and retrieve the full text of the *Wall Street Journal* and continuing through transcripts of the TV programs *Charlie Rose* and *Talking with David Frost*. It also offers the full text of *Forbes*, *Time*, and the many local newspapers covered by the DataTimes database.

DJN/R offers tons of things that the average online user or small-business owner would love to have.

And I haven't even told you about DowQuest, the incredible, artificial-intelligence-based search engine from Thinking Machines that lets you enter your searches as plain English sentences. Nor have I mentioned //CLIP, the newsclipping service that automatically looks for instances of names, companies, or whatever else you specify and puts the relevant articles or newswire pieces into your online mailbox.

Your Best Bets In short, DJN/R is not easy to use. It is anything but cheap. But it has dozens of absolutely wonderful things to offer. That's why I suggest that you first send for a free information kit.

If you like what you see, opt for the $29.95 start-up offer that includes three free hours of usage, plus your annual membership fee ($19.95). Be sure to ask for a copy of the TextSearch Plus software package to help you use DJN/R's incredible text databases. In fact, you might want to wait until you have that program before using up your three free hours.

Finally, if you want to use DJN/R for investment information, I strongly recommend doing so with a Dow Jones program like Market Manager, Market Analyzer, Spreadsheet Link, or other products. These programs can save you money by automatically going into the service, retrieving the stock quotes or other information you need, and signing off.

NewsNet: The Best-Kept Secret

NewsNet, the Bryn Mawr-based electronic purveyor of industry and professional newsletters is simply too good a resource to share with anyone but your closest friends and allies. You'd have to be out of your mind to tell a competitor about it.

The newsletters offered on NewsNet are the type whose print editions normally carry subscription prices of $100 to $500 or more a year. They offer current, high-quality, highly concentrated expert information. And, by virtue of being on NewsNet, they are available within *minutes* of leaving their creators' word processing programs.

NewsNet is simply too good a resource to share with anyone but your closest friends and allies.

NewsNet can cost several dollars a minute to use, depending on the newsletter you are reading. But if you are familiar with the kind of information you will find in newsletters of this sort, you know that it's worth it—particularly since you can search all at once through every issue of a single newsletter, or an entire group of newsletters, for a certain person, company, or topic of interest.

Resources

NewsNet
800-952-0122

Nexis

I have to admit I was thrilled during the 1992 presidential campaign to hear Ross Perot suggesting that reporters fire up their computers and do a "Nexis search." I doubt that most of his listeners had any idea of what he was saying, but I know the reporters did. At long last, this service from Mead Data Central (a division of the famous paper company) has come into its own.

As I write this, however, Mead has announced that its Nexis/Lexis service is for sale. (Lexis is the legal information service that competes with WestLaw.) The company apparently wants to concentrate on forest products and papermaking. The database operations accounted for only 12 percent of Mead's operations anyhow.

Resources

Nexis
Mead Data Central
800-227-9597

Certainly, someone will purchase these assets. After all, Nexis is the sole source of the full text of the *New York Times,* plus all kinds of other goodies. Indeed, the keyword that best applies to the Nexis service is "full text." For many years, while most comparable services offered only bibliographical citations and possibly brief article abstracts, Nexis was alone in offering the complete, full text of a given article or item.

Orbit Online Service

Orbit, like BRS, was caught up in the late Robert Maxwell's acquisition plans regarding online services. And, like BRS, it too has been spun off since Mr. Maxwell's death. The company is now owned by Questel.

As with BRS, the high quality of information Orbit offers has not changed. But, if BRS can be said to specialize in databases of interest to the medical community, Orbit has always had a special orientation toward patent and trademark databases and databases of interest to the scientific and technical communities.

Resources

Orbit Online Service
Questel
800-456-7248

It is impossible to know what the future will bring, but if these areas are of interest to you, you should probably give Orbit a call and request an information packet.

Services to Watch For

Only Rip Van Winkle could be unaware of the frenetic activity the online world has been treated to since mid-1993 or so—mergers, acquisitions, and rumors of same; communications and entertainment company giants wrestling with each other to stake their claims; and of course, everywhere, talk of the "Information" super-you-know-what.

In the meantime, Ziff-Davis, Apple Computer, and AT&T have entered the fray in very real ways. And Microsoft Corporation is rumored to be not far behind. Only time will tell whether these and other new services become services to watch, as opposed to merely watch for. But here's a quick summary of the majors at this writing.

Ziff-Davis's Interchange Online Network (ION)

At this writing, "Interchange Online Network" is the working name of a service scheduled to appear soon from Ziff-Davis. The press kit I've seen is quite impressive. But most of all, I'm impressed by the fact that "ION" is coming from Ziff-Davis, publisher of *PC Magazine*, *PC Week*, *MacUser*, *Computer Shopper*, and many other leading publications—as well as the creator of the present ZiffNet online system.

Resources

Interchange
Ziff-Davis Interactive
617-252-5000

It isn't quite clear yet, however, that even Ziff-Davis itself is sure what the service will offer. But two things seem certain. First, the company will take full advantage of its print-based assets, making its magazines and newsletters available for searching online. Second, savvy company that it is, Ziff-Davis will go GUI with the interface, as the figure "Interchange" shows.

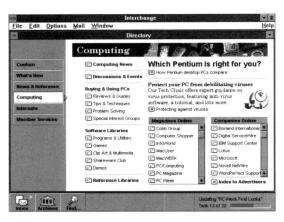

Ziff-Davis's Interchange.

Apple's eWorld

Introduced in late June 1994, Apple Computer's eWorld service is colorful, graphical, and, for the time being at least, available to Macintosh users only. Using the increasingly popular metaphor of a graphical "town," the eWorld opening screen depicts buildings offering different services. Click on a building like the town library, for example, and you are instantly transported to Grolier's *Electronic Encyclopedia.* You get to your e-mail via the post office building, of course. And so on.

Resources

eWorld
Apple Computer
800-775-4556

The subscription cost is $8.95 a month, and that includes two non-business connect-time hours. After that, the cost is $7.95 an hour during business hours and $4.95 an hour during evenings and weekends.

AT&T's PersonaLink Services and General Magic's Telescript

For all the obvious reasons, AT&T has long wanted to get into the online services business. The company took its first real step in doing so when it acquired the EasyLink system from a troubled Western Union Corporation several years ago. AT&T also has extensive experience offering e-mail services to companies.

Early in 1994, AT&T announced that it plans to introduce PersonaLink Services as the foundation for an electronic community. The notion seems to be that PersonaLink could be used to access an online service. But initial plans call for it to offer mainly a pipeline and means of access to users of hand-held personal assistants, with conventional modem access becoming available later.

I'm hoping to be pleasantly surprised. But right now, the most remarkable thing about the plans for PersonaLink is its use of Telescript, a product of General Magic, an alliance that includes firms like Sony, Phillips, and Motorola. The key concept in Telescript is the use of intelligent software "agents" you can launch into the networks to go get the information you want. This may be more power than most people can absorb, but it should be fun to watch.

Resources

PersonaLink Services
AT&T
800-936-5465

General Magic
415-965-0400

four

E-Mail Basics

26

I've long been convinced that anything human beings can conceive, can indeed be accomplished. Look at the Martian death rays in War of the Worlds, *a book published in 1898, more than half a century before the invention of the laser.*

Electronic mail or "e-mail" fulfills an even older dream—that of instant, any-time communication with anyone on the planet. The ancient gods had their winged messenger, Mercury. We today have MCI Mail. And, frankly, though Mercury may have worn shoes that were the Air Jordans of his time, I'd put my money on MCI, CompuServe, Prodigy, America Online, GEnie, Delphi, and the Internet any day.

The E-Mail Concept

Suppose you want to send a letter to your daughter who's spending her junior year abroad studying in Japan. Let's assume that you're one of the people whose hard work feeds the rest of us. Let's assume you raise corn in Indiana.

Okay, it's seven in the evening, and you've just finished supper. You sit down at your Macintosh, load your word processor, and key in a chatty, newsy letter to your daughter. You save it to disk as pure ASCII text. Then you fire up your comm program and tell it to dial the CompuServe packet-switching network node in Indianapolis.

You log on, key in `go mail`, tell your comm program to upload your letter, and, when prompted for "TO:" you key in your daughter's CompuServe account number, which also serves as her e-mail address on the service. You sign off, and shut your computer down for the day.

Time-wise, Tokyo is 14 hours ahead of Indianapolis. So while you're sound asleep at one in the morning, your daughter is taking an afternoon break at 3 P.M. She boots up the cute little Compaq

E-Mail Factoid

The Electronic Messaging Association (EMA) estimates that the number of people sending and receiving e-mail will grow by 50 percent in 1994, to a total of around 60 million people. The majority of those e-mailers will be using internal corporate systems, but it's a short step from sending e-mail to your boss on the 14th floor to sending it to a co-worker in Bombay, India via the Internet or some other world-girdling network. In fact, it's really no step at all.

The EMA is a trade organization that seems to list every e-mail provider among its members. It doesn't offer much a private individual can use, but if you're charged with implementing or improving e-mail operations at your company, the EMA can be a wonderful resource.

Resources

EMA
703-524-5550

Contura you got her for Christmas and logs on to CompuServe by dialing the local CompuServe node number in Tokyo.

She sees the CompuServe notification, "You have electronic mail waiting," as soon as she signs on, and her heart skips a beat. Or maybe not. But we all like to get mail, even if it's from Mom and Dad and not from a special friend doing his junior year abroad in Vienna.

By keying in `go mail` and selecting "1. Read mail" from the resulting menu, your daughter can read the letter you wrote. She can then key in a reply or sign on again later to "message" you back.

And the Cost?

E-mail can deliver a document anywhere in the world, instantly, for far, far less than Emory, AirBorne, UPS, or Federal Express. And as for comparing it to an international phone call, not only is e-mail a lot cheaper, you don't have to worry about time differences. You transmit at a time that's convenient to you, and your correspondent picks up at a time convenient to her. And vice versa, of course.

So just how much did this Indianapolis-to-Tokyo message cost?

Delivering the Mail

The hows and whys of electronic mail don't really matter. But it's worth knowing that there are at least two ways of delivering the mail. The most common is the "store-and-forward" system. You call CompuServe in Dublin, Ohio and leave a message for your daughter. CompuServe stores the message until she calls to pick it up. Packet-switching networks make the calls affordable. Whether it's CompuServe or AOL or some other service, the store-and-forward technique revolves around the central hub of the main computer.

Messages sent via the Internet, in contrast, actually travel to the location you specify as part of the address the moment you send them. The computer at that location then stores the message until your correspondent picks it up.

It's hard to know precisely, but I'd be very surprised if it cost much more than 20 cents—for everything:

- Your local call to Indianapolis was free.
- The basic CompuServe subscription entitles you to send a certain amount of e-mail at no cost, so there's no charge there.
- Your daughter made a local call in Tokyo, which I'm going to assume cost her nothing. And her connect time to CompuServe itself, reading mail, is covered by her membership fee.

The only cost is in the $12 per *hour* CompuServe charges for using the CompuServe packet-switching network from Japan. That's 20 cents a minute.

At 9600 bps, only about five seconds are required to display the equivalent of two double spaced pages of text. Your letter may be double or triple this length, and it's not going to have much impact on the cost. Your daughter could still sign on, pick up your letter, and sign off in a minute, without rushing.

It's true that I have not included the cost of two CompuServe subscriptions, yours and your daughter's. And it's true that all kinds of other variables could throw off this estimate. But folks, we're dealing with pennies here. Suppose the actual cost is closer to $1 or $2? It's still chump change when you consider that you are in effect sending a long, chatty message halfway around the world—instantly—at any time of day or night. No postage. No stickers. No slow boats to Japan. No long-distance phone call charges.

The Internet Connection

It's just possible that you can cut your international correspondence costs in half, thanks to the Internet.

The Internet began as a government-subsidized means of linking defense contractors, the Pentagon, and the scientists at colleges and universities in a communications network. Consequently, most college students, whether in the U.S. or abroad, can get an Internet connection and mailbox for *free*.

Assume that your daughter in Tokyo can get an Internet address through her Japanese university at no charge. If the two of you want to correspond via CompuServe, your cost will be $8.95 per month for your CompuServe subscription, as usual.

Sending mail to her Internet address will cost you nothing. But CompuServe charges 15 cents to *receive* the first 7,500 characters of mail from the Internet. That's about four double-spaced typed pages. After that, CompuServe charges five cents per 2,500 characters.

Other services offer similar deals. Your best bet? Pick the domestic service you want to use for other reasons. Then contact customer service or consult "The Online Cookbook" at the back of this book to figure out how to use it to correspond with your progeny, friends, relatives, etc. Although most of the leading consumer services have been slow to offer full Internet access, all of them offer a mail connection to the Internet.

The Best Services to Choose CompuServe certainly isn't the only service that can make it possible for you to quickly and cheaply correspond with someone in Japan—or Africa, Australia, or anyplace else on the globe. If international e-mail is your primary interest, I suggest you consider three services: MCI Mail, GEnie, and CompuServe. These three services operate their own national and international packet-switching networks, with access numbers in most major cities. Other services can be accessed using SprintNet, Tymnet, and other IRCs (International Record Carriers), but it's simply not as convenient, or as cheap.

> **If international e-mail is your primary interest, I suggest you consider three services: MCI Mail, GEnie, and CompuServe.**

Quick-Start Guide to E-Mail

I have done my best here to make this complicated. After all, like lawyers, doctors, and CPAs, we computer writers have a vested interest in making everything seem as convoluted as possible. If it were simple, why would you need us?

Unfortunately for my profession, however, e-mail really is simple. Once you've got the concept, it's just a matter of seeing how that concept is applied on various services. But here are a few pointers you won't find covered in most manuals:

1. Do your writing offline.

The absolute best way to send mail is to prepare your letter with your favorite word processing program *before* you go online. Don't waste your time trying to master the clunky, old, "line-oriented" text editing programs some services offer for composing mail online.

2. Set your margins for 0 and 65.

In other words, do not set your left margin at 10 or otherwise indent your entire text. And do not set your right margin at 80, even though everyone's screen can display 80 characters.

3. Use upper and lower case.

Don't ever send a message using all capital letters. Full caps are hard to read, and in the online world using them for anything is considered SHOUTING.

4. Keep it short!

When you're writing to a relative or good friend, go as long as you want. But when writing to a business associate or acquaintance, think in terms of leaving a phone message. Like, "Hi, John. Here are the figures you asked for. Call me or message me if there are any questions. I'll be in Denver on Friday, but will be checking my mailbox over the weekend. Here are the nums ..."

5. Don't ever just dump text files into someone's mailbox.

If you have a lengthy file you think someone should see, send a quick message asking permission to send that file. You won't get into trouble if you follow this simple rule: Treat your correspondent's electronic mailbox as an extension of his or her home, and behave accordingly.

6. Be careful!

Remember that e-mail letters can easily be copied, forwarded, collected, and transmitted to other services. Therefore you may want to be cautious about what you write since it could one day appear elsewhere.

7. Use only pure ASCII text.

When you tell your word processing program to save your letter to disk, make absolutely certain that the file is saved as plain, pure, unformatted, non-document mode ASCII text! If you don't, the italics you use in WordPerfect or the boldface you use in Word will show up as garbage on your correspondent's screen. Most word processing programs today have a "text only" option, but it is not their default. So you will have to tell them to use that option.

If your word processor does not have this feature, get a shareware text editor program and use it to prepare e-mail messages. (Text editors do not insert the strange formatting codes used by many word processing programs.)

Sending and Receiving

Let's assume that you've written your letter and saved it to disk as a plain ASCII text file. Now you're ready to send it. If you're using Prodigy or AOL, you'll find that their software includes an option for transmitting a text file from disk, so what I'm about to say does not apply to you.

But, regardless of your service, make sure you have the e-mail address of your correspondent handy. Then sign on and get to your service's mail feature.

Don't "Upload"

Now for the trick most new users miss: specifically, *don't* pick the mail system's "upload" option, even though you will be uploading your text file from disk. Things will go much faster, and your correspondent will be much happier, if you instead select whatever option the online service offers to make it possible for you to *compose* mail online.

This will put you into the service's text editor. Then use your comm program to transmit your ASCII text file to the service. The service's text editor, if it thinks about you at all, will simply assume that you're a very fast typist.

When your own computer has transmitted the last line, key in whatever command the online service's text editor requires to tell it that you're done. It will be a slash or "/ex" for exit or some such command.

Finishing Up

Online services differ as to when they ask you for the address of your correspondent, the subject line you want to use, and so on. Some do it before you enter the message, some after. But they'll all finish with a prompt saying, "Is everything okay? Shall I send the letter now?"

Answer "yes," and your letter is "on its way." Two points here, though. First, the letter may not be available to your correspondent immediately. The online service may "post" new messages to recipient mailboxes in batches every five or ten minutes. Second, once a letter has been sent, for all practical purposes, it cannot be recalled.

And You Shall Receive ...

Receiving mail is the easiest step of all. When you sign on and see you have mail waiting, open your comm program's capture buffer or otherwise do what you must to save incoming mail to disk. Then get the online service to show you your mail. Since you are capturing it to disk, you can print it out later, after you are offline.

All e-mail systems have an option to let you reply to the message you've just read. And, in general, I recommend taking advantage of it. It's just much easier to key in `reply` or `answer` and dash off a few lines on the spot than it is to sign off the service, print out the letters, compose replies to each, sign back on, and transmit the replies.

If your reply must be carefully worded or if it requires you to do some research, of course you will want to compose it offline. In which case, reply to the letter with something like, "Got your message. Let me look into it and get back to you." That way the sender will know that you did indeed receive his or her letter.

One other tip regarding replies: An e-mail exchange is very much like a conversation. The difference is that you can't always assume that the person you're replying to will remember exactly what topic or question you are responding to. That's why it's always a good idea to recap the original question before you respond. Instead of saying "Turn it twice to the right," say "In regard to your question about the proper adjustment of the eyebolt on the Framus 7, turn it twice to the right."

Conclusion

See? I told you e-mail was essentially simple. Each online service has its own way of doing things. And each comm program or front-end program has its own commands. But the *concepts* are the same, and now that you've got them, you've got everything you need to outpace Mercury sending messages around the world.

But, of course, there's more. You really and truly don't need to know anything that's not in this chapter to use e-mail on any online service with confidence. But, should e-mail become a part of your private and professional life, you'll be glad to know about the little time-saving "extras" discussed in the next chapter.

Fax and Advanced E-Mail Techniques

27

Plain old e-mail can be a powerful tool all by itself. Heck, just learning the basic techniques presented in Chapter 26 will put you miles ahead of the vast majority of people and make you seem like a real e-mail expert.

But once you get into it, you'll begin to say things like, "Hey, wait a minute. It's a pain to have to look up and key in Sue's number every time I want to message her online. And I'm not too crazy about keying in ten separate e-mail addresses at the "cc:" prompt whenever I want to make sure everyone in Marketing gets my memo. There's got to be a better way!"

There is, of course. Actually, there are lots of better ways. And that's what I'll show you in this chapter. One brief word of warning, though: You will appreciate this chapter more *after* you've had some experience with your favorite service's e-mail feature.

Not that the stuff you'll find here is difficult, it's just that it will make more sense to you once you've actually used an e-mail system. If you have yet to do so, concentrate on the general concepts here. Then check your favorite online service, the instructions for the software you use to access it, and "The Online Cookbook" section at the back of this book for specifics.

Personal Phone Books and Mailing Lists

Many e-mail systems give you a "phone book" feature that lets you key in a person's name and e-mail address once. From then on, you can respond to the "TO:" prompt with "John" or "Sue" or whatever, instead of the person's full e-mail address on that system. This is an incredible timesaver and well worth looking into and exploiting.

Similarly, it is usually possible on an e-mail system to send the same letter to many people with a single command. The key lies in creating a mailing list on the system. Once you have given the list a name and keyed in the e-mail addresses of all people on the list, you can use the list name as your address. Thus if you had a list called "Sales," you

Member Directories Online

Since communication is what the online world is all about, it's not surprising that many online services have taken steps to make it easy for one member to locate the e-mail address of another. Generally, there are three places to look when you want to find out how to e-mail a particular person:

1. The main member directory

This feature lets you search for members and add your own name to the database. Entries typically include your e-mail address, your geographical location, and whatever interests you choose to specify. You can search the database on any of these items.

2. Special Interest Groups (SIGs)

Every Forum on CompuServe, for example, has its own membership directory. This operates just like the main directory, but the two do not exchange information. A member who wants to be listed in a given Forum's database must take steps to do so.

3. The "Whois" command in Chat

The command may differ from one service to another, but all services offering real-time, CB radio-style chat have a command that tells you more about someone whose "handle" you see on the screen. America Online does this best, since at any time you can click on someone's handle and be presented with a brief bio. Nothing will appear, though, if the person has not taken action to see that his or her biography or profile is added to the database.

All such directories are *voluntary*. So there is no guarantee that you will be able to find someone in particular. If you don't take steps to tell the service to add your name, location, e-mail address, and interests to the database, you will not appear in the directory. Simply subscribing to a given service does not automatically put you into its member directory.

could simply specify "Sales" as the address to receive your message and everyone on the list would automatically get a copy. Again, some time and effort will be required to set up this feature, but the convenience in months and years to come is likely to be worth it.

Simplicity and Binaries

Like everything else about computers, e-mail systems have been continuously evolving over time. It used to be that sending a file to someone via a consumer online service was a royal pain in the modem.

Fortunately, most e-mail systems now make this simple. That means two things.

First, the e-mail system simplifies your life if you find that you are constantly sending the same file to different people. It could be a price list, a corporate backgrounder, information about the club for which you are the membership chairman, or whatever.

Instead of transmitting this "boilerplate" file from your own personal computer each time it must be sent, you may be able to store a copy on your favorite online service and simply tell the service to send that file to the e-mail address you specify. If this feature is of interest to you, among the main consumer-oriented services, CompuServe offers the best implementation. And these days, thanks to the Internet, you can send mail to all major online services.

Stop Me Before I Upload Again . . .

Sorry folks, I just can't help myself. This is really cool. Remember how I spoke of messaging your daughter in Tokyo in the last chapter? Well, suppose you wanted to send her more than just a chatty letter. Suppose you wanted to send her a picture of her four-year-old brother, a sound file of him saying "Hi, happy birthday, Mary," plus a letter from you and your wife?

If you have a PC, you'll need two things you probably do not yet have. You'll need a Sound-Blaster (or compatible) sound board and either a digital camera or a friend with a good digital "scanner." Use the camera to take your picture and record it on disk as a file. Or take a conventional photograph to your scanner-owning friend.

Use the SoundBlaster's microphone jack and a microphone to record the child's birthday greeting and save it as a file. Prepare your letter and save it, too, as a file.

You've now got three files (image, sound, and text), and you can pack them all into a single compressed archive using a program like PKZIP. Send the archive file to your daughter as a binary file via CompuServe's e-mail system. (The techniques and concepts are the same for Mac users, though the hardware and software differs.)

When she downloads it, she can unpack it with PKUNZIP, read your text file with her word processor, listen to the sound file on a desktop system equipped with a SoundBlaster, and view the picture with a graphics viewer program. I know it's not simple. But it's cheap!

The cost of sending this "multimedia" file, which will be about 200K in size, to Tokyo will be about 75 cents. A voice call to Tokyo, in contrast, is likely to cost you around $3 for the first minute and about a dollar for each additional minute. And, of course, with a 14-hour time difference, a voice call may not be easy to arrange.

Second, the "file send/receive" feature means you can exchange *binary* files with your correspondents. That means you can send programs and sound files (.WAV, .SND, .SEA, .SIT, etc.) and graphic image files (.GIF, .TIF, .PCX, .JPG, etc.) as easily as you send a text message. In fact, you can usually enter a text message like "Hey, Joanie, take a look at these neat images I just modified with Photostyler. Tell me what you think." and then "attach" a binary file. Your recipient will see the text message and be prompted to download (or skip) the attached file.

Once text, sound, or graphic or video images are transformed into computer files, all kinds of wonderful things can be done with them.

But, you know what else? You can also send and receive *compressed* files. You'll learn how easy it is to work with compressed files in Chapter 41. For now, all you need to know is that with freely available compression programs, you can reduce the size of a given file by as much as 50 percent. That means it can be transmitted in about half the time. Your recipient downloads the file and then decompresses it with the same compression program once he or she is offline.

Fax, Paper, and "Exotic" Options

Even if you are a brand-new computer user, let alone a new online communicator, you may be getting a sense by now of the "magic" of digitization—specifically, that once text, sound, or graphic or video images are transformed into computer files, all kinds of wonderful things can be done with them.

Consider MCI Mail, a service that most people agree is the leader in the e-mail field. When you prepare a letter on your word processor and transmit it to MCI Mail, there are quite a few ways you can have that letter delivered:

1. As plain e-mail, of course.
Your correspondents can include any one of the 20 million or so people worldwide with an Internet address. That includes most of the world's college students and every subscriber to every consumer-oriented online service, since they all handle Internet mail.

2. To any of the 2 million telex or TWX machines in the world.

Telex machines are plugged into the old telegraph network. It's slow and it's limited in capabilities, but it's still the lowest common denominator worldwide. Places so primitive that they don't even have telephones often *do* have telex service. (TWX, or "twix," machines are basically faster versions of telex machines.)

3. To any fax machine anywhere in the world.

MCI Mail will perform the conversion from text file to fax image and transmit wherever you say. And it will keep trying, should the fax line be busy. A confirmation of delivery will appear in your MCI Mail mailbox.

4. As paper printouts.

If your recipient does not have an e-mail account, you can have the service print a copy of your letter and send it via regular mail or overnight delivery. On MCI Mail, the printouts are done by laser printers on 25-pound bond paper, at the location nearest the addressee.

For about $35 a year you can opt to keep a black-and-white image of your company's letterhead and your personal signature on file. You can tell MCI Mail to use your letterhead and signature in any message you want to have printed and delivered as "paper mail."

Other online services and e-mail services offer similar features. AT&T's EasyLink service even offers text-to-speech capability. If one of your message recipients doesn't have a computer or does not have easy access to one, you can use EasyLink to convert your ASCII text to speech and make it possible for the person to call in and pick up your message, just as if it had been recorded on an answering machine.

Resources

MCI Mail
800-444-6245

AT&T's EasyLink
800-242-6005, Dept. 4950

Fax from Your Computer

At the back of this book you'll find a coupon good for 10 percent off any Zoom Telephonics modem purchased through the well-respected mail order firm PC/Mac Connection. This is a coupon I've negotiated especially for you. It means that for a little over $100, you can get a 9600 bps internal data/fax modem, and for a little more you can get one that will do 14.4 or 28.8 Kbps.

Zoom data/fax modems come with all the software you need to send a fax anywhere in the world, but you can also use your own comm program. The software sits in memory waiting for an incoming fax. When one comes in, it notifies you that it is receiving. Since any fax you *receive* can be printed out on your computer's printer, adding a fax modem gives you a "plain paper" fax.

All that's missing is the ability to scan in a paper document you want to fax to someone. But you can solve that with a $200 hand scanner or a $900 flatbed scanner. It all depends on what else you want to do with a scanner. But in my opinion, the best solution is to forget scanners. Get a data/fax modem and use it to send and receive whenever possible, printing the results on your laser or other printer. Get a stripped-down regular fax machine for faxing newspaper articles and the like. If you have two phone lines, you can even use the fax machine as a scanner by sending a fax to your computer's data/fax modem.

Encryption and Security

Most e-mail messages on most services consist of plain text sent to one or more individuals. But, of course, your mail is stored somewhere until your recipient signs on to pick it up. In an age when government agencies have the technology to locate and monitor a specific phone conversation transmitted via microwave among thousands of others, it is foolish to assume that your mail is "private."

To which you may say, "Who cares? It doesn't matter a whit to me if someone wants to read my love letters to my fiancé or the bread-and-butter notes I exchange with my co-workers." And I agree. But there may be times when you want to convey crucial information to a colleague that really should not be seen by others. That's when it is well worth your time to encrypt your message.

It's easy to do. And the software you need is free. What's more, the results are so good that a Cray supercomputer would have to labor long and hard before even approaching a solution. In the "Glossbrenner's Choice" section at the end of this book, you'll find a disk with everything a DOS or Windows user needs to keep the National Security Agency guessing. It includes Philip Zimmermann's famous Pretty Good Privacy (PGP) program. Versions for the Mac are available on the Internet and elsewhere.

Basically, you prepare your file. Then you run an encryption program against it. The encryption program will ask you to supply a "key" that it can use to control just how it scrambles the file. The key might be "whale" or "xyzzy" or anything else. As long as your recipient has the same program and as long as you give the person the key (either by voice phone or by a separate e-mail message), he or she will be able to transform the gibberish you send into readable text in an instant.

E-Mail on the Internet

28

The Internet is everywhere—both literally and figuratively. It is both the physical, world-spanning master network that links thousands of smaller networks and systems and the one online system everyone refers to when offering an e-mail address.

From mid-1993 to mid-1994, we went from a nation where virtually no one had even heard of electronic mail to the point where it became common for everyone from radio program hosts to manufacturing companies to political parties and activist groups to routinely offer their Internet e-mail addresses.

Most of the time, they don't even say, "You can reach us via the Internet at ..." They say, "You can reach us online at goodies@aol.com." Or they simply publish an address like that or include it in their ads. The notion clearly is that if you don't already know what an address like that means, it is irrelevant to you anyhow, so there's no need to explain.

What's it All About?

You don't actually need to know what an Internet mail address means. All you have to do is be able to recognize it as such—the "at" sign (@) is the tip-off. After that, it's just a matter of figuring out how you have to enter the address when sending mail from your particular online service.

On CompuServe, for example, you would send a message to jsmith@company.com by entering the following when prompted for an address: `>internet:jsmith@company.com`. On Delphi, you'd key in `internet"jsmith@company.com"`. Prodigy and AOL, user-friendly systems that they are, let you simply use the person's Internet address.

Actually, you don't even have to figure out how to handle Internet addresses on different services. All you need to do is consult "The Online Cookbook" section at the back of this book.

The "Domain" System and All That

Books about the Internet love to blather on about the intricacies of the "Domain Name System" that was developed to make it easy to specify Internet addresses. But here's all you really need to know:

I. An address like goodies@aol.com is pronounced "goodies at a-o-l dot com." In other words, you pronounce the "at" sign (@) as "at," and you pronounce the period as "dot."

Internet "Zones"

So what do things like ".com," ".edu," and ".org" mean when you see them in an Internet address? These are called "zone" name extensions. They exist so you can look at an address and know what type of organization it represents. Here are the main possibilities:

.com	U.S. commercial businesses
.edu	U.S. college and university sites
.gov	Governmental bodies
.int	International bodies, like NATO
.mil	Military organizations
.net	Companies or organizations that run large networks
.org	Nonprofit organizations and others that don't fit anywhere else

Addresses for international users typically end in a country zone code. For example, .AU is Australia, .KH is Cambodia, and .NP is Nepal.

Finally, although you will probably never need to use a site's numerical address, you should be aware that the Domain Name System is actually a user-friendly (sort of) cover-up for each system's "Internet Protocol" or "IP" address. The English address jsmith@bigcompany.com actually gets translated into something like jsmith@123.45.67.89, the numbers being the IP address of bigcompany.com. The Internet will accept either form of address. But who wants to remember a bunch of numbers?

2. The reason addresses like this are divided by an "at" sign is that the information to the *left* of that symbol is your personal e-mail address, and the information to the *right* is the name of the service you are on. The service you are on is your "domain" or "sub-domain."

3. When delivering mail, the Internet drops the message off at the domain (the computer system) farthest to the right in the address. Thus if you were sending to the address jsmith@genie.geis.com, the network would drop the message off at the system called geis.com. GEIS (General Electric Information Systems) is the parent company of the GEnie service. Once the GEIS computer got the message, it would know to route it to the GEnie computer. And the GEnie computer would know to post it to the mailbox "jsmith."

Internet Exotica

Well, not exotica, really. But there are some tips, tricks, and limitations about using the Internet that you should tuck away for future reference. Let me just tick them off for you quickly:

1. The 64K limit.

No message sent on the Internet, whether via e-mail or to a newsgroup can be larger than 64K. That's about 35 pages of double-spaced text, assuming 65 characters per line and 28 text lines per page.

2. Everything must be 7-bit ASCII text.

That's another way of saying "plain, pure text," and you already know how important it is to use plain text in any kind of e-mail.

3. Binary files *can* be sent on the Internet.

But they must be converted to 7-bit ASCII text first. You can send graphics, sound, and compressed files via e-mail. But you've got to convert them to text using a program called UU-ENCODE first. For technical reasons, this increases the amount of data that must be sent by about 30 percent. Your recipient must capture your message as a disk file and then run UU-DECODE against it to convert it back into binary form. Versions of UU-CODE are available for nearly every kind of computer.

Instant Internet E-Mail

The people who create and manage Internet sites can be a bit "bytehead" in their approach at times. But many of them have a great sense of humor, as you will see if you use the "send moral support" option. Be sure to check your service's current policy regarding any charges for receiving mail from the Internet. As noted elsewhere, for example, CompuServe charges 15 cents for the first 7,500 characters, and Prodigy charges 10 cents for each 6,000 character block.

Then turn to "The Online Cookbook" section at the back of this book to learn how to send Internet mail to the address almanac@oes.orst.edu. Prepare a note containing a single line starting at the far left margin. The line should read "send moral-support." Send the message. Wait an hour or two. Then check your mailbox to see what you find. (I'm not going to spoil things by telling you what to expect.)

4. Send a floppy or call direct.

Because of the 64K limit on message sizes, the UU-ENCODE program often cuts a file up into numerous parts, each of which must be sent as a single message. Most versions of UU-DECODE have no problem identifying and reassembling the parts, but what a hassle!

You can get a DOS version of the UU-CODE programs from the "Glossbrenner's Choice" section at the back of this book. But, really, you will be much better off sending your friend a floppy disk containing the file. Or ask your correspondent to put his or her comm program into "host" mode; then dial their computer and log on to make a direct transfer. If the two of you plan to do a lot of file exchanging, you should both agree to get accounts on the same consumer service and use that instead of the Internet.

Chat and Real-Time Conferencing

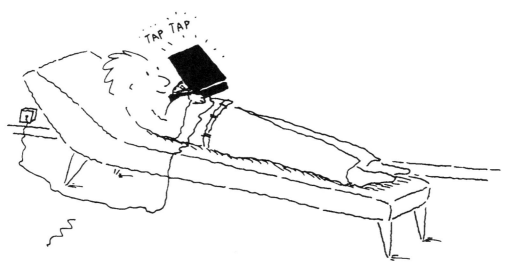

29

THIS IS MY FIRST TIME ON "PSYCHOTHERAPY SIG."
HAD FAIRLY HAPPY CHILDHOOD (FOR DOS USER), BUT
WASN'T MODEM-TRAINED TILL WELL AFTER PEERS.
⟨embarrassed⟩

E-mail is certainly the most common way to reach out and touch someone. But you can often make even more direct contact.

Almost from the beginning, mainframe computers have offered a feature that allowed one user to "talk" with some other user who was logged on to the same system at the same time. The other user could be across the street or across the country. As long as both people happened to be on the same system at the same time, they could "talk" by typing messages back and forth.

As far as I know, CompuServe was the first commercial service to take this notion of one-to-one communication and expand it into a full-blown "CB radio simulator" that made possible real-time, multi-person conversations. The citizen's band radio fad that was the original namesake for this feature faded long ago, so offerings of this sort are normally called "chat features" today. But the CB concept is still the most convenient and accurate paradigm here.

What's Your "Handle"?

Different services implement chat slightly differently. But in general, when you opt for a chat feature, you will either be asked to key in the handle by which you would like to be known for the current session, or the service will automatically use your service logon name. No one will know your real name (unless you tell them), but everyone will be able to see your user ID if they choose to with a "whois" command.

When you've selected your handle, you will be asked to choose the "band" or "channel" or "room" you wish to enter. To help you make a choice, most services will show you how many people are currently tuned to each channel. And, on some services, you may find that each channel is limited to a certain number of users. On America Online, for instance, only 23 people can be logged on to a single "room" at a time.

Candygram ... Pizza Delivery ... Land Shark!

You've got to be a fan of the original *Saturday Night Live* to get the title of this sidebar, but even if you're not, the key word is shark! Under no circumstances should you ever key in your password when using a chat feature—even if some official-sounding notice appears on the screen requesting you to do so. Such a notice might read, "Sorry for the interruption, but there's trouble on the node. Can you key in your password to verify?" or some such nonsense.

No online service *ever* asks users to key in their passwords at anytime other than at sign-on. If you see such a message, rest assured some shark is trying to rip you off. The person knows your account number, thanks to the "whois" command. So if you give him or her your password, you're basically passing over your credit card and saying, "Here, have some connect time on me."

Channel Differences and Tracking Multiple Conversations

Entering a well-populated channel can be like entering a noisy room. Lines of text will immediately begin appearing on your screen, each one beginning with a person's identifying handle, followed by whatever it is he or she has just said. Multiple, overlaid conversations are the norm, and it can take a little while to get used to all the chatter.

The best advice is to simply plunge right in. Some services permanently label their channels with names like "New Users," "Teens," and "Gays and Lesbians." On other services, channels are numbered, but, by custom, certain channels are allocated to particular categories of users. The only way to find out which is which is to plug into the chat community. (Try Channel 19 on CompuServe, for example, since it is the general channel and a good place to ask questions.)

"The Duke and Duchess of Canterbury ..."

When you enter a channel or a chat "room," the service you are using will almost certainly announce the fact that you have joined the group, much like a wizened old butler announcing your entrance at a formal English ball.

Until you're known on the channel or known to other users, most won't pay much attention to this announcement, so don't be concerned that the spotlight has suddenly been turned on you. On the other hand, it is considered good form to key in a greeting like "Hi, all!" or "What's happening?" or something else to personally acknowledge the fact that you have entered the room.

Chat users who simply sit in the background and watch—like Peter Sellers in *Being There*—are called "lurkers" and "lurking" is generally frowned upon.

More than likely, some or all of the people will fire off a quick word of welcome. They may then return to their conversations or invite you to say where you're calling from or otherwise start to chat. Usually you'll want to watch the conversation for a bit to gauge its drift and then add a comment should the spirit move you. If nothing interests you on one channel, you can easily tune to another. Indeed, on some services you can opt to monitor two or three channels while actually participating on another.

To Love, Honor, and Go Online

There isn't a chat system going that has not developed its own community, complete with its own characters, heroes, villains, history, and squabbles. On services like CompuServe, chat regulars upload scanned pictures of themselves and store them in the data library of a related Special Interest Group.

That makes it easy for you to see what the person with whom you are chatting looks like. (Or at least, what he or she wants you to think is a real image. "Role playing" of every sort is common in the world of chat.) The really hard-core users on some services hold parties, for which people fly in from all over the globe.

And, as you might guess, numerous weddings have resulted from chat-originated friendships. And in more than one case, the wedding ceremony was held online. The minister was in one state, the parents in two other states, and the happy couple in a fourth. Guests attended—online—from all over the country. And when the ceremony was over everyone showered the happy couple with rice by hitting their hyphen keys: --------.

It may also be possible to move to a different channel or room for a private conversation with one or more individuals. What makes it private is that, with a certain command, you may be able to limit access to only those you want to let in. Or you may be able to enable encryption so that everyone who is not part of your group sees nothing but gibberish coming from you, but all group members can read what you say.

Chat, Thoughtfully Considered

Chat systems are very popular—at least with a hard core of inveterate users. You can even find chat on the Internet, where it is called "IRC" (Internet Relay Chat), pronounced "irk." And, since consumer online services know a good moneymaker when they see one, all offer some form of chat.

There is a strong sexual component, to be sure. People meet and passionately chat in private and presumably have a satisfying experience. But it all takes place on the screen and in the mind, and as a lapsed Presbyterian, I find it impossible to criticize such behavior. As long as love—any kind of love—remains electronic it is difficult to see how anyone can be hurt or harmed by it.

After all, isn't sex mostly in the mind? If so, what better medium than online chat to talk to and get to know the person within? Freed of all the sexist, ageist, culturally biased baggage we all carry around, you can really get to *know* someone via online chat.

Here Comes the Wet Blanket!

But you can also waste a lot of time on chat systems. I've been on systems all over the electronic universe, and, I'm sorry to say, most of the conversations are vapid and inane. I know those are harsh words, but they're the truth. No doubt, the sense of community is crucial to some, and I know that the "regulars" look forward to chatting with each other several times a week. But to become a "regular," you've got to spend a lot of time online chatting about, well, about nothing at all.

So, naturally, I've got some advice. First, I firmly believe that every online communicator should at least *try* a chat feature. Log on and just

Cool Chat Applications

The fascination with chat for chat's sake wore off on me a long time ago. There are all kinds of ways I'd rather spend my time, none of which involve sitting in front of a computer.

But I'm really enthusiastic about the other ways chat technology is being applied. As you'll see in Part 5, "Special Interest Groups (SIGs)," all online services offer Special Interest Groups, or SIGs, devoted to specific topics. And most SIGs include a conferencing feature that makes it easy for SIG members to chat.

But that same feature is often used to present guest speakers to SIG members. Imagine being able to key in a question for best-selling author Tom Clancy or Apple genius Steve Wozniak to answer. Talk about rubbing shoulders with the great!

Or how about this: You're an avid National Public Radio listener who happens to hear a guest on NPR's daily afternoon program, *Talk of the Nation.* You feel passionately about what the guest has said. So you sign on to AOL, go to the NPR area, and use AOL's chat feature to register your opinion and make comments—pro or con. A minute or two later you hear the host say, "We've just gotten a comment from a user of America Online who wishes to point out that ..."

Wow! And double wow! It only works because AOL provides the service and because the NPR host pays attention to the AOL chat screen. There is no guarantee that your comment, or comments made by anyone else chatting at the time, will be picked up. But this is about as close as any of us will ever come to "talking back" to the radio or TV.

"lurk" for a while to get a sense of what it's all about. Second, if chat is a strong interest, check out America Online's version since AOL clearly does it best. Not only does AOL have what at this writing is the most attractive user interface going for it, the service also offers a number of neat chat-related features.

AOL Does It Best

The figure "America Online - [Red Dragon Inn]" provides a good idea of what it's like to chat on AOL. You can click on the List Rooms icon to get a list of all the available channels, and you can easily get a list of who is in each room. If the individual has put profile information on file, you can retrieve that also.

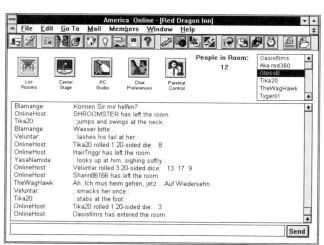

"Chatting" on America Online.

When you're actually chatting, the names of your fellow chatters in the room appear in the box at the upper right. You can click on a name to get the person's profile or send a private message. Finally, you prepare your messages in the box at the bottom of the screen, but nothing gets sent until you hit Enter or click on the Send button.

If you are using a regular comm program to access chat on Delphi, CompuServe, GEnie, or some bulletin board system that offers this feature, check to see if your software has a "chat" mode. Usually this will divide the screen into two sections—one for incoming text and one for whatever you choose to key in and send. Since nothing you key in will be sent until you hit your Enter key, this makes it easy to prepare and edit chat comments without having the text seem to be disrupted by other "chatters."

"Smileys" and Online Slang

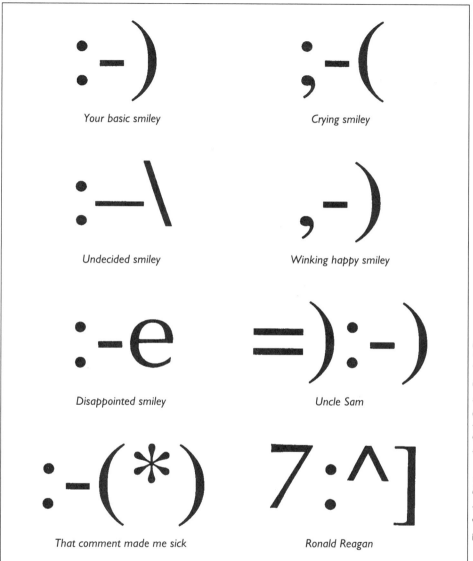

Your basic smiley

Crying smiley

Undecided smiley

Winking happy smiley

Disappointed smiley

Uncle Sam

That comment made me sick

Ronald Reagan

30

From *The Smiley Dictionary* by Seth Godin, Peachpit Press

The human urge to communicate is irrepressible. The popularity of e-mail and chat services is certainly evidence of that. But there are two special ways of communicating that drive the point home even further. Both were born solely of online communications. You won't see them used anyplace else. And both are used in e-mail and in online chat.

I am speaking, of course, of "smileys" and online slang abbreviations. Curmudgeon that I am, I don't approve of either of them. But then, I'm not really crazy about Windows and Macintosh icons, either.

After all, there are so many icons that it's impossible to remember what each means. It would be so much simpler if there were a button labeled "Printer" or "Scanner" instead of some abstract drawing of a machine eating a piece of paper. Or is it disgorging a piece of paper? Impossible to tell until you click on it. (That's efficiency for you!)

The Short Course

In any event, I can't send you out into the world of e-mail and online chat without a basic grounding in smileys and online slang abbreviations. But, even though I have a file called "All the Smileys in the World," I'm going to limit myself to the basics. And so should you, since, like icons, some of the more obscure smileys and abbreviations can actually impede communication instead of assisting it.

Your Basic Smileys

Smileys are pseudo facial expressions made up of text characters. They are sometimes called "emoticons." To "see" them, you have to turn your head 90 degrees to the left and look at them that way. Thus, the basic smiley consists of a colon, a hyphen, and a right parenthesis, all of which combine to represent eyes, nose, and a smiling mouth like this: :-).

You really can't blame people for using smileys. After all, online communicators are deprived of physical gestures, facial expressions, and voice tones when talking to or messaging someone online. Before smileys came along, users who wanted to soften an apparently harsh comment might include "<grin>" or "<smile>" at the end of a line of text. Many still do. But ever since someone discovered "Mr. Smiley," smiley symbols have gotten completely out of hand.

There are now literally hundreds of smileys symbolizing every shade of human emotion you can think of. There are also smileys that are jokes, like `<<<<<(:-)` for "hat salesman." They're all good fun, but if you want to be understood, stick to the basics:

`:-)`	Don't take it too seriously
`:-D`	Laughing
`;-)`	Winking
`:-(`	Frowning
`:-X`	My lips are sealed
`:-O`	Surprise

Abbreviations Galore

I certainly haven't done the research, but my sense of things is that abbreviations originated with online chat services. During a really active discussion, text can scroll up and off the screen so fast that it makes a lot of sense to key in `BTW` instead of `by the way`. And, of course, ROTFL ("rolling on the floor laughing") makes little sense in an e-mail letter but a lot of sense if someone is commenting on what some fellow chatter has just said.

In any event, here are the basic abbreviations used in e-mail and chat. But be warned: They're addictive. More than once I've found myself saying "BTW" in face-to-face conversation, instead of "by the way." The only thing I would add is that some abbreviations listed here, and others that are not, are more popular on some services than others. So, when in doubt, ask. That's what chat is for. Here's the basic list:

AFK	Away from the keyboard
BAK	Back at the keyboard
BRB	Be right back
BTW	By the way
GMTA	Great minds think alike
IMO	In my opinion
IMHO	In my humble opinion
LOL	Laughing out loud
ROTFL	Rolling on the floor laughing
TTFN	Ta-ta for now

five
Special Interest Groups (SIGs)

The Special Interest Group (SIG) Concept

31

SARAH SPENT MANY SATISFYING
HOURS ON THE KITE CLUB SIG.

Let me be frank, or Bob or Bill or whomever. The feature

known as a "Special Interest Group," or "SIG," is the

single best reason for most people to get a modem and go online.

Forget online encyclopedias and headline news stories. Forget cruising library card catalogues on the Internet. All of these features have non-computer, non-online equivalents. But the only way to take advantage of all that a SIG has to offer is to go online. You can't get the goodies any other way.

Many Guises, Many Names

"SIG" is the generic name for features that on CompuServe are officially called "Forums." On GEnie, they're called "RoundTables," or "RTs." On America Online, they're called "Clubs." Prodigy offers "Bulletin Boards." Only Delphi calls its SIGs "SIGs."

And just what is this miracle of rare device? It's essentially a place for people who are interested in the same topic to meet online. The topic can be anything you can imagine, and the people can come from all over the world.

That makes for an environment rich in opinion, knowledge, and resources. With literally tens of thousands of people using the IBM Forums on CompuServe, for example, the chances of one of them being both able and willing to answer any hardware or software question you might have are very good indeed.

This kind of environment simply could not exist any other way. It can *only* exist online. And—here's the kicker—it can be created for any topic in the world, whether it's "Making the Most of Your PowerBook," "Scuba," or "Real Estate and Home Improvement."

Learn One and You Learn 'Em All

Certainly the basic SIG design is the product of many influences, but the programmer who pulled everything together and put the first SIGs into place was John Gibney. He did so as one of CompuServe's original employees. Later, he did so for Delphi, too. Bill Louden, who went to work for CompuServe shortly after Gibney, was eventually hired away by General Electric to design and run GEnie.

What's So "Special" about Special Interests

Why is an online feature apparently named after the kinds of organizations that employ lobbyists to roam the halls of Congress in Gucci loafers?

No one could blame you for assuming that a "Special Interest Group" is an organization like the tobacco lobby, the National Education Association, the National Rifle Association, and others known for making their influence felt on Capitol Hill.

The term only makes sense once you know that it comes quite innocently from the computer-user-group movement. Computer user groups typically have a group meeting to discuss club business and, possibly, to listen to a guest speaker. Then they divide up into separate SIGs, each of which is a smaller group devoted to some specific topic: Lotus, Excel, WordPerfect, dBase, telecommunications, and so on.

The idea is that these interests are "special" compared to the larger, broader interest of the user group as a whole, which may be generally devoted to Macintosh computers or to IBM compatibles and DOS machines.

I mention this not only because both men are personal friends and because both are among the unsung heroes who helped create today's electronic universe, but also because this is clearly the reason why CompuServe's Forums, Delphi's SIGs, and GEnie's RoundTables are so similar. America Online paid attention, added some improvements, and made its Clubs an integral part of its easy-to-use graphical interface. Prodigy went its own way and decided to offer Bulletin Boards, or "Boards," instead of a fully developed SIG feature.

Thus, if you learn the basic layout of one service's online SIG, you pretty much know them all. The key point to keep in mind is that, like computer user groups, the main purpose of any online SIG is to facilitate the exchange of information among its members.

The Floor Plan of Your Basic Special Interest Group

Entering a SIG is like strolling into a fraternity or sorority house. You walk in, and there's a message board on your right where members post information and questions about tickets wanted or for sale, rides to distant colleges or home, and so on. As you walk down the entrance hall toward the staircase, you notice members engaged in discussions of various topics in the rooms to your right and left. You go up the stairs to the club library, a room divided into several alcoves. The books, programs, and other materials in each alcove are devoted to one particular aspect of the topic that is the main focus of the club.

That's basically it. All true online SIGs have three main areas or components:

1. A message board
The message board is for the posting and answering of questions. To make it easy to locate messages of interest, most boards are divided into several topic or subject areas. A message and a series of replies and replies-to-replies is called a "message thread."

2. A conference area
The conference area is for real-time discussions, chat, and guest speakers.

3. A library
The library offers software, text files, transcripts of SIG conferences with guest speakers, and particularly outstanding message threads.

The greeting screen for the Home Office and Small Business Round-Table on GEnie is shown in the following figure. Notice that the first

```
GEnie                       HOSB                  Page   370
                   Home Office/Small Business RT

   1.    HOSB RoundTable Bulletin Board
   2.    HOSB Real-Time Conference
   3.    Business Software Library
   4.    About The HOSB
   5.    How to use the Bulletin Board..
   6.    Announcements
   7.    Send Mail to RoundTable Staff

   8.    Home & Small Business Answer Book Excerpt
   9.    Featured File
  10.    Download Adobe Acrobat Reader Software

Enter #, <P>revious, or <H>elp?
```

The greeting screen for GEnie's Home Office and Small Business RoundTable.

three items are the message board, the conference area, and the library.

Consider the Possibilities

Pick a topic, any topic, and with just a bit of imagination, you can see how the SIG concept and floor plan could be applied to it. Think of a hobby and ask yourself what questions new and experienced users might ask on the message board or what items they might offer to buy or sell. What recognized authority in the field might be invited for an online conference with SIG members? What "How-to" files, price lists, personal recommendations, and so on, would ideally be available in the libraries?

A Taste of What You'll Find: Message Board Subjects

I'll use the Home Office and Small Business RoundTable on GEnie as an example. Here are some of the permanent subject categories you will find on this SIG's message board:

- Starting a Business: Questions, Tips, and Brainstorming
- Finding Customers: Sales, Marketing, and Advertising Tips
- Business Finances: Loans, Leases, Credit Cards, and Getting Paid
- Accounting Questions
- The Legal Side of Business
- Office Technology: Equipment, Supplies, and Software
- African-American and Minority Business
- Shareware and Your Business
- Doing Business Internationally
- Mail-Order Business and Mail Regulations
- Multi-Level Marketing
- ## Women's Business ## (Contact NADINE.K for access) *PRI-VATE*
- Trade Show by Service and Occupation
- Businesses by Geographic Location

And the Libraries . . .

And here are some of the permanent sections of this RoundTable's library. These are the places to look for information files and software:

- Sales, Marketing, and Ad Strategies
- Management Tips and Techniques
- Planning and Start-Up Information
- Tax Information and Tips
- Business Law and Legal Issues
- International Business
- IBM Windows Business Programs
- IBM Business Software and Clip Art
- Macintosh Business Software and Clip Art
- Franchises and Franchising
- Entrepreneurs' Digests

Sample Files Finally, within the various library areas of the Home Office and Small Business RT on GEnie, you'll find the following kinds of files:

- Advice on Getting Merchant Status for Visa and MasterCard
- Tips on Buying Business Insurance for Your Home Office
- Mentors for Women-Owned Business
- The Basics of a Direct Mail Piece
- Cut Your Postage Costs by Up to 30 Percent
- Advertising with Card Decks
- Good Books on Marketing
- Women in Business (transcript of SIG conference)
- Tips for Planning a Brochure
- Advertising in the Yellow Pages (transcript of SIG conference)

Go Get It!

And this is just one SIG on one service. With just a little imagination, you can easily see how this concept can be applied to any topic that interests you. In fact, the SIG you want to join probably already exists. CompuServe alone has over 600 of them! And on Delphi, you can instantly create your *own* SIG on any reasonable topic.

It's all there waiting for you. And once you try a SIG or two, I think you'll agree that Special Interest Groups are the single best reason for going online.

How to Make the Most of Any SIG

32

MEETING OF THE
"CONCEPTUALLY-CHALLENGED
DESKTOP PUBLISHING SIG"

To make the most of any SIG, you first have to find it on your service. It's quite common for a service to list relevant SIGs as items on topic-specific menus. Thus, a menu offering features concerned with stock quotes, Securities Exchange Commission filings, investment advice, and online brokerage services might very well include an item for the "Personal Investment SIG."

But why not take the direct route? Use "The Online Cookbook" section at the back of this book to uncover the commands needed to search your service's index of keywords or "jump words" for "Forums," "Clubs," or whatever name your service uses for its SIGs. That'll give you a complete list from which you can pick and choose.

How to Instantly Get a "Sense of the SIG"

Getting lists is also the key to making the most of any SIG. Thus, the first thing you should do when entering any SIG for the first time is to go to the message board and get a list of its permanent topics. Then go to the SIG file area and get a list of its permanent libraries or library subdivisions. This will give you an instant snapshot of what the SIG is all about.

A CompuServe Example

Let's use the Gardening Forum on CompuServe as an example. Your first step in getting a sense of that SIG is to open your capture buffer or otherwise set your comm program to log to disk. That way you won't have to worry about missing anything.

Then key in `go gardening` to get to the Gardening Forum's greeting screen. (On CompuServe, you are always given the option of joining the SIG. Do so. It costs nothing, and you won't be able to download files from the libraries of the SIG until you do.) After you join, you will see the main Forum menu.

When you choose "Messages" from that menu, you'll be taken to the message board of the SIG, where you'll be able to select "Read by section and subject." On CompuServe *that's* the option that will produce the list of permanent SIG message topics.

```
Gardening Forum+ Forum Menu

 1 INSTRUCTIONS
 2 MESSAGES
 3 LIBRARIES (Files)
 4 CONFERENCING (0 participating)

 5 ANNOUNCEMENTS from sysop
 6 MEMBER directory
 7 OPTIONS for this forum

Enter choice !
```

Gardening Forum main menu.

Real, Live Subjects In the figure "Gardening Forum Sections Menu," the "subjs" number indicates the number of initial messages with subject lines that people have posted. The "msgs" number indicates the number of replies to those messages. A section with only a few "subjs" and lots of "msgs" is one where you can expect to find long message threads. That's usually good, because it connotes an active discussion.

I picked the category "Vegetable Gardening" to get a better idea of the kinds of subjects being discussed there at

```
Gardening Forum+ Sections Menu

Section names (#subjs/# msgs)
 1 Forum News/Help!   (33/69)
 2 Vegetable Gardening  (53/167)
 3 Flowers/Bulbs   (55/194)
 4 Herbs/Recipes   (8/18)
 5 Fruits/Berries/Nuts   (21/43)
 6 Ponds/Hydroponics   (14/34)
 7 Lndscp/Trees/Bonsai   (69/191)
 9 Nature/Ethics/Bees   (7/32)
10 Pests/Disease/Weeds   (47/158)
11 Tools/Books/Software   (7/20)
12 Houseplants/Orchids   (31/92)
13 Seed and Photo Swap   (4/4)
14 Roses   (40/175)
15 Lawns/Groundcovers   (20/59)
16 Compost/Soil/Fertlz   (11/27)
17 Over the GardenGate   (24/127)

Enter choice(s) or ALL ! 2
```

Gardening Forum message topics.

the time. The figure "Gardening Forum Subjects Menu" shows what I saw. Remember, each of the items on this numbered list is the subject line from a person's initial message.

The numbers in parentheses next to each entry tell you how many answers or replies other Forum members have uploaded. It gives you, in effect, the length of the message thread. You can select any of these items and begin reading with the first message in the thread.

```
Gardening Forum+ Subjects Menu

Subject (# msgs)
Section 2 - Vegetable Gardening
 1 Onions going to seed!  (11)
 2 tomatoes, peppers--dying  (1)
 3 Cantelopes  (3)
 4 Plum/Roma Tomato Prob  (3)
 5 Blossom Drop on 'maters  (3)
 6 Growing Garlic  (4)
 7 Overripe Snow Peas  (1)
 8 Cilantro Harvest  (2)
 9 Organic pesticides?  (1)
10 JAPANESE EGGPLNT SETTING  (1)
11 Pumpkins  (3)
12 How to estimate yield ?  (1)
13 No Broccoli heads  (1)
14 BEAN Problem  (2)
15 Birds eating tomatoes  (4)
16 All Tomato Seed catalog?  (4)
17 beans won't germinate  (1)
18 growing from seed  (1)

Enter choice(s) !
```

Gardening Forum message subjects.

Getting the Library List

On any CompuServe SIG, getting a list of the available data libraries is as easy as selecting "Libraries" from the SIG's main menu. The CompuServe Gardening Forum has libraries devoted to everything from flowers and bulbs to swapping seeds and photos. As you'll see in Chapter 40, once you select a library, you can browse through the file descriptions or search for files on a specific topic. This is true on all SIGs on all services.

Tapping the Message Board

Since the conference areas of all SIGs are the same within each online service, they're of interest only when a conference is actually taking place. SIGs typically use a variation of their host system's "chat" feature to make real-time, multi-user conferencing possible. And often the

SIG sysop (the person who manages the SIG) will post a schedule of who will be the guest speaker and when. Some SIGs hold regular weekly conferences devoted to one issue or another.

Since I've covered chat features in Chapter 29, I can skip the conferencing feature and go straight to the SIG message board. Typically, SIG message boards are divided into several permanent categories. This makes it easier to find and post messages. It also makes it easy for you to block out message categories so you won't be shown them when you enter the board area.

Regardless of your online service, there are five things to remember about SIG message boards:

1. They are not official databases.

If someone has raised a question like "Why aren't my bush beans coming up?" and one or more members have replied, that thread will be on the board. Great if you have the identical problem; not so great if you're really interested in preventing your cucumber plants from being eaten alive. In short, when searching for information on any SIG database, you take potluck.

2. Message boards tend to be *very* responsive.

So, if you don't find the answers you seek, *post* your question to the board! Check back in 24 hours and see if you don't get several helpful suggestions.

```
Gardening Forum+ Libraries Menu

 1 New Uploads/Help!
 2 Vegetable Gardening
 3 Flowers/Bulbs
 4 Herbs/Recipes
 5 Fruits/Berries/Nuts
 6 Ponds/Hydroponics
 7 Lndscp/Trees/Bonsai
 8 NGA Youth Project
 9 Nature/Ethics/Bees
10 Pests/Disease/Weeds
11 Tools/Books/Software
12 Houseplants/Orchids
13 Seed and Photo Swap
14 Roses
15 Lawns/Groundcover
16 Compost/Soil/Fertlz
17 Over the GardenGate

Enter choice !
```

Gardening Forum library list.

People frequent SIGs both to get and to give answers. Every SIG has its egomaniacs who know everything. But these toads are far outnumbered by knowledgeable folk who genuinely enjoy helping others by sharing what they know. This fact is the absolute *essence* of online SIGs.

3. On active SIGs, messages "scroll off the board" pretty quickly.

There are limits on how many messages can be stored. Imagine a SIG with 10,000 members that stores only 500 messages on its boards. Imagine that the SIG is devoted to Microsoft Windows. When a new version of Windows comes out or some other momentous event takes place, literally thousands of messages may be posted in a day. And since each new posting pushes the oldest message off the board, you may have to check back several times a day!

4. Most SIGs keep track of the messages you have read.

That way you are shown only the messages that are new to you each time you enter the board. (Software is available that will automate the process for you, as you'll see in the next chapter.)

5. Do not rely on the search function of a SIG's message board.

A search function can only be as good as the raw material it's got to work with. On most SIGs, that means the "subject" line of each message. If the person who posted the message was less than precise in the words he or she put there, you may not find the message—even if it is exactly the message you want.

You'll be better off if you keep your capture buffer open and opt to look at *all* the subject lines of all the messages on a particular topic. You can then quickly decide if a given message is of interest.

Full Automation!

33

Psssst! You there. Yes, you. Over here so no one over-hears. What would you say if I said there was a way to completely automate your interactions with the mail sys-tems and the SIGs on CompuServe, GEnie, and Delphi?

That's right! Full automation. Software robots, auto-pilot—the works! How 'bout it?

Well, don't all shout at once.

The Three "Autopilot" Programs

Actually, by the time you finish this chapter you will indeed be shout-ing—shouting for joy. Because, in the online world, time still means money, and the programs I'm going to tell you about can save you a great deal of both. Here's the breakdown:

- CompuServe users want TAPCIS.
- GEnie users want Aladdin.
- Delphi users want D-Lite.

TAPCIS (tap the CompuServe Information Service, get it?) and D-Lite (Delphi Lite) are shareware. That means they are freely available online, through the "Glossbrenner's Choice" section at the back of this book, and elsewhere. But it also means that if you like and use the program, you are honor-bound to send its authors the registration fee they request.

Aladdin started out as shareware, but several years ago, GEnie it-self bought the program and began making it available to everyone for whatever it cost to download. I supply the latest DOS version with every copy of *Glossbrenner's Master Guide to GEnie* ordered through Glossbrenner's Choice. However you get Aladdin, no contribution or registration fee is required.

At this writing, all three programs are available in DOS versions, which means they ain't pretty. But then, good looks have nothing to do with how efficiently a robot functions. In fact, graphical good looks merely get in the way.

D-Lite is the only one of the three that is also available for the Mac-intosh. There are currently no Windows versions, though that may change in the future. Nor are there similar programs for AOL and Prodigy, the two online services that require you to use their own pro-prietary software.

The Essence of Autopilots

By now, I'm sure you're wondering what in blazes I'm talking about. Well, here it is. All three of these programs can be used to automatically:

- Log on to a service.
- Pick up any e-mail that's waiting for you.
- Upload any e-mail you want to send.
- Move to each of your favorite SIGs and pick up any private messages that have been left there for you by fellow SIG members.
- Download all of the public messages on the SIG's board that you have not yet read, excluding and including subject areas as you please.
- Upload the replies you have typed in—offline—to the last batch of SIG messages you retrieved.
- Download any files in the SIG library that you told it to get.
- Upload files to the SIG library that you want to contribute.

Cost Savings and More for Your Money

And just why would you want to do this? To save money, of course! Think about it: There are some things you have to be online to do, but reading and composing messages aren't among them.

For example, it's true that CompuServe offers a package of basic services that you can use as long as you want as part of your monthly fee. But you and I know that the really good stuff is not part of that package. To use most Forums on the service, you'll pay eight cents a minute for 2400 bps access or 16 cents a minute for 9600 bps or 14.4 Kbps access.

The creators of TAPCIS, D-Lite, and Aladdin feel that it's just stupid to sit there composing a wonderful reply to each message of interest while the connect-time meter is ticking. Far better to have a robot program go in, quickly pick up what you want, and sign off. Read and compose at your leisure, then turn the robot loose again to sign on, blast your missives into the service, and sign off.

Many Other Features, Too

Each of these programs can be used as a regular terminal program, and each includes standard features like split-screen "chat" mode and download protocols such as Zmodem and Xmodem. But each is really tuned to its respective service, and that makes all kinds of things possible. The program "knows" its host system intimately and can thus offer all kinds of service-specific features.

These include tracking your online time and giving you an instant summary of how much money you've spent so far this month, even before the service posts charges to your credit card or other account; a scheduling option to let you tell the program to automatically sign on and do its thing during the cheapest hours of the day; an address book that lets you send mail to other users based on their names instead of having to key in their IDs; and the ability to send Internet mail and take advantage of other kinds of e-mail features offered by the service.

And, of course, there's more. But I don't advise working with any of these programs until you have used the e-mail feature on Delphi, CompuServe, or GEnie and until you have used a SIG, Forum, or RoundTable. Get a human feel for the features D-Lite, TAPCIS, and Aladdin are manipulating first. Then you'll not only have a better idea of what they can do, you will appreciate them all the more.

Where Your Interests Lie: SIGs on the Major Services

34

G.W.: THOMAS, LET'S STALL ON THE DECLARATION 'TIL WE HEAR FROM OUR POLLSTERS. CAN WE MEET ON THE THIRD?

T.J.: GETTING HAIR DONE, GEORGE. HOW 'BOUT THE FOURTH?

You now know everything you need to know about Special Interest Groups, the feature many feel is the best reason to go online in the first place. You've got the concept. You know how to quickly extract the essence from any SIG. And you know about how your interactions with SIGs can be fully automated to save you money. All that's missing is a "what's where" treatment of the SIGs on the five main services.

The Limits

You'll find "what's where" here—within limits. Limit Number One is that SIGs do come and go. The sysop develops other interests or feels that the compensation is not commensurate with the work involved in operating the SIG. The company that sponsors the SIG falls on hard times or goes out of business or simply decides that running a SIG to support its hardware or software product is not worth the expense. So what you'll find here can be only a snapshot of the SIGs available at this writing.

And it can be only an incomplete snapshot. That's because of Limit Number Two—space. One could do an entire book devoted to nothing but the Special Interest Groups available via the Big Five online services. As it is, there simply is not room to describe each SIG available to you on each service. But then, most SIG names make it pretty easy to figure out what they cover.

Leaving Out CompuServe To offer the most information possible in a reasonable number of pages, I am leaving out the more than 600 Forums on CompuServe.

Instead, let me say that, as the originator and most vigorous promoter of the SIG concept, CompuServe offers a Forum for just about any topic you can imagine. And, in addition to having more SIGs than anyone else, CompuServe appears to be the preferred place for hardware and software companies to sponsor a SIG devoted to supporting their customers.

In short, if you can find a SIG someplace else, an equivalent is probably also on CompuServe. And if you can't find a SIG someplace else, it is almost *certainly* on CompuServe, if it exists at all. In any case, I strongly advise you to use your free time on CompuServe to key in `go index`, open your comm program's capture buffer, and search the service's index for the word "forum." That will give you the current complete list of CompuServe SIGs.

America Online Clubs and Forums

Adult Literacy
Astronomy
Aviation
BBS Sysops
Baby Boomers
Better Health and
    Medical Forum
Comedy
Cooking
Debate
disABILITIES

Dolby Audio and
    Video
Emergency Response
Environment
Ethics and Religion
Free-Form Gaming
Gadget Guru Elec-
    tronics Forum
Gays and Lesbians
Genealogy
Giftedness
Ham Radio
Military and Vets
Pet Care

Photography
ProSel
Role-Playing Games
Science Fiction
Scuba
Star Trek
Substance Abuse
Teachers
Travel
Trivia
Writers

Delphi SIGs

Amiga
Apple II
Atari Advantage
Aviation
BBS
Business
Close Encounters
Color Computers
Commodore
Custom Forums
D-Lite Support
Desktop Publishing
Environment
GameSig
Golf
Graphics

Hobby Shop
Internet
Languages and Cultures
Macintosh ICONtact
MensNet
Midrange Systems
Music City
New Age Network
OS9 Online
PC Compatibles/IBM
Person to Person
Photography and Video
Portable Place
Radio
Science Fiction

Seniors
Software Reviews
Sports Connection Online
TI International Users' Net
TV and Movies
Tandy PC
Theological Network
U.S.A. Gymnastics
WCF (World Community Forum)
WIDNet (Disability Network)
World of Video Games
Writers
Yachting

Delphi's Unique "Custom Forums"

Whether an online service can be "lovable" or not is up for debate. But if you're attracted to innovation, you can't help but have a warm feeling in your heart for Delphi. Unlike its competitors, Delphi has always been willing to try something new and different. Not every effort succeeds. But, thanks to Delphi's Bob Adams, the service's "Custom Forums" feature is going gangbusters!

Any Delphi user can easily and inexpensively set up a Custom Forum on virtually any topic. If the SIG attracts a regular audience, Delphi will pay the originator a percentage of the total connect-time dollars spent in the Forum. No one's saying you're going to get rich, but you might. And no other online service makes it so easy to set up a Forum. Here are the Custom Forums in existence at this writing (an asterisk [*] means that admittance to the SIG is by "Application Only"):

Adventure and Recreational Sports
All Star Sports
Anglo-File
Animal Rights and Vegetarian Living
Arabnet: The Arab-American Forum *

Art Critics
Art Therapy Professionals
Audacity Alternative Music
Bonding Place *
Book and Candle Pub
Bridge Players
Building Community
Cafe Gourmet

Call of the Highlands
Callahan's Saloon
Career Center
Chat and Chat Games
Child Care Support Net
Christchurch
Code-3

Delphi's Unique "Custom Forums" (continued)

Codependency Support Group
Comedy Club Online
Comics
ComicSig
Computer Online Real Estate Service
Cooks' Nook
Creative Real Estate
Death and Dying Online Exchange
Delphi Flea Market
Department 56 Collectibles
Desolate Weyr *
Disney
Dittoheads Unlimited
Divorce Support Board
Doctor Who
Domestic and Family Violence Issues
Dragonet
Earl Weaver (Sports)
Edge
Educational Technology
Electronic Books
EPN *
Family
Fathers and Families
Fisherman's Net (Christian) *
Flight Simulator
Flush Limbaugh *
Friends Of Bill *
Fundamental Forum *
Furry Forum *
Get Organized Group
Go Players
Good Samaritan Net *
Good Soldier Magazine
Hallmark
Handicap Forum
Healing Place At Delphi
Hearth and Home
Home Theater
Homeopathic and Holistic Health

In Full View (Gay) *
Infotech
Inner Study Network
Inventors and Inventions
Irish Roots
Jacob's Ladder
Job Complex
Kidsfirst
Lady Sally's House *
Lavender Wolves Family Home
Law
Law and Investigative Forum *
Linksville, U.S.A.
Living Healthy
Men and Women: Are They Too Different?
Men Against Circumcision *
Metaphysical Universe
Military *
Mommy Track
Multimedia
Murder Online—Mystery
NASCAR Fans
National Online Media Association
National Online Quilters *
National Philosophy Forum
Nether Realms™ *
Network Television Connection
New York . . . New York
Northern Michigan Connection
Nvn Refugees Meeting Place
OJ Simpson Opinion Forum
Online Auction
Online Naturists *
Oracomm Users
OS/2
Parrothead Madness
Path To Peace *
Pen Pals
Pet Lovers
Pitt *

Plant-Lovers
Politinet
Programming
Public Health
Respiratory Care World
Roissy—Le Maison De Plaisir *
Rotary Club *
RPG
Scadians On Delphi
Scotland Online
Scout
Scuba
Seagear Sailing
Searching For Roots
Single Parents Network
Singles
Soap Operas
Star Trek
Statuesque and Rubenesque
Teachers' Lounge
Teens and Youth
Textile Arts
TNT's Lies and Cons
TQM Help Desk
Travel Talk
12 Step Recovery—Sex and Love Addiction *
Unitarian Universalink—Uulink
United Methodist Idea Exchange *
Upper Room *
Vector 001
Wargaming and Military Strategy
Weather Watchers Online
Windows NT
Windows Users
Wits End (Comedy)
Women's Network *
Work At Home
X-Files
Yellow Submarine *
Zeitgeist

GEnie RoundTables

Air Force Small
  Business
Aladdin Support
American West
Amiga Aladdin
Amiga
Apple II Programmers
Apple II
Astrology
Atari 8-Bit
Atari Developers
Atari-ST Aladdin
Atari-ST
Autodesk Retail
  Products
Automotive
Aviation
BBS and Telecommu-
  nications
Bitstream
Borland
CP/M
Canada
ChipSoft
Collectibles
Comics
Commodore
Computer Game
  Design
Computer Press Asso-
  ciation
Consumer Electronics
DTP (Design to Print)
Data Communications
  and Interconnec-
  tivity
Database
Deutschland

Digital Publishing
disABILITIES
Disney
ENABLE
Education
Family and Personal
  Growth
Fantasy Sports
  Leagues
First Science Fiction
  & Fantasy
Food and Wine
FreeSoft
GE-MUG (Macintosh)
GEnie Users
GEnie for MAC
GEnie for Windows
Gadgets by Small
Games
Gardening
Genealogy
Geoworks
Graphic Images
Hayes
History
Home and Real Estate
Home Improvement
  and Do-It-Yourself
Home Office and
  Small Business
IBM and Compatibles
  Product Support
IBM PC
ICD
Internet
Investors' RoundTable

Japan
Jerry Pournelle
Laptops
Law Enforcement
Law
MIDI and WorldMusic
MPGames
Mustang Software
Mac Developers
Macintosh Product
  Support
Medical
Microsoft
Military
Mini and Mainframe
Modeling
Motorcycling
Multimedia Desktop
  Video and Virtual
  Reality
Music
Needle Arts
New Members' Prac-
  tice
Newton
OS/2
Outdoors
Pet-Net
Photo and Video
Portfolio
PostScript
PowerPC Program-
  mers
PowerPC
Pro-Am
Programming and
  Programming Lan-
  guages

GEnie RoundTables (continued)

Public Forum Non-profit Connection
Radio and Electronics
Religion and Philosophy
Rensselaer Polytechnic Institute
Romance Writers' Exchange
Scuba
Second Science Fiction and Fantasy
Show Biz
Soft Logik

Softronics
Space and Science
Sports
Stamp Collecting
TI and Orphan
TSR Online
Tandy
Tax
Third Science Fiction and Fantasy
TimeWorks
Timeslips
Travel
UNIX

U.S.A. East
U.S.A. MidWest
Video Games
Virus and Security
VisualARTS and Crafts
White House
Windows
WordPerfect
WorkPlace
Writers' Ink
Zymurgy

Prodigy Bulletin Boards

Books and Arts
Careers
Cars and Motorcycles
Collecting
Comedy
Computer
Computer Support
Crafts
Education
Food
Foreign Languages
Games
Genealogy
God of the Book
Health
Hobbies

Homelife
International Business
Internet Forum
Lifestyles
Marketplace
Medical Support
Member Exchange
Money Talk
Movies
Music
News
Office
Pets
Radio
Religion Concourse
Science Fiction and Fantasy

Science and Environment
Seniors
Service Clubs
Singles
Sports
Sports Play
Teens
The Club
Trading Cards
Travel
TV
Veterans
Wine, Beer, and Spirits

Internet Newsgroups and Mailing Lists

35

WE UNDERSTAND THAT YOU AND SUSIE SHARE AN INTEREST IN THE INTERNET.

You can't walk into a bookstore these days without stumbling over a pile of books about the Internet. I'm not criticizing. Certainly I have done my best to raise high the roofbeams of bookstores across the land with every Internet book I could nail down and then nail together. I hope, however, that my carpentry is better than most.

Of all people, I know how vast the Internet is and how futile it is to attempt to capture its scope in a single book. That's why in this chapter I want merely to perform an introduction. I want you to know about the wonderful phenomenon of Internet newsgroups and mailing lists, what they can mean to you, and how to learn more.

You'll have to see another book, perhaps one written by me and/or my co-author and life's partner of 20 years, Emily, for real, hands-on details. But I can't leave the topic of Special Interest Groups without alerting you to their Internet equivalent.

Glorious Anarchy!

As you will recall, the Internet consists of the physical phone wires and cables that link thousands of computer systems around the world and the software that turns this linkage into a network. No single orga-

```
Usenet Discussion Groups
Page 1 of 3

1    PERSONAL FAVORITES                                          Menu
2    Access Any Newsgroup (by typing its name)                  Usenet
3    DELPHI Newsreader Help                                      Text
4    READ BEFORE POSTING TO ANY NEWSGROUP!!!!                    Text
5    New User Topics and FAQS (NEW USERS, START HERE!)           Menu
6    How to Create Signature, edit Personal Favorites           Text
7    How to Create New Newsgroups (FAQs)                         Menu
8    Usenet FAQs (Frequently Asked Questions files)             Menu
9    Other Usenet servers (by gopher)                           Menu
10   DELPHI Command Summary                                      Menu
11     ================NEWSGROUP LISTS =====================     Text
12   Search for (but not connect to) Newsgroups, Mailing Lists  Menu
13   Newsgroup Lists (Delphi lists: 6/29/94, others: 06/02/94)  Menu
14                                                               Text
15     ================SELECTED NEWSGROUPS==================     Text
16   Best of Internet--Don't post!See FAQ (alt.best.of.internet) Usenet
17   Commercial Online Services (alt.online-service)            Usenet
18   Computer Underground Digest (comp.society.cu-digest)       Usenet

Enter Item Number, MORE, ?, or EXIT: 12
```

Delphi makes it easy to locate and read newsgroup articles with screens like this one. This screen appears when you select Usenet from the Internet SIG menu. To find out if there's a newsgroup or mailing list on a given topic, select "Search for (but not connect to) Newsgroups, Mailing Lists" from this menu.

nization controls, rules, censors, or otherwise has dominion over the information that appears on "the Net."

Like a metaphysical deity, the Net simply *is*. No one controls it or controls what can appear, although the service you use to access the Net may control which things you are permitted to see.

The Essence of Newsgroups

Internet newsgroups and mailing lists have a lot in common with the SIGs you'll find on the Big Five consumer services. But to any "SIG-meister," they will appear as crude as a dull bronze sword. That's because Internet newsgroups are nothing more than veritable "piano rolls" of messages, one tacked onto the other.

Although "newsreader programs" abound, none can match the features of TAPCIS, D-Lite, or Aladdin. And newsreader programs can only be used with the type of Internet connection that can cost you $20 to $200 a month. If you tap the Net through Delphi, Compu-Serve, or America Online, you must use the news-reader programs they offer.

There are currently about 10,000 newsgroups. That's right: *ten thousand!* Groups exist to discuss any topic you can possibly imagine, and some you'd rather not be told about. The record for the largest

```
"Search Academic email lists (alt. Kovacs)" is an indexed
service.  Please specify a word or words to search.

Search for: gardening

Search Academic email lists (alt. Kovacs)
Page 1 of 1

1   GARDENS on LISTSERV@UKCC                         Text
2   econ-dev        Contact: majordomo@csn.org       Text
3   econ-dev@csn.org                                 Text
4   alt.bonsai  For discussion of Bonsai gardening.  Text
5   rec.gardens  Gardening, methods and results.     Text

Enter Item Number, SAVE, ?, or BACK:
```

Just follow the "Search for . . . " menus from the main screen, and eventually you'll be asked for a keyword. Here, I specified "gardening" and located two newsgroups (alt.bonsai and rec.gardens) and two mailing lists (LIST-SERV@UKCC and econ-dev). The text files that appear when you select one of these items give you more information.

number of SIGs on any *consumer* online service is held by CompuServe with more than 600.

What You Need to Know

Here in quick, bulleted fashion are the facts you need to know about Internet newsgroups:

- Not all Internet sites subscribe to all available newsgroups. Delphi and CompuServe get them all; America Online offers a selection.
- All messages transmitted must consist of plain, 7-bit ASCII text (ASCII codes from 0 through 127), and no single message may be longer than 64K.
- The quickest, easiest, cheapest way to gain access to all news-groups is to subscribe to CompuServe or to Delphi Internet Ser-vices. On CompuServe, key in `go usenet`. On Delphi, sign on and key in `internet` to get to the Internet SIG. Then use the menus to get into newsgroup reading. (On Delphi, select the Del-phi Newsgroup Reader. Do not waste your time with the "nn" newsgroup reader; it is absolutely terrible!)
- Like SIG message boards, the "articles" posted to newsgroups scroll off over time. The number of days the articles in a given newsgroup remain on a given service is determined by that ser-vice's administrator. If you plan to follow a particular group, you may have to check it every day or so.
- Like SIG software, the newsreader software you use on a given ser-vice keeps track of the articles you have read. So once you get into the swing of things, you can keep current without a lot of effort.

  My advice: The first time you select each newsgroup, use the service's newsreader command to set all articles as "already read." Otherwise, you could be facing 1,400 articles or more per newsgroup. Once you've done this, the next time you enter the group, you may find only a few score (or a few hundred) articles that are "new" to you.

- Watch for FAQ (Frequently Asked Questions) files or articles. Dedicated individuals have taken it upon themselves to upload FAQs to given newsgroups on a regular basis. Among other things, a group's FAQ will tell you where to go to get files con-taining archives of previously posted articles—if such archives have been kept by someone somewhere.

Mailing Lists

In addition to newsgroups, there are mailing lists. The difference is that you can pick and choose the newsgroups you want to read and the individual articles within them you want to see. You can read or not read at any time.

Once you subscribe to a mailing list, however, you automatically get in your mailbox every article any other list subscriber posts to the list. If you are really interested in every aspect of a given topic, this is enormously convenient. If you like to be more selective, you'll be better off focusing on newsgroups. You'll thus be glad to know that many newsgroups exist to "mirror" mailing lists.

Mailing lists are clearly ideal for project teams and other small groups of people who are focused on a particular subject or task. But they're not a very good way to publicly discuss some issue. So why are there so many public mailing lists?

Mailing lists exist because Bitnet, one of the major networks that the Internet links to the world, cannot support newsgroups. The software just can't handle it. As it happens, Bitnet is the network that links many colleges and universities. And you know how much people at those institutions love to talk. So, since newsgroups were not a possibility, they invented "mailing lists."

People connected to non-Bitnet portions of the Internet saw this and began implementing mailing lists of their own. The only reason for making a distinction is that to subscribe to any mailing list, you must send your request by e-mail. When sending to a Bitnet address, you've got to tack on a ".Bitnet" to the Internet address.

Decoding ROT-13 Messages

Some newsgroups use an Internet-developed technique to prevent unsuspecting users from being shocked by what they find when reading articles in a newsgroup. The technique is used most often in the jokes-oriented group, rec.humor.funny. When someone wants to contribute a joke that some readers may find offensive, he or she encodes it with ROT-13, a simple code that rotates the letters 13 places.

The phrase, "Why did the chicken cross the road?" thus becomes "Jul qvq gur puvpxra pebff gur ebnq?" and that is what everyone looking at the joke will see.

To decode the joke, you can use commands built into the newsreader you are using. Or you can capture the joke as a text file and run a program called ROT13.EXE against it. This program is widely available on the Internet in versions for every computer. The DOS version is available from the "Glossbrenner's Choice" section at the back of this book.

Conclusion

Internet mailing lists, newsgroups, and SIGs are united in that they all offer a mechanism for exchanging information among lots and lots of people—most of whom you'll never meet in person and would never encounter any other way.

As crude as they are, Internet newsgroups and mailing lists are an incredible resource. I want you to know about them. I want you to use them. And, if you happen to see a book called *Internet Slick Tricks* by Emily and me, I wouldn't mind at all if you were to whip out the old Visa card and buy a copy.

The key point is to be aware that Internet newsgroups and mailing lists are out there and that they cover nearly every subject under the sun. If you're interested in SIG-like interactions, and if the anarchy and bytehead-complexity of the rest of the Net leaves you nonplussed, these are two features you don't want to miss.

six

Games Unlimited!

Online Games: The Concept

36

In the Beginning . . .

"You are standing at the end of a road before a small brick building. Around you is a forest. A small stream flows out of the building and down a gully."

I will never forget the first time I encountered those words. I'd read about the game *Adventure* in Tracy Kidder's 1981 book, *The Soul of a New Machine*. I was writing with a CPT word processor at the time, but when IBM introduced its first PC in the fall of 1981, I had to go see it. It was quite a drive to get to a store that carried it, and when the salesman suggested I try playing *Adventure* on the thing, I was thrilled.

Those opening words appeared, and two hours later, I was convinced that I had to have one of these strange new boxes. I just hoped that their little 5.25-inch disks would be big enough, since I was using man-sized 8-inch disks on my CPT.

What makes *Adventure* so fascinating is that it talks back to you. I knew I was hooked when, unable to figure out how to open a locked grate, I keyed in "abracadabra," and the computer responded with "That is a very old magic word, and it does not work here." I clapped my hands like a kid on Christmas morning, I was so surprised and amused.

The Importance of Computer Gaming

If the truth were told, I'll bet more than one original IBM PC (or Apple II or Commodore 64) was bought with the secret intention of using it to play games. And that's really my point here.

Computers of every size and sort have *always* been used to play games. It's something we all now take for granted. But in retrospect it is very significant that the only three packages you could buy for the original IBM PC, other than DOS, were IBM BASIC, VisiCalc, and Microsoft *Adventure*, which were, respectively, the most popular programming language at the time, an IBM PC version of the spreadsheet program that made the Apple Computer company, and a game.

Clearly, someone had concluded that many people would see game playing as a good enough reason to buy an IBM PC. Or at the very least, people would see it as a sweetener. "With this machine you can write your own programs, calculate your taxes, and . . . play a wonderful game that calls for skill and wit."

Games as an Online Driver

Although we're not there yet, it seems entirely likely that game playing will fill a similar role in getting people to go online. More important, it will get "online" into the home. Don't forget that you and I are among the happy few who are even aware of the electronic universe.

Consider: There are about 5 billion people in the world, and 25 million or so are on the Internet or one of the consumer online services.

That's less than one half of 1 percent of the world's population. I could be off by 100 percent—say there are actually 50 million people on the Internet and other online systems worldwide—and that's *still* not even 1 percent of the entire population!

If you accept the fact that the wiring—or cabling via fiber optic threads—of the industrialized world is inevitable, you have got to ask "What is going to be the driving force? What's going to persuade people to buy the equipment and pay the monthly fees to bring 'online' into their homes?"

The answer is games!

Why Games? People may say they want "information," but the truth is that we all get more information—for free—via television, radio, magazines, and newspapers than we can absorb. People may say they want to shop online. And some will do so. But sitting in front of a TV set or computer doesn't in any way compare to the human experience of going to the mall, seeing people, and handling the goods before whipping out the plastic.

But think about this. It's the middle of the week and you're bored with what's on TV. You don't feel like reading, and you've done your chores for the day. You want . . . you want, oh I don't know, something . . .

The ImagiNation Model

So you turn on your computer and sign on to the ImagiNation Network (INN). Using your mouse, you click on SierraLand and go to Dogfight Downs. In the Waiting Room, you do some more mouse clicking to set flags telling anyone who's interested that you'd welcome a game of *Red Baron* or *PaintBall*. In less than a minute, someone halfway across the country invites you to join him in the skies over Europe to fight to the death; you use your joystick to pilot your World War I vintage biplane.

You can also access INN through the "GamePoint" feature on Prodigy's Games page. As of this writing, ImagiNation is only available to DOS and Power Mac users.

The Product is *Entertainment!*

It's interactive. It's graphical. It's intense. It's also noisy, thanks to multimedia sound. When the combat has been decided, you can chat with your opponent and swap lies about your previous encounters. Then you can enter MedievaLand and assume your character of Elric, the wise elf, as you once again join forces with other players to combat Evil. The music and graphics are wonderful. Or you can mouse over to CasinoLand for a quick game of blackjack, poker, or roulette.

Here's the future: Mouse to a building or location and click ... and you're there!

And the bill? The cost is $2 per hour. That's about what you'd pay to rent a movie that was not a "Hot Hit" at a video store. Since the typical movie runs for about an hour and a half, a real one-to-one comparison would be $3 for an hour and a half of connect time versus whatever it costs to rent a movie.

But these are nickels and dimes. The point is that entertainment is the product. And for about what you'd spend to rent a movie, regardless of where you live, you can have a real-time interactive experience online, playing against real people, not against some computer.

With all due respect to Vice President Gore, *this*—and "movies-on-demand"—will build and finance the "Information Superhighway," not access to the Library of Congress, every Supreme Court decision, or every speech ever made by any American politician anywhere.

Resources

The ImagiNation Network
800-462-4461

The Multi-Player Games Network (MPG-NET)

The ImagiNation Network isn't the only game in town. There is also the Multi-Player Games Network, which is available to both DOS and Mac users. Accessed via a local call to your nearest CompuServe network node, MPG-NET offers a smaller selection of games than INN. But its offerings are impressive and include *Drakar, Empire Builder, Star Cruiser*, and *Operation Market-Garden*: fantasy, adventure, interstellar war, and World War I simulation!

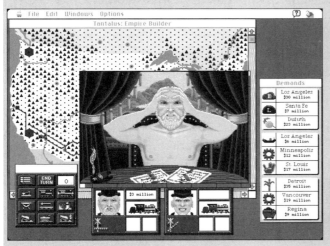

The Empire Builder just lost his empire on MPG-NET!

Resources

Multi-Player Games Network
800-438-4263

Games Online and Off

Created as an experiment in artificial intelligence at the Stanford Artificial Intelligence Laboratory (SAIL), *Adventure* has long been available via many online services. But it's also available on disk in many shareware and public-domain software collections. So why pay connect-time charges to play it online?

There's really only one reason to do so, and that's if the online service is smart enough to keep track of your scores so you can see how you stack up against other players. Whether it's blackjack or *Cyberstrike*, the opportunity to compete or play with others is the main attraction of online games.

Although everyone should play *Adventure* at least once (Hint: The key you need to unlock the grate and get into the Colossal Cave is in the little house), text-based games of this sort have been relegated to the backwater by multimedia titles.

Multimedia Raises the Bar

With a SoundBlaster (or equivalent), a pair of speakers, and a double-speed CD-ROM drive, you can play *Lands of Lore* on your own PC. (Available from Virgin Interactive, the list price is $75.) Movie-like sequences, hours of speech, digitized sound effects, and professional actors like *Star Trek*'s Patrick Stewart, who provides the voice of King Richard, make it impossible to ever be satisfied with a plain text game again.

Trouble is, this kind of experience has yet to become available online. And surely we will one day see CD-ROM–based games that you'll be able to play both as a single user locally and as part of a group gathered online. As long as everyone owns a copy of the same CD-ROM, the only data that has to travel over the phone lines are simple commands telling the software which images to display or which sounds to play.

Resources

Virgin Interactive
714-833-8710

Where We Are Today

If you're accustomed to playing games on your PC, your Mac, or your Nintendo, you will probably be disappointed by what you find online. There are some bright spots. The ImagiNation Network, a joint venture of AT&T, General Atlantic Partners, and Sierra On-Line, incidentally, comes close. But be warned—the INN software requires 585K of free conventional (640K) memory and a whopping 12 megabytes of your hard disk space, and it's only available to PC and Power Mac users. Another bright spot is GEnie, which, among the Big Five online services, is the standout for graphical, truly interactive multi-player games.

There are essentially two types of games available online: text-based and graphical. Text games can range from *Adventure*-style games—where you key in a simple command like `look` or `get` and the computer responds with a few sentences—to trivia games you can play with others. Graphical games tend to be "shoot-'em-ups," and they vary greatly in quality and cleverness. Some can be played only against the computer, while others are designed for multiple players.

In the next two chapters, I'll take a quick survey of both types of online games.

Text-Based Games

37

Text-based online games are kind of like black and white television. In their day, they were quite remarkable. Now, they are quite unacceptable. For example, the figure "Starting 7 Card Stud" shows what text-based online poker looks like on Delphi as you play against "Max-the-Vax" and his relatives.

```
Starting 7 Card Stud
Ante up - 1 each.
Pot now has 4 chips.
3 Maxessa is dealer. Shuffling... (44 card deck - no 2s or 3s)
You hold [AS 7S] 4S (3-Flush)

1 ALFRED       shows 4S (Four High)
2 Max-Fax      shows 4D (Four High)
3 Maxessa      shows 6D (6 High)
6 FlexMax      shows 5H (Five High)

3 Maxessa shows the high hand - Open, please.
3 Maxessa opens with 1.
6 FlexMax sees it
(You can enter F to fold or S to see.)
>>> Your bet? (Between 1 and 11, pot 6)
```

Text-based online poker on Delphi.

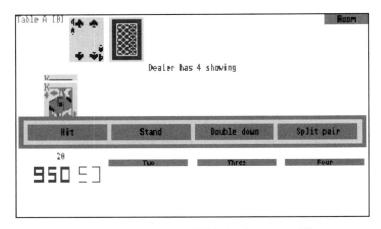

Here's a shot of the graphical RSCARDS Blackjack game on GEnie.
Much, much better than trying to play cards via text.

The Best of Text

Text-based games can be quite elaborate. CompuServe, GEnie, and Delphi, for example, all offer multi-player text games that require you to do things like build your own spaceship, fight battles, and eventually manage the economies of entire planets.

If you love complexity, for example, try *MegaWars III* on CompuServe or *Federation II* on GEnie. The attraction that keeps players coming back again and again is that as you become more skilled, you rise in the ranks and acquire even more power. And, of course, there is the camaraderie of your fellow players.

Trivia and Other Quizzes

Probably the most enjoyable text-based games, however, are the quizzes. Most are based on some version of "trivia," but I *like* trivia and could play *The Twilight Zone Quiz* on CompuServe all day. Graphics would be nice, but what would make it more fun would be to compete with others. And that you can do on CompuServe by playing *You Guessed It!*, a TV game show-style quiz.

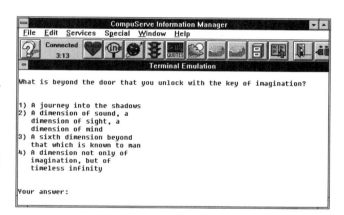

The Twilight Zone Quiz *on CompuServe. The graphics of WinCIM, CompuServe's Windows-based terminal program, can't change the fact that the essence of this game (and CompuServe itself) is still text.*

NTN Trivia: A Text Program Goes Graphic!

And speaking of trivia, you haven't lived until you've played *NTN Trivia* on GEnie. This used to be a text game, but when I signed on I found that text is no longer supported.

Instead, you spend about two minutes at 9600 bps to download a self-extracting compressed file containing a special *NTN Trivia* front-end program. From then on, you can play the game whenever you like. Versions of the software are available for IBM-compatibles, Amiga, Atari ST, and color Macintosh computers.

When you tell GEnie you want to play, you are told to run the *Trivia* front-end program. (For DOS users, this means "shelling out" to DOS and keying in `trivia`, though there are other ways to do things.) The results are shown in the figure "Countdown," a screen shot taken in the middle of a rousing game.

The sooner you answer the question correctly, the more points you win. Competitive results are posted after each question, so you can see how you're doing against the other players. And you can chat with other players during and after the game. (A version of this game is also available on the ImagiNation Network.)

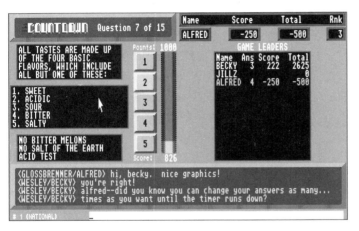

Countdown NTN Trivia *on GEnie.*

NTN Trivia also schedules *Topix,* a theme-oriented trivia game played each Wednesday and Friday night at 10:45 P.M., Eastern. One night might be devoted to horror show trivia, another to famous firsts and lasts, and still another to inventions.

Plus, there are real prizes. The top player each month gets $90 in free GEnie connect time, good anywhere on the service. Players who score a total of 3,600 points get a "trividend" usage credit worth $30. Other prizes, awarded for achieving specific point totals, include T-shirts, hats, Sony Walkmen, cordless telephones, CD-ROM players, and VCRs.

In short, *NTN Trivia* is a perfect example of what *can* be done with what is fundamentally a text-based game. As such, it offers a nice transition to the next chapter, where we'll look at online games that were designed to be graphical from the beginning.

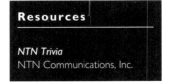

Resources

NTN Trivia
NTN Communications, Inc.

Graphics Galore!

38

INLINE, ONLINE, FELINE

Really good online graphical multi-player games (MPGs) are fantastic. With the addition of sound, animation, and joystick control, online play can be almost as good as an arcade game. Better, in fact, since with an MPG you get to play against one or more other people.

There are just four things you need to know:

1. The bulk of all online graphical games is always located on your hard disk or on a disk in your CD-ROM drive.

2. GEnie has far and away the best selection and the best implementation of online graphical games.

3. Many BBSs offer a nice selection of games, but as a new user, you'll be better off sticking to the offerings of the Big Five (AOL, CompuServe, Delphi, GEnie, and Prodigy).

4. You'll want to set a kitchen timer and place it next to your computer before you begin any online game. Otherwise, you're likely to become so engrossed that you'll spend far more time (and money) playing than you had planned.

How it Works

The reason the bulk of a graphical game must reside on your disk or CD-ROM is that, even at 14.4 Kbps, your telephone line can't deliver all the necessary data to your computer to make a graphical game playable. The "pipeline" connecting you to a remote host computer is just too narrow to pump sound, graphics, animation, and the like to you fast enough in real time.

Instead, once you have the necessary game software on your disk, the online service can send a short, simple command to tell it to display a certain frame, picture, or picture element, or to play a certain sound file. This is exactly how Prodigy and America Online run their entire services. It is why installing the software needed for either of them eats up a couple of megabytes of disk space.

The point here is that if you want to play *Air Warrior*, *RSCARDS Blackjack*, or even the much inferior *RabbitJack* casino games on AOL, you've got to first download the necessary software. Once you do that, you'll be all set to play at any time.

Winners and Losers in the Big Five

Who has the very best graphical online games? The answer clearly is the services that *specialize* in games: The ImagiNation Network and the Multi-Player Games Network, both of which were discussed in Chapter 36. So if games are your main interest, these are the places to check first.

Your next choice would be those distinctly graphical services, Prodigy and America Online, right? Well, no. You'd think these two would be far ahead of their competitors in graphical games. But their offerings are really quite thin, at least at this writing.

Off the Board: AOL and CompuServe

I wish I could be more upbeat about games on AOL, but there's just not much there. The one exception is *Neverwinter Nights*. This is a *Dungeons and Dragons*—or "DND"—type game that offers sound and 3-D graphics. If you can stand another "gamer" abbreviation, it's a role-playing game or an "RPG." But the first roll you'll have to encounter is your bank roll, since you've got to buy the shrink-wrapped version of *Neverwinter Nights* for $15 before you can play.

It may be that AOL is less than enthusiastic at this point about offering any feature that would encourage users to stay online for the amount of time required to play a good game. After all, the service's fantastic growth rate has often exceeded its capacity to handle all who want to sign on at a given time. So for now, at least, AOL is pretty much off the board as far as graphical games are concerned.

Delphi on the Move!

For most of its history, Delphi's games offerings have been mediocre at best. But in late August 1994, some dramatic changes took place that have the potential to lift Delphi to the top spot. In a word, *Air Warrior* arrived at Delphi!

This occurred shortly after Rupert Murdoch's The News Corporation bought Kesmai, the little Charlottesville, Virginia, firm that created *Air Warrior*. The game is still available on GEnie, the service that introduced it several years ago, and that brings up one of the most interesting points of all: Through the magic of telecommunications, Delphi users and GEnie users can play each other in real-time.

Other graphical games are scheduled to appear on Delphi in the not-too-distant future. Although it is far too early to tell how things will turn out, clearly the powers that be at Delphi are making a serious attempt to become a top graphical game service.

So, too, is CompuServe. At this writing, the only graphical game available via CompuServe is *Sniper,* a game that pretty much requires the downloadable "Scope" program. Other than that, it's all text.

The Prodigy Approach

All of which leaves only two services, Prodigy and GEnie. Prodigy doesn't do a bad job, but its "graphical" games have the same look and feel of the Prodigy service itself. That's because all of them build their images using the same frame and picture-element information that is used for the main service. In other words, no special, game-specific software is involved. This is adequate, if not spectacular.

The Carmen Sandiego *world view.*

As examples, see the figure "Prodigy service – Carmen Case" from the game *Where in the World is Carmen Sandiego?* and the figure "Prodigy service" from *MadMaze. Carmen Sandiego* is the kid-oriented geography-teaching game that sends you all over the world in search of clues to help you solve a mystery. *MadMaze* is an *Adventure*-style game that starts in a torchlit passageway of stone walls that eventually leads out into the "world."

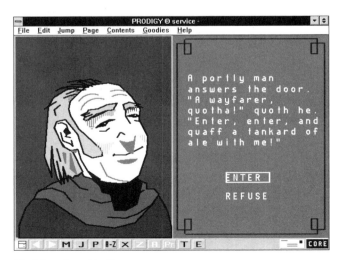

MadMaze *"graphics."*

Both games feature sharp, smartly written text, which is a good thing since there's a lot of it. *MadMaze,* in fact, is your basic *Adventure*-style quest with a few supplemental graphic images thrown in. A nice idea, but you will find yourself wishing that there were a *lot* more graphics like the one shown here.

Before leaving Prodigy, there are four points to make:

1. Prodigy does have an elaborate 50-player RPG about stellar conquest called *Rebel Space.* But playing it costs you $25 per game.

2. Accolade's *Jack Nicklaus Gold Signature Edition* golf program can also be played, though you must buy the shrink-wrapped package to do so and your Prodigy "greens fees" will be $8 a month.

3. At this writing, the best games on Prodigy are the ones you can access through its GamePoint feature—a gateway to the gamer's heaven of the ImagiNation Network.

4. But Prodigy is always getting better. As I was writing this chapter, for example, Prodigy added "sound." If you have a sound board, you can now actually hear, say, thriller author Clive Cussler discussing his latest book. With this technology in place, Prodigy could easily add sounds to its online games.

How to Get the Most Out of Online Games

As has been emphasized repeatedly in this book, the key to the online world is *people,* especially people-to-people communication. That's why your best bet when getting into any game on any service is to seek out the relevant SIG or other Special Interest Group. Not only can you post questions on the message board ("How can I do thus and so?" or "The snake kills me every time! What am I doing wrong?"), you can also tap the SIG's file libraries.

In most gaming SIG libraries, for example, you'll find shareware games you can download and play on your own system. And, you will almost certainly find "cheat" or "hint" files telling you how to beat or rack up a high score in a given game. Read these at your own risk, since a single file of this sort could forever spoil a given game for you. But, if you're desperate, they can be a big help. Particularly if you can ask your significant other to read the file for you, revealing *only* what you're desperate to know about—the Pirate, say, or the Troll, or whatever.

And the Winner is ... GEnie!

Yes, GEnie. This is the very same service that makes no apologies for the fact that in recent years its mission has been to sop up and sell excess capacity on the main General Electric network, as opposed to playing a leadership role in the online world. Yet no one in the industry would seriously contest the fact that GEnie has—and always has had—the best selection of online games.

The jewel in the GEnie crown is *Air Warrior*, an incredible, graphical, sound-using simulation of flight combat. Imagine, for example, that you're sitting at your computer with *Air Warrior* loaded. You start the engine of your Vought F4U-1D Corsair. The room rocks as digitized sound pours out of the speakers you have plugged into your sound board. You give the plane full throttle, and it begins to roll down the runway. The scenery flashes by as you pick up speed and gently rise into the air.

The view from an Air Warrior *cockpit.*

No sooner are you airborne than a black spot appears on the horizon—it's an enemy plane. Quickly you clear your guns, and the room is filled with the sounds of a .50 caliber machine gun burst. You push the joystick to the right and you're off to engage in desperate combat with another player, or players, since you could find yourself in a World War II dogfight to end all dogfights.

Other Games on GEnie

If flying is not to your taste, or you merely want a bit of a change, you may also opt to take command of a tank or an anti-aircraft battery to roll over buildings and shoot down enemy planes. And how do you know who's the enemy and who is on your side? The answer lies in the campaigns that are regularly waged each month. One month it may be the Battle of Britain, the next it may be Midway or something else in the Pacific theater. And, of course, you don't want to miss the debriefing (and bull) sessions in the ready room after the battle.

If air combat is not on the agenda, how about *MultiPlayer Battle-Tech?* Based on the *MechWarrior* series, this game lets you do mortal

Modem-to-Modem Gaming

If games are an interest, you should know that you can also play "mano a mano," as it were, with another person who owns the same piece of software. Actually, "modem-to-modem" or "MTM" is a better term here.

If you're equipped to communicate, only two things are necessary. You'll need a copy of a gaming program that includes a "modeming" option, and you'll need to find an opponent who is similarly equipped. The key thing is the software. As long as you both have the same modem-capable game, the computers you use do not matter.

Probably the best way to go MTM is to do so via Delphi or CompuServe. Both of these services have a special feature designed for just this purpose. And there are lots of advantages to doing things this way. For one thing, the applicable connect-time rate will almost certainly be lower than what you'd pay your long-distance carrier for a direct connection with your opponent. Also, you can preserve your anonymity, since there is no need to give a stranger your name or home phone number. And, since both services have so many subscribers, finding a qualified opponent is rarely difficult. Add to this the camaraderie of a SIG devoted to MTM on each service, and the option is all but irresistible.

On CompuServe, at this writing, you can play the following games:

- BattleChess
- Vette!
- Command HQ
- Tank
- Faces
- 3-D Helicopter
- Flight Simulator
- PC Othello
- Populous
- Dots-Dashes
- Stunt Driver
- Battleship
- Tracon II
- Knights of the Sky

Delphi does not publish a set list at all. Instead, there's a list of MTM games that "have been tested and have been found to perform reliably in Delphi's Game Room." These include the following commercial and shareware games:

- Battles of Destiny
- Global Conquest
- ChessNet
- The Perfect General
- Command HQ
- Spectre
- Conquered Kingdoms
- Falcon 3.0
- Empire Deluxe
- Conquest (shareware)
- Telego (shareware)
- Telecards (shareware)

battle with gigantic fighting machines. And then there's *Cyberstrike*, where you pit yourself against hunter-killer robots. When you add *RSCARDS Backgammon, Checkers, Blackjack, Bridge*, and *Poker*—all of them graphical, all of them multi-player—you've got a very attractive games offering. And I haven't even mentioned *Gemstone III* and *Dragon's Gate*, two non-graphical, text-only games that have attracted a culture all their own.

FREE Software and Other Files

seven

Yours for the Taking: Shareware Online

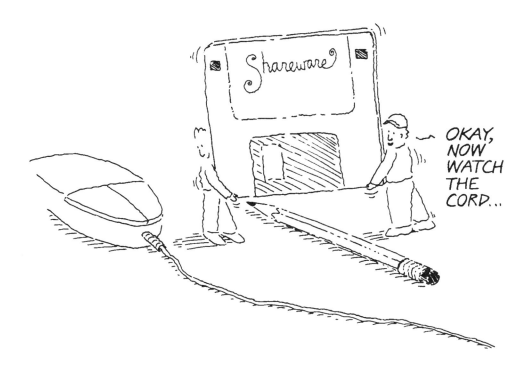

39

OKAY, NOW WATCH THE CORD...

Shareware software and the online world have always had a close relationship for a very good reason: distribution. Shareware authors don't advertise, and their products do not normally appear on the retail shelf. So to put their programs before the public, they send them to computer user groups and to mail-order firms specializing in shareware. And they upload them to online services and bulletin boards.

It was through the online world that I first discovered public-domain (PD) and shareware software, or as it used to be called back then, "freeware." Since then, I've written three books about it—and saved a ton of money. I've also had a lot of fun and saved a lot of time. And, now that you're online, you can, too.

The Facts About Shareware

Shareware is "software on the honor system." The men and women who create shareware programs make them freely available to all who want copies. But if you like and regularly use a shareware program, you are duty-bound to send the programmer the requested fee. This isn't likely to be much of a burden, since the fees typically range from about $10 to $40, though some registration fees are higher and some are lower.

Shareware programs typically come with a complete on-disk manual that's ready for you to print out. But as an encouragement to register the program, many authors send you a printed version of the manual when you send in your fee. In addition, once you register, you are usually entitled to telephone support, free or low-cost updates, and similar benefits.

Other things you should know include the following:

1. Shareware and commercial software are of comparable quality.
You don't need an office and a factory to produce a great program. All it takes is a computer and a very talented programmer.

2. Some shareware is absolutely awful. Some is brilliant.
The same can be said of commercial programs. But just try returning a lousy commercial program to your friendly local retailer.

3. The price difference between commercial and shareware programs is no longer as great as it once was.
This is because of ferocious competition and the emergence of "office suite" application bundles. On the other hand, telephone support is becoming an extra-cost item in the commercial market. With most shareware products it is included when you pay your registration fee.

The Association of Shareware Professionals

As you explore the shareware world, you will encounter the term "ASP," short for the Association of Shareware Professionals. These are programmers who have agreed to meet certain standards: to supply only fully functional versions of their software (no demos or "crippleware"); to supply all the documentation needed to install and run their program; and to guarantee that all their registered users will receive support.

The ASP imprimatur on a program is thus an assurance that the programmer is serious about the product. But it does not mean that the program is the best, or even that it is particularly good. Understandably, the organization steers clear of making value judgements about the products of its members. And some really good programmers refuse to pay the annual membership fee, even though their products meet all the criteria.

A Few Examples, If You Please ...

Finding, downloading, and running shareware programs can be as addictive as any aspect of personal computing. I have spent hours with *Wolfenstein 3-D* and *Doom*, just two of a dozen or so absolutely incredible VGA shareware games from Apogee and Id Software. The smooth-scrolling graphics are amazing, and if you've got a sound card and joystick, you'll think you're in an arcade. In *Wolfenstein*, you'll hear the prison doors clank open and the pistol report as you shoot a Nazi guard. In *Doom*, there's this chainsaw ... Anyway you slice it, you're in

for hours of fun. Or consider Apogee's *Word Rescue*, a cute, McDonaldLand-style adventure, designed to teach word meanings to kids while offering a lot of fun in the process.

But I digress. For examples of truly wonderful and *productive* shareware, you have only to look at the figures nearby. In the figure "The Software Vision Newsletter," you will see EnVision Publisher, a DOS-based desktop publishing program on a par with Ventura

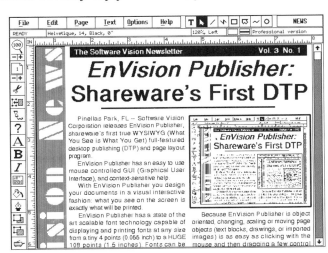

The award-winning DOS-based EnVision Publisher program.

Bruton Parish Church seen via the Neopaint program.

Publisher and PageMaker.

In the figure "Video Mode," you will see a screen from Neopaint, a program that runs rings around PC Paintbrush. (And I say that as someone who paid good money for the PC Paintbrush package.) The image being edited is a photo of the Bruton Parish Church in Williamsburg, Virginia—which happens to be one of Emily's and my favorite places—and which we found as a .GIF file on CompuServe.

Finally, in the figure "Jigsaw for Windows - Eiffel.Jig," you'll see a nifty Windows-based program called Jigsaw. Give it a file, and it will shatter the image into jigsaw pieces that you move about by dragging them with your mouse. What a great way to keep your young children or grandchildren busy (and quiet!) for an hour or two.

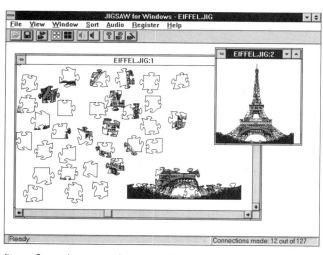

Jigsaw fun and games with any graphic image.

I can't show you everything. Indeed, I don't have room to show you even the tiniest fraction of all the good stuff that's available. So you will just have to take my word for it that really outstanding DOS and Windows software is available for a song, if you know where to look and what to look for.

Macintosh Titles

Although the Apple Macintosh holds only about 13 percent of the personal computer market, tens of thousands of shareware programs are available for Mac users. In 1993, for example, the magazine *MacUser* listed the following among its Shareware Awards:

- **Maelstrom**
  An addictive, commercial-quality, arcade-style, outer-space shoot-'em-up with streaking meteors, gyrating alien spacecraft, vortexes, and other dangers flying at your ship from all sides.

- **Bolo**
  A splendid tank war game in blazing color. You maneuver a tank around heavily defended terrain, blasting your opponents into submission.

- **Tetris Max**
  Simply the best freeware *Tetris* clone available for the Mac. It's color-filled and awesome—and best of all, it's free.

- **SpeedyFinder**
  A System 7-only control panel and extension that speeds up various aspects of the Finder. It turns off window zooming and energizes file copying. The extension also lets you colorize floppy-disk icons, rebuild the desktop without restarting your Mac, add keyboard command equivalents to the Finder, and much more.

- **MenuChoice**
  Turns the flat Mac menu into a hierarchical system complete with cascading menus, making the System 7 Apple menu everything it should have been to begin with.

- **WindowShade**
  A super desktop spacesaver that keeps window clutter to a minimum by letting you "roll up" open windows so only the title bar shows.

- **FileBuddy**
  A file-management utility that files Type and Creator codes, lets you change Finder flag info (toggles that make a file locked or unlocked, visible or invisible), and more.

- **Calculator II**
  A replacement for Apple's Calculator desk accessory. Offers a snazzier look and feel and offers more number-crunching options than the desk accessory that comes with your Mac.

- **GIFConverter**
  Lets you view and print images in .GIF format and translate many other graphics formats.

Available Nowhere Else!

With the exception of DOS, Windows, and possibly Visual BASIC, you really can run a business or an office using nothing but shareware programs. But even if you've already got all the major applications programs you need, the shareware world still has much to offer. That's because there is a shareware or PD program for nearly every purpose you can imagine, including many, many functions that are either not available or impossible to find through commercial channels.

Certainly, limited shelf space is part of the problem. Most stores have room to stock only the best-selling commercial packages. But the low price is a problem as well. You might be willing to pay $5 for a program that will make it easier to play your audio CDs on your computer's CD-ROM drive. But you probably wouldn't pay much more than that for a single-function program. Even if you'd pay $10, a retailer couldn't generate enough profit on the item to make it worth stocking.

That's why you'll find programs like these Windows packages in the shareware world, and probably nowhere else. And, as we'll see in the next chapter, you'll find them online:

- **CIMRater**
  An add-on to WinCIM that keeps track of your CompuServe usage charges.
- **Eye on the Sunrise**
  Displays the time of sunrise, sunset, moonrise, and moonset for any location.
- **Metrix**
  Converts U.S. measurements (length, volume, temperature, etc.) to metric. Over 1,000 different conversions are covered.
- **Activity Monitor**
  Records a program's open, working, idle, and close time in a text file.
- **Shoot the Messenger**
  Shows you every type of Windows message presented by a program as it runs and lets you suppress those you don't want to see any more.

How to Find the Files You Want

40

Shareware and online services of every sort have a symbiotic relationship. Programmers are happy to have online services distribute their products, and online services are happy to do so because a rich collection of downloadable shareware makes them attractive to users like you and me.

The Art of File Finding

But shareware isn't the only thing you'll discover in the file directories and libraries of BBSs and the Big Five consumer services. You'll also see graphic images—and on some BBSs, *porno*graphic images. There are sound clips and animation files, recipes and joke collections, interview transcripts, preserved message threads, and the full text of the U.S. Constitution.

In short, just about any fact, figure, type of program, or piece of information you want is available online. The trick is to *find* it when you need or want it. It's a trick anyone can learn. And, as with all skills, the more you practice, the better you'll become.

Seven Steps to Getting the File You Want

The most important concept to be aware of is what I've called the "Universal Four-Part Online File Format" as described in the sidebar. The second most important thing to remember is that file finding and getting is a two-phase process. First you find, then you get, and to save on connect-time dollars, you sign off in between. In other words, if you care about your online bill, don't do your looking online.

Here are the seven steps to follow to find and get any file:

1. Sign on to your chosen service.

2. Move to the free software treasure rooms—those sections of the service where the goodies are kept (normally, the SIG libraries).

3. Download either a list of all the keywords used to reference the files or a list of all the file names in the library. (Some SIG sysops offer single files that contain lists of all the *other* files in the library.)

4. Sign off the service and search these lists of keywords or file names on your own machine, noting file names or keywords of interest.

5. Sign on again, and return to the treasure room.

The Universal Four-Part Online File Format

The key to searching for anything is knowing what it looks like. In the case of the files on the Big Five online services, BBSs, and even most high-octane information services like Dialog and the Knowledge Index, the package that is a file consists of four parts. The actual layout and length vary with the service, but all use these parts: a file name header, a list of keywords, a descriptive paragraph, and the file itself. As an example, consider this from CompuServe:

```
[73510,3550]
CONSTI.ZIP/Bin  Bytes:  44844, Count: 1427, 28-Dec-93

   Title   : The Constitution - Windows Help File
   Keywords: CONSTITUTION RIGHTS UNITED STATES WINDOWS

   The Constitution of the United States of America compiled as a
   windows help file featuring hypertext jumps, struck text for
   portions superseded or amended with jumps to the amendment,
   browse sequences, explanatory notes, quick access guide, and
   over 200 search terms and phrases. Shareware. v 1.04.
```

This is your target. You can hit it by telling CompuServe to look for any one of these items: the ID number of the uploader (73510,3550), the name of the file (CONSTI.ZIP) or its file name extension (.ZIP), and the date the file was submitted. Or you can combine two or more of these items, telling the service to find only those files that qualify on all counts.

But frankly, none of this is likely to do you much good. The only time it is at all helpful to be able to search on the name of a file is if you have learned the name from some other source. That's how "Archie" works on the Internet. Indeed, the *only* thing the Archie program finds is file names.

The key to finding files on any non-Internet system is the list of *keywords* attached to each one. Some services will also search the descriptive paragraph (CompuServe does not), but they all search the keywords field for something to match the word you've specified.

6. Use your selected file names or keywords to call up expanded descriptions of your candidates.

7. Download the programs you want using an error-checking protocol (Zmodem, Xmodem, etc.), and sign off the service.

Where the Files are Kept

On Prodigy, ZiffNet provides the files, each of which is priced separately. But, as discussed in Chapter 12, on CompuServe, Delphi, and GEnie, the treasure rooms are the SIG libraries. That means that you will have to think about which SIG libraries to search. You can make things easier on yourself by searching the service's index for whatever it calls a SIG. See "The Online Cookbook" section at the back of this book for service-specific instructions.

Here's how you tell AOL's Software Center what you're looking for. This is completely mouse-driven and very well done. Notice that I have clicked on "All dates," "Games," and "Windows," and that I have specified the keyword "poker."

America Online and CompuServe make it especially easy to search for files. AOL keeps all its files in a single, system-wide library called the Software Center. So there's no need to think about which SIG or Club library would most likely have a given file. CompuServe has not completely eliminated that necessity, but it has gone a long way with its "FileFinder" feature. The IBM, Macintosh, and Graphics FileFinders search the libraries of scores of CompuServe SIGs all at once.

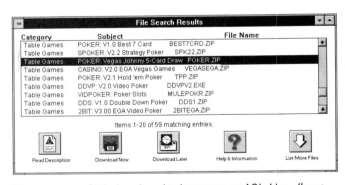

There are lots of Windows-based poker games on AOL. Here, I'm at Vegas Johnny's version. Notice that I can click on buttons to "Read Description" or "Download Now." Or, if I wanted to do all my downloading all at once, I could mark the file "Download Later."

Clown in a Cage: Keyword Searching

Online searching is a lot like attending a carnival and trying to throw a baseball at a target that will dump some good-hearted clown into the water. The difference is that at the carnival, you've only got one target that can be hit. When you're online, you can hurl a bunch of keywords at multiple targets surrounding the file, and if any one of them hits, the file will be dumped out of its protective cage.

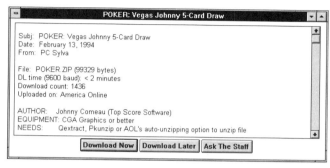

I decided to look at a description of AOL's Vegas Johnny poker game program. And here are the first few lines of a very lengthy and meaty description. The keywords attached to the file showed up next.

Unfortunately, it's not quite as easy as it looks or sounds, especially when you're dealing with shareware and other computer-related topics. First, there's the fact that so many common words can have so many completely different meanings: Is it "type" as in "type of file" or "type to the screen," or "type" in the sense of "font"?

Second, the person who uploads the file is the one who is prompted to select the keywords and prepare the extended description. In the information business, professional indexers and abstracters study for years to master this skill. When you or I attempt it, it is not uncommon for our keywords to be less than

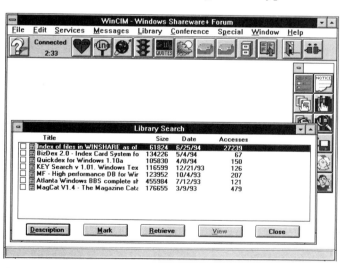

Though not nearly as smooth as AOL when it comes to finding files, CompuServe's WinCIM front-end program does a pretty good job of making it easy to find, mark, and download files. But you've still got to know which Forum (SIG) to check. And if cost is a concern, you will be much better off operating from the command line as discussed in "The Online Cookbook" portion of this book.

precise or for us to make typing or spelling errors, all of which can make the file difficult or impossible to find.

Give Yourself an Edge That's why you should take the easy way out. On CompuServe and Delphi, you can quickly get a list of every keyword that's been used to tag every file in a given SIG library. The list will even tell you how many times each word has been used in the library. Armed with this list, searching for files in these libraries is like shooting fish in a barrel, since you already know that every word will turn up a file. (On CompuServe key in `key` after you've entered any SIG's library. On Delphi, select "Databases" from a SIG menu and continue until you can opt to Search by keyword. When prompted for a keyword, enter a question mark, and the entire list will be displayed.)

The other alternative is to see if the sysops of a given SIG maintain a list of all the files in its libraries. The sysops of the computer-oriented SIGs on CompuServe, GEnie, and Delphi tend to be pretty good about this. But that may not be the case on your favorite SIG. (To find out, send a message to the sysop. You'll see his or her name in the greeting screen.)

Following is the kind of thing you'll find on a really well run SIG. This example comes from the Windows Shareware SIG (WinShare) on CompuServe. This is the beginning of the index file covering all the libraries in the Forum. These are just the first seven of some 2,500 files in this SIG:

```
=========================================================
File Name  Lib  Size  Date     Description
NEWUPS.TXT  1    20K 24-Jun-94 New Uploads (last 30 days)
INDEX.ZIP   1    60K 11-Jun-94 Index of files as of 06/11/94
PK204G.EXE  1   198K 03-Feb-94 PKZIP 2.04g
MSA11.ZIP   1   561K 17-Aug-93 MS Access DLLs for Visual BASIC Apps.
VBRUN3.ZIP  1   227K 16-Jun-93 VBRUN300.DLL
VBRUN2.ZIP  1   215K 21-May-93 VBRUN200.DLL
VBRUN.ZIP   1   170K 21-May-93 VBRUN100.DLL
```

Do Your Searching Locally

The most effective and most economical way to locate the files you want to download is to obtain either a list of the keywords used in the SIG, or an index or summary file, or both. Sign off the service to stop any connect-time meter from running. Then load the information into your favorite word processor or a program like Vernon Buerg's LIST and search to your heart's content.

This technique works best on CompuServe, GEnie, and Delphi. You can't do it on Prodigy, but if you're trying to keep connect time down, you can certainly capture a bunch of file descriptions from America Online—without pausing to read them while the connect-time meter is running.

You may suspect that this procedure is far more elaborate than necessary. And you may be right, if all you're looking for is a game—any game—to download and play right now. But, if you're really interested in finding files online, the seven-step process outlined here will stand you in good stead.

How to Download—and What to Do Next

41

With apologies to Thomas Magnum of Magnum, P.I., *"I know what you're thinking. You're thinking 'Gad, but getting files from online services and BBSs is an elaborate process. I thought I was done, and now there's a whole 'nuther chapter!'"*

I truly sympathize. And I have to confess something. Finding, downloading, and decompressing files is something I've been doing for so long that it's second nature to me. I plead guilty to forgetting how intimidating and complicated the process can seem to anyone encountering it for the first time.

Except it's not the process itself that's complicated. There are a lot of steps to take between the birth of a desire for, say, a program to help you learn a foreign language or improve your touch-typing skills and the moment when you can be blissfully sitting at your computer learning Spanish or trying to better your previous record on a typing drill.

But the total time involved between these two stages could be literally a matter of *minutes!* And only a very few commands or mouse clicks are involved. But they've got to be the *right* commands or mouse clicks. For that to be possible, you've got to understand what's going on. It is here that the complexity enters the picture.

Sprinting to the Finish Line

But let's see if we can slash through the Gordian knot and simplify things. The topics covered in this chapter include:

- Error-checking file transfer protocols
- Calculating the cost of downloading a file
- Compression programs
- Anti-virus procedures
- What to do once you've decompressed a file

This sounds like the Mother Lode of Technobabble. But, trust me, you'll soon understand it.

Error-Checking Protocols

A protocol is nothing more than an agreement between two machines on the procedures they will follow to transmit a file from one to the other. It covers questions, like, "How are we going to make sure that a file gets from me to you error-free? You know how noisy some phone lines can be. And what shall we do if a bit of static or other noise garbles some data? In fact, how are you going to know if a chunk of data I send you has been garbled or not?"

That's really all you—or almost anyone else—needs to know about what error-checking file transfer protocols do. The actual techniques that are used to insure an error-free file transfer, whether you're uploading or downloading, are pretty much irrelevant.

To use error-checking protocols, here is all you have to know:

1. The protocols you and the remote system use *must* match.

You cannot use Ymodem to upload to a remote system that is using Kermit. It's square-peg-in-round-hole time!

2. Zmodem is the best protocol to use. Period.

Not only is it the most efficient, but should you need to interrupt your download before it is finished, Zmodem will pick up right where you left off when you arrange to download the same file again! (The Compu-Serve B+ protocol will also do this.)

3. Xmodem is the lowest common denominator.

Available on most systems, it is offered by nearly every comm program you can name. There is nothing wrong with it, per se, it's just not as fast and robust as Zmodem.

4. The best protocol to use on CompuServe is the B+ protocol, if your comm program supports it.

Otherwise, you're pretty much stuck with Xmodem. Though it has been placed in the public domain, the B+ protocol is used only on Compu-Serve. If you are using any version of CompuServe's CIM or Navigator programs or TAPCIS, there's no need to worry. All support B+.

5. If you are an America Online or Prodigy user, there is never a need to think about protocols.

Your software and the host system know exactly what to do without bothering you.

6. Only binary files (.EXE, .COM, .ZIP, .SIT, etc.) *must* be transferred with a protocol.

Text files can be transferred this way also, but it's cheaper to open your capture buffer and tell the remote system to "type" or "list" the text file to your screen. Using a protocol adds about 15 percent to the time required to transfer a file, due to the conversations that take place between the two computers: "Did you get that chunk? Did it check out okay? Alright, here's the next chunk." and so on.

Calculating the Cost

Online services offer two very powerful features to anyone interested in finding a program that will perform a particular task, a graphic file of some image, or whatever. First, they offer a searchable database that makes it relatively easy to *find* the files you want. (With a little practice, of course.) Second, they offer near-instant gratification. Sign on at 9600 bps or 14.4 Kbps, and you can pretty much have the file right *now*, any time of day or night.

The drawback is the cost. Online services are not charitable institutions. They want to make money, and every one of them knows that offering files for downloading is the best way to boost profits. Same with the phone company, whose wires you use to log onto a distant BBS and tap its file collections.

To their credit, Prodigy and ZiffNet tell you exactly what it's going to cost you to download a given program. Usually the price is $3 to $5 *per program.* And to *its* credit, AOL tells you right up front how many minutes of connect time you'll have to spend to download each file at a given speed.

Divide by Ten! So what do you do if you want a file on a service or a BBS and want to figure out how much it's going to cost you to get it? You divide by ten, is what you do. To figure out the number of bytes you will receive per second, divide your modem speed by ten. Thus, if you're connected at 9600 bps, you can expect to receive a file at a nominal rate of 960 bytes per second.

So how long will it take you to download a 100K file? Divide 100 kilobytes (100,000 bytes) by 960 to get the bytes per second. The answer is about 105 seconds. Divide that by 60 to get the number of minutes, and you're looking at 1.75 minutes. Add about 15 percent or so for the overhead imposed by an error-checking protocol, and you're at about two minutes. Then just figure the cost per minute of using a given service, and you'll know the cost of downloading a given file. More or less.

If your connection happens to be noisy, the error-checking protocols may have to resend some pieces of the file two or more times. If the host system is particularly busy—heavily loaded—it may not pump the data your way as quickly as it could when only a few people are using it.

Prodigy and ZiffNet excepted, there is simply no way to know precisely what you'll have to pay to obtain a given program online at any given time.

You can come close, and for files that are relatively small (say, 360K and under), it doesn't much matter. But when you get into the 720K to 1MB range (as is frequently the case with Windows and Macintosh programs), it's worth considering membership in a computer user group so you can tap its disk library. Or order the software on disk through the mail.

Compression Programs

Speaking of saving money, that's exactly what compression programs were created to do. They are truly simple to use, once you know the basics, which are:

1. Compression programs or "file archivers" today perform two tasks.
They compress individual files, and they bundle groups of files into a single archive file. The archive file typically ends in .SIT, .ZIP, .LZH, .ARC, .ZOO, or .ARJ (more about this in a moment).

2. Compression programs work by scanning a given file for repeated patterns.
They replace multi-character patterns, like the word "the" in a text file, with single non-text characters. Then they create a substitution table showing which non-text characters stand for which multi-character patterns in the file. The result is a much, much smaller file—smaller by 50 percent or more.

3. Files are typically compressed for "shipping" (via modem) or for "storage" on disk.
When you need to actually use the contents of a compressed archive or file, you "decompress" it with the appropriate program. Said program looks at the substitution table created by the compressing program. It then goes through the file or files substituting the correct multi-character patterns for the non-text characters. (I've used a text file as an example here, but the same technique applies to binary files.)

The Tools for Dealing With Compressed Files

Here is a list of the file extensions you are most likely to encounter online and how to handle such files. The "Compression Tools" disk in the "Glossbrenner's Choice" section at the back of this book offers most of the DOS and Windows tools you are likely to need.

File Extension	What It Is and How to Handle It
.ARC	Compressed archive. Requires ARC from SEAware; PKARC; or Vernon Buerg's tiny, free ARCE or ARC-E program to extract. Macintosh program ArcMac will also work.
.ARJ	A compressed archive requiring the ARJ program to decompress. Not very common.
.COM	A DOS program file. Type the file name at the DOS command line to make it run.
.CPT	A Macintosh file created by Compactor 1.21.
.DD	A compressed Macintosh file created by Disk Doubler.
.DOC	A text file ("document" or "documentation"). View on screen or with your word processor when offline.
.EXE	A DOS program file that is usually larger than a .COM file. To run it, key in the file name at the DOS command line. (Note: Self-extracting archive files created by PKZIP and LHA may also have this extension. Just key in the file name at the command line. No need to use—or even own—PKZIP or LHA.)
.GIF	A Graphics Interchange Format file. CompuServe created this format to make it possible to exchange graphic images among different computer systems. Look at the file with a "viewer" program that can handle .GIF (pronounced "jiff") files.
.HQX	Macintosh compression format. Requires the Mac program BinHex 4.0 or the DOS program XBIN23 to convert.

The Key to Compressed Files As you might imagine, the people who have created the most popular compression and archiving programs are *very* involved with their work. Their programs include all kinds of features, as if all everyone did all day was to compress and decompress files. Fortunately, you don't have to worry about 90 percent of these features.

(continued)

File Extension	What It Is and How to Handle It
.JPG	A graphics file in the Joint Photographic Experts Group (JPEG) format. Can be viewed on any system with a JPEG-compatible viewer program.
.LHA or **.LZH**	DOS compressed archive requiring the use of the public-domain program LHA, which can also handle archives created by its predecessor if you specify the "/O" (for "old version") switch.
.MPG	A video file in the Moving Picture Experts Group (MPEG) format that can be viewed on any system with the right software.
.PICT	A Macintosh-format picture file.
.PAK	A DOS compressed archive created by the PAK program. Rarely seen these days.
.PIT	A file created by the Macintosh program PackIt 3.1.3.
.PS	A PostScript document (in Adobe's page description language). Make ready your PostScript printer and simply "copy" such a file to the printer. The results are often desktop-publishing-quality pages.
.SEA	A Macintosh self-extracting archive.
.SIT	A compressed archive created with the Macintosh StuffIt or StuffIt Deluxe program. DOS versions are available.
.TIF	A graphic Tagged Image Format File (TIFF). TIFFs come in many flavors, and not all viewer programs can display all types.
.ZIP	Compressed archive created by the DOS program PKZIP.
.ZOO	Compressed archive created by the ZOO program, which is required to decompress it. Versions of ZOO exist for most platforms. Historically popular on GEnie.

It is usually much cheaper to download a file in compressed form since only about half the time is required. It is also enormously convenient to be able to get just one compressed archive file that contains everything you need to run a given program. (I well remember the days when you had to download a program and its documentation files separately.)

Once you get the compressed archive file on your disk, the rest is simple. The crucial thing is to make sure that you have on your disk the correct "decompressing" program. (See the nearby table of file extensions and required decompression programs.) Once you are sure of that, you can put the compressed file (say, a .ZIP file) and the correct decompressor (PKUNZIP) into a single disk directory and enter a single command—`pkunzip *`—to decompress and dearchive the file.

Folks, unless you plan to prepare .ZIP archives yourself, that is the only ".ZIP" command you ever need to learn. The same procedure works for all the other compression and decompression programs.

Anti-Virus Procedures

There are four things you need to know about computer viruses. First, they are much rarer than the *New York Times* and other layman's media would have you believe. Because it fundamentally does not understand computers, the general press has always been cyberphobic. Thus any negative story about "what computers are doing to us" always gets far more play than it deserves. But what can you say?—it helps to sell papers.

Second, you cannot get a virus from a *text* file. Only executable program files—which in the DOS and Windows world means those ending in .COM or .EXE—can infect your system.

Third, all consumer online services, and most reputable bulletin boards, check programs for viruses before they make them available to the public. If they didn't, they would soon be out of business.

Fourth, if you have downloaded a file from a BBS, and you're not certain whether the BBS sysop checks uploaded files for viruses before making them available for download, you can easily run an anti-virus program against it before giving it a chance to infect your system. Starting with DOS 6, Microsoft began including an anti-virus program as part of the operating system. Competitors have followed suit. Shareware anti-virus programs are also freely available on CompuServe and elsewhere.

Your best protection is either to get your software through the mail or to download it from an online system that you know screens user-uploaded programs before making them available to all callers. "Joe's Dewdrop Inn" bulletin board system across town may not pass muster on this, though it's hard to believe that any sysop these days would not make every effort to operate a "virus-free" board.

After You Get the File

There are just a few more things you need to know about what to do once you have a file on your disk.

Personally, I believe it's best to create a new directory or folder for a downloaded file. For DOS users, I suggest that you decompress it with the appropriate program, and then delete both the compressed file and the decompression program to preserve disk space. (You can create a UTILS directory somewhere, put all your decompression programs into it, and add UTILS to your path so that the programs are always available to you. If you need help with creating directories and paths, check your DOS manual. Or get *DOS 6* or *Power DOS!* by yours truly.)

The key thing is to give your new arrival its own space. That way you can zero in on just this package. In doing so, you'll want to look for files ending with .DOC, or files beginning with "READ" like READ.ME or README.DOC or README.TXT. These files will tell you all about the program and what you should do to install it or to print the manual.

eight

Information at Your Fingertips

News, Weather, Sports, and Entertainment

42

As you may know, in the early days of personal computing, it was common practice to answer the question, "Why should I spend over $2,000 for a personal computer?" with "Well, you can keep track of your recipes and use it to balance your checkbook..."

Right! I'm going to give you two grand for a machine to balance my checkbook and keep track of my recipes when I could buy a pocket calculator and a recipe card box for $20 or so? Besides, who's going to type in all my recipes so I can keep track of them—me?

The Truth About Online News

I'm sorry folks, but I feel the same way about online news, weather, and sports. When the daily paper is available for 30 to 50 cents, why would any sensible person pay good money to read the same news online?

Heck, forget the paper. Now there are CNN, Headline News, and C-SPAN, all included as part of your monthly cable TV subscription. There are radio stations that deal in nothing but news and talk, also available at the push of a button or a remote-control clicker. In addition, there are magazines and trade journals.

Even if cost were not an issue, why would I go to all the trouble of booting my computer and signing on to a service to get news, weather, and sports? It's not like I can do this and also putter around my wood-shop for half an hour or so, the way I can with a portable radio tuned to an all-news station, or a TV tuned to CNN.

And what am I supposed to do with the news photos it takes two minutes to download at 9600 bps? Print them out? Send them to my friends? Use a paint program to draw a mustache on Hillary Clinton? Using an online, dial-up service to track current news, weather, and sports stories and images simply makes no sense.

The Secret of Online News

On the other hand, using newspapers, television, or radio to locate a *particular* news story is equally futile. Trying to find a weather forecast or a movie review doesn't work very well either. There are no buttons to press. You're at the receiving end of a pipeline that flows only one way—toward you.

Locating that same news story online, however, makes perfect, and perfectly economical, sense. Why riffle through the newspapers in your recycling bin hoping to find a review of a movie your spouse or significant other has suggested you go see this weekend? Maybe the movie review you want will be there, maybe it won't. But one thing's for certain: You will spend at least 15 minutes on your quest, and you will emerge with newspaper ink all over your paws.

It's merely a question of the appropriate application of the available technology. The online world is a poor substitute for CNN and TV and radio news. But it's a wonderful alternative to diving into a pile of newspapers or magazines looking for whatever. After all, helping you search for and surgically extract what you want from a huge collection of information is what the online world does best.

Your Own Electronic Clipping Service

The online world can also deliver a feature today that's available nowhere else: a low-cost, automated clipping service. Online services got into offering news online because the newswires were already there and because news was a feature everyone could understand.

But systems like CompuServe and GEnie took the next logical step—selecting news stories based on the keywords they contained and channelling them to a person's electronic mailbox. Now that is a powerful and entirely appropriate application of the technology.

Suppose, for example, that you want to be able to read every story that appears on the UPI newswire about IBM's involvement with the PowerPC chip. On CompuServe, you can set up a search profile in about two minutes that will automatically select just those stories and route them to your personal electronic mailbox. Once you get your profile set up, all you have to do is sign on to CompuServe once or twice a day. The service will notify you as soon as you sign on if there is any mail waiting.

The same thing is true with GEnie, though GEnie charges a pretty penny for this service. GEnie's rates for its QuikNews Clipping Service include a charge of at least $25 a month. On CompuServe, the clipping service is included as part of the Executive Service Option. At $10 per month, the Executive Service Option is only a dollar more a month than the basic plan, and it includes many other benefits as well.

If an electronic clipping service is of interest, go with CompuServe. GEnie's alternative is grossly overpriced and very difficult to use. CompuServe's has gotten better and better through the years. And, at this writing, none of the other Big Five online services offers anything comparable.

The Journalist: A New Twist on News

The PED Software Corporation has a most interesting and unusual Windows-based product. It's called The Journalist, and it's available in versions for Prodigy and CompuServe users. Basically, The Journalist lets you design your own personal newspaper from the ground up.

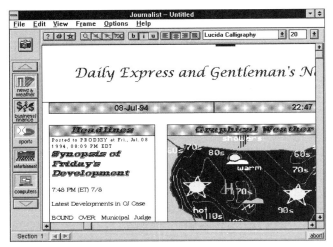

Welcome to the Daily Express and Gentleman's Newsletter, *a personal newspaper I just created for use with Prodigy and PED Software's The Journalist.*

You decide which topics will be covered (news, sports, business, etc.). You decide which weather reports for which cities and which weather maps will be included. You decide which stock quotes and relevant news stories will be retrieved. And so on.

Then you decide where each type of story will appear on the page. You can pick the fonts and point size, too. Then you turn the sucker loose and let it sign on to Prodigy or CompuServe and start "filling" its pages with the textual and graphical information you have requested.

A "Personal" Newspaper

The result is a completely customized and totally personalized newspaper, complete with weather maps, news photos, stock market charts, and anything else you might want. Best of all, perhaps, The Journalist can work in the background. If your machine normally boots into Windows, and you're accustomed to working exclusively within Windows, then you will be pleased to know that The Journalist is designed to take advantage of Windows "multi-tasking."

Just set it and forget it. Tell The Journalist when you want it to sign on to Prodigy or CompuServe to update your personal newspaper, and it will do so automatically when the time comes, regardless of the task you yourself are performing at the time.

I have installed and tested The Journalist, and I have found it easy to use, intuitive, and very, very well done. If I wore a hat, I would tip it

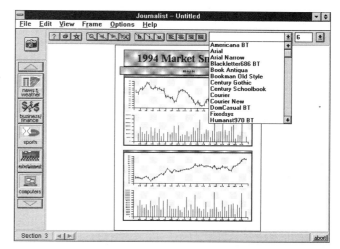

Stock quotes and charts! The raw data comes from Prodigy. The charts are prepared by The Journalist.

gladly to the people at PED Software. But, while it is great fun to design your own newspaper, I'm not sure that such a publication will ever replace a cup of fresh-ground mocha java and a copy of the *New York Times* and the *Wall Street Journal.*

In any case, if this concept is of interest, I urge you to check it out. There are just two caveats. First, The Journalist can take a while to update or "fill" its pages. On the other hand, since it runs under Windows, it can run in the background and not put your machine out of commission for the duration. Second, the Journalist-created newspaper is not really designed to be read on the screen. It is designed to be printed and read in its paper form. Nothing wrong with that, but it is something you should know.

Resources

The Journalist (for Prodigy or CompuServe)
PED Software Corporation
800-548-2203

That's Entertainment!

I freely admit to having strong opinions about what makes sense and what does not. For example, 23 hours a day my local cable company scrolls the weather forecast across the bottom of the screen, while the audio channel carries the National Weather Service forecast for my area. Yet, for some reason, whenever I am truly interested in tomorrow's weather, I tune the channel and find some kind of local piano recital or senior citizens' awards banquet being broadcast.

Aggravating as it is, I never think of going online. Instead, I pick up the phone and dial the number for the recorded weather forecast. I don't know what it costs. A dime . . . a quarter . . . maybe it's free. But it gives me the information I want, when I want it, with a minimum of hassle and expense.

Thus, while online headline news does not make sense at all, in my opinion, the opportunity to go online and search for reviews of movies, books, or music makes perfect sense. I simply love the fact that I can sign on to CompuServe, key in `go ebert`, specify "Thompson" as my search term, and come up with a list of every movie Emma Thompson has ever appeared in, or at least every movie that Roger Ebert has ever reviewed that listed Emma Thompson as one of the players.

Each of the Big Five services has its entertainment sections. (Prodigy has even begun to offer 30-second sound clips of authors or entertainers talking about their latest books or productions. It's a gimmick, but it's cute.) There are so many entertainment-related features online, in fact, that there isn't room to even cite them all here. But they are well worth scouting out. Just follow the instructions in "The Online Cookbook" section of this book to search your service's index for "movies," "books," "music," or some similar term.

An Information Sampler: Knowledge Index, PaperChase, the Internet, and More

43

What do you do if you need information—real informa-tion? Perhaps you want to know what's been published in the Journal of the American Medical Association *about a particular new drug or treatment. Maybe you're scheduled to have lunch with an executive you hope will become a client. Sure would be interesting to scan several years' worth of* Business Week *and* Forbes *to see if he or she has been mentioned. Or maybe you've got a paper to write for school on the latest develop-ments in carbon-carbon composites, their use, and their manufacture.*

Whatever piece of information you want, it's almost certainly online somewhere. But where? Dialog, Nexis, and the other services intro-duced in Chapter 25 are great places to look, but they can be expensive to use, and you've got to have a subscription. Fortunately there are alternatives. There is the Internet and there are the vast databases on CompuServe. (You might also want to check out the Database Center on GEnie for gateway access to Dialog.)

Gopher It on the Internet

At this writing, you can search the Internet through Delphi or America Online. If you take this route, follow my advice and go immediately to the Gopher feature each service offers. As explained in "The Online Cookbook" portion of this book, a Gopher is a menu system designed to make it easy to access Internet resources of every kind.

But each Gopher is a unique creation of the system administration staff at its home site. So you may have to search several Gophers

Scaring the Crows

Sometimes you really do find exactly what you're looking for online. And that event makes up for all the times you come close or come up empty.

Emily, my wife and uncredited co-author, is so good at searching that "Let's check the Net" has become a frequent response to any question we can't immediately answer. That's how she solved our crow problem.

Perhaps it's because we live on a river, but for some reason, a murder of crows has taken up residence in the tops of our trees. That'd be okay if it weren't for the noise they make each morning at about 5 A.M. We've tried everything, from high-pitched horns to firecrackers, to encourage them to leave, all to no avail.

So at 5:02 one morning, having been thoroughly awakened by the cawing, Emily tapped into the Net. Figuring that the PENpages feature published by the Penn State College of Agricultural Sciences would be a likely place to look, she discovered that this was one database on the Net that could actually be searched by keyword.

The word "crows" didn't do it. But "wildlife and birds" found 27 articles, including:

- How to Attract Hummingbirds
- Philadelphia Birdline
- Study Measures "Non-Consumptive" Uses of Outdoors
- Wild Birds, Your Cat, and You
- Water for Wildlife: Bird Baths
- Blackbirds—PA Wildlife Nuisance and Damage Control
- Blackbirds-Crops—PA Wildlife Nuisance and Damage Control
- Blackbirds-Feedlots—PA Wildlife Nuisance and Damage Control
- Quoth The Raven

The "Blackbirds" articles specifically addressed our problem. Apparently the solution is to get a tape of crow distress calls and play it on a boombox in the evenings just before the crows come home to roost for the night.

But where do we find such a tape? "Let's check the Net!"

before you find what you want. As explained in "The Cookbook," however, a program called Veronica can search all the Gopher menus in "Gopherspace" to produce an ad hoc customized Gopher menu for you. Even better are the Gopher Jewels, a feature you will also find discussed in "The Cookbook."

Catch as Catch Can

There may very well be more "real" information stored in the thousands of computers accessible via the Internet than in the computers of Dialog, Orbit, WestLaw, and the other commercial information vendors combined. We'll never know. Information on the Net is so widely scattered and each site's collection is so eclectic that it's impossible to treat the Internet as a dependable source of answers, at least for the general public.

But lack of coherent organization is only one problem. There is also the fact that you generally cannot search the contents of a file or group of files. In fact, you usually won't find any file descriptions, either. There are features like Wide Area Information Servers (WAIS) and the World Wide Web (WWW) that attempt to address this problem, but they don't really work very well and are available on only a limited number of Internet-connected systems.

My advice is to stick with Gophers and with the Gopher Jewels. If the information and answers you seek do not appear to be "on the menu," as it were, you might as well conclude that the Internet can't help you this time out. (Incidentally, don't wait till the need arises—go "a-Gophering" as soon as you can so you'll have an idea of what's available when you really do need something.)

The *CompuServe Companion*

The absolute best tip I could give anyone who wants to tap CompuServe's databases is to get a copy of *CompuServe Companion: Finding Newspapers and Magazines Online* by Glenn and Ruth Orenstein. Published by BiblioData, the cost is $29.95 plus postage. The book introduces you to the major full-text databases on CompuServe, helps you plan your search, and keeps a careful eye on the dollars.

I was amazed to find that the cost of the identical search of the *Books In Print* database could range from $1.31 (on Knowledge Index) to $18.80 (on IQuest) to $40.80 (if you choose to use CompuServe's access to the *Books In Print* database). With tips like this, the book pays for itself many times over. Plus, with the Orensteins' help, you are much more likely to find the information you seek.

Resources

CompuServe Companion
BiblioData
800-247-6553

The CompuServe Connection

As mentioned, GEnie does offer a gateway service to Dialog. But by and large, CompuServe has far outpaced its rivals among the Big Five services in offering "industrial-strength" information. Among many other things, CompuServe offers:

- PaperChase
- Knowledge Index
- IQuest
- Computer Database Plus
- Business Database Plus
- Magazine Database Plus

PaperChase

PaperChase offers you a friendly, menu-driven way to tap the world's largest biomedical database, Medline. Prepared by the National Library of Medicine, Medline has more than 7 million references to articles from 4,000 journals. Approximately 8,000 new citations are added each week. Coverage goes back to 1966.

PaperChase also taps into the Health Planning and Administration (HEALTH) database, which includes references to articles on all aspects of health care planning, facilities, insurance, management, personnel, licensure, and accreditation.

Medline, known as MedLARS on other services, corresponds to the *Index Medicus,* and, in part, to the *Index to Dental Literature* and the *International Nursing Index.* Please note that PaperChase and Medline give you bibliographic citations, not the full text of an article, although abstracts are available for about 60 percent of these citations.

When accessing PaperChase, the following surcharges are added to your normal CompuServe connect-time rate:

- $18 per hour from 7 P.M. to 8 A.M., your local time, during the week and all day on weekends
- $24 per hour from 8 A.M. to 7 P.M., your local time, during the week

Resources

PaperChase
Beth Israel Hospital
800-722-2075, 617-278-3900

Knowledge Index

As mentioned in Chapter 25, Knowledge Index, or "KI," gives you non-prime-time access to over 125 of Dialog's most popular databases. Some of the databases give you full-text articles; some offer only bibliographic citations. But you can easily order a reprint of any article via KI.

Welcome to Knowledge Index!

Knowledge Index offers one of the easiest, least-expensive ways to get *real*, in-depth information. Accordingly, rather than simply recite the number of magazines and publications it covers, it's worth taking a moment to look at some of the 27 subject areas on the service and the databases they hold.

I want to emphasize that this is a partial list, intended only to give you a flavor of what to expect:

Subject Area	Databases
Arts	*Art Bibliographies Modern:* comprehensive coverage of all modern art from 1974 to the present; worldwide historic coverage of Western art from 1973 to the present.
Biology, Biosciences, and **Biotechnology**	Worldwide coverage of research in biology, medicine, biochemistry, ecology, and microbiology from 1978 to the present.
Books	*Books In Print:* currently published, forthcoming, and recently out-of-print books.
Business Information and **Corporate News**	ABI/Inform, *Harvard Business Review,* Trade and Industry Index, Businesswire, PR Newswire, Standard & Poor's News, etc.
Chemistry	Chapman and Hall Chemical Database: physical property data on over 175,000 substances; Kirk-Othmer Online: online encyclopedia of applied chemical science and industrial technology.
Computers and **Electronics**	Inspec, Microcomputer Index, Computer Database, Business Software Database, and complete articles from *Computer-World* and *Network World.*
Drug	International Pharmaceutical Abstracts, Drug Information Fulltext, and The Merck Index Online.

KI is available to you only after 6 P.M., your local time, and during the weekends. The cost is 40 cents a minute ($24 an hour), and it *includes* your CompuServe connect time, even if you're connected at 9600 bps or 14.4 Kbps.

(continued)

Subject Area	Databases
Education	ERIC: research reports, articles, and projects significant to education from 1966 to the present; Peterson's College Database; A-V Online; and Academic Index.
Government Publications	GPO Publications Reference File: publications for sale by U.S. Superintendent of Documents.
History	Historical Abstracts: article summaries of the history of the world from 1450 to the present.
Legal Information	Legal Resource Index: Index of over 750 law journals and reviews from 1980 to the present; BNA Daily News: daily, comprehensive news coverage of national and international government and private-sector activities.
Magazines	Magazine Index: index to articles in over 400 American and Canadian publications from 1959 to March 1970 and from 1973 to the present.
Mathematics	Mathsci: research on pure and applied mathematics from 1973 to the present.
Medicine	Medline; Cancerlit; Sport: coverage of sports medicine research and fitness; AIDSline: provides complete access to the medical literature related to AIDS from 1980 to the present.
News	Full text of *USA Today, Washington Post, Philadelphia Inquirer, Los Angeles Times, San Jose Mercury News, Chicago Tribune, Boston Globe, San Francisco Chronicle, Newsday, New York Newsday, Akron Beacon Journal,* and scores more!
Psychology	PsycInfo: leading source of published research in psychology and the behavioral sciences.

IQuest and Ziff-Davis's "Plus" Databases

There are at least four other major-league information services available via CompuServe: IQuest, Business Database Plus, Computer Database Plus, and Magazine Database Plus. The first is a product of Telebase Systems, Inc. The other three come from Ziff-Davis's Information Access Company (IAC) subsidiary.

IQuest When you go to the IQuest feature, it will ask you a series of questions to help you specify and refine your search. Then, when you're satisfied that the search that will be done is close to what you want, you tell IQuest to go look. IQuest takes just a moment to connect to services like Dialog, NewsNet, or BRS to conduct your search.

It then returns with the first batch of hits. For about a dollar a hit, IQuest will give you a preliminary idea of what each hit is all about. If the hit looks promising, you can tell IQuest to go out and conduct the same search again, but this time come back with the actual article or abstract.

IQuest is not cheap, so be sure to look at the rate table it provides before plunging in. On the other hand, IQuest is quite friendly; it offers live, online help; and it saves you the cost of subscribing on your own to the systems it taps.

The Ziff-Davis Plus Databases The Ziff-Davis Plus databases are priced differently. But they have at least two points in common. First, the information they contain is almost exclusively full-text. Second, you can get a list of the publications each covers by going to the free Ziff Support Forum (key in `go ziffhelp`). Check Library 8 for BDPPUB.TXT (Business Database Plus publications), Library 11 for MDPPUB.TXT (Magazine Database Plus publications), and Library 9 for CDPPUB.TXT (Computer Database Plus publications).

Business Database Plus lets you retrieve full-text articles from two complementary collections of business-oriented articles from regional, national, and international sources. You can search Business and Trade Journals for access to five years' worth of articles from more than 500 business magazines, trade journals, and regional business newspapers. And you can search Industry Newsletters for access to a year's worth of articles from a variety of specialized business newsletters issued by various news services and industry watchers.

The cost is 25 cents per minute ($15 per hour) over and above your CompuServe connect time, plus $1.50 per article viewed on the screen or downloaded to your computer. All articles are full-text.

For its part, Magazine Database Plus lets you retrieve full-text articles from more than 140 general-interest magazines, journals, and reports. The database covers magazines like *Time, The Atlantic, Forbes, Kiplinger's Personal Finance Magazine, The New Republic, National Review, Good Housekeeping,* and *Cosmopolitan.* Coverage for most magazines begins with the January 1986 issue.

There is no additional charge above your CompuServe connect time. But you will be billed $1.50 per article viewed or downloaded.

Finally, there is Computer Database Plus, a service that lets you search over 230 computer-related magazines, newspapers, and trade journals. It's the place to look for news, reviews, product introductions and more, in areas such as hardware, software, electronics, engineering, communications, and the application of technology.

Magazines covered include *InfoWorld, PC Week, Macworld, PC Magazine, Computer Shopper,* and just about any other similar publication you can imagine, all of them full-text. Coverage typically starts with January 1987.

The cost is 25 cents a minute ($15 per hour) on top of your normal CompuServe connect rate, plus $2.50 per full-text article viewed or downloaded. Abstracts are also available; the charge is $1 per abstract viewed or downloaded.

Keyboard Commerce: Buying and Selling Online

44

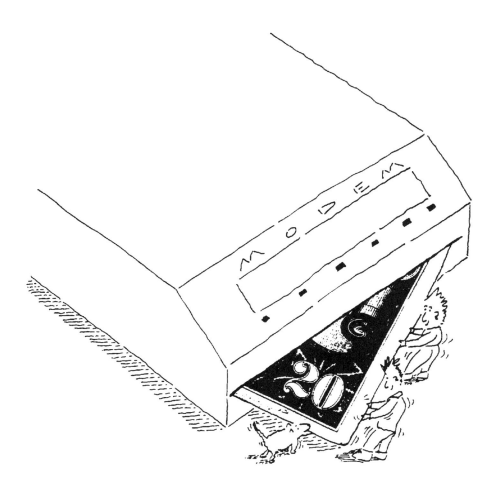

In the 1953 science fiction classic, The Space Mer-
chants, *authors C. M. Kornbluth and Frederik Pohl pos-
tulated a future society in which absolutely every aspect
of daily life has been subsumed by advertising. Posters*

on subways and buses don't hang passively on the wall waiting for you to notice them—they project electronic images on your retina, regardless of where you are standing. Coffee is no longer drunk only at breakfast and dinner; people drink it throughout the day, even at bedtime. But then they have little choice, thanks to the addictive alkaloid secretly ground into each pound by the manufacturer.

Unfortunately, at times, the electronic universe bears more than a passing resemblance to the world imagined by Messrs. Kornbluth and Pohl. Often it seems that for every company motivated by a desire to provide a superb online service, there are ten others who see the medium primarily as yet another way to sell you things.

This is by no means bad, particularly if you're interested in the merchandise they're pushing. But it does lead to a great deal of hyperbole on the part of online retailers about the joys of electronic shopping. This chapter will help you sort out the good from the bad or the just plain stupid!

The State of Play Today

Shopping is really too limiting a term. Let's instead refer to the buying and selling of things online as the area of "electronic transactions," or "keyboard commerce." That broadens the scope to include a whole range of possibilities, not all of which make a great deal of sense:

- Shopping
- Banking and bill paying
- Stock trading

The Fallacy of Online Shopping

Let's start by considering online shopping. I don't know. Maybe I'm being too harsh. But if I'm going to buy something, I like to touch and feel the merchandise. I want to be able to physically compare items. I also like to wander around Sears and other stores just browsing.

Yes, it's true that Emily and I tend to avoid the real-life mall and order most of our stuff from catalogues. And it's true that you can't touch and feel a piece of soft luggage from Lands' End. But you trust them, and you can at least see a color picture of what the item looks like.

Catalogues Online? Okay, suppose that Lands' End were online. Well, as a matter of fact, it is, on Prodigy and GEnie. Suppose the technology advanced to the point where you could quickly and easily display a color photo of each item online. What then? Wouldn't that be just like the catalogue you get in the mail?

Lands' End on Prodigy.

Yup. Sure is. But that paper catalogue is sitting on my kitchen table where I can easily pick it up and leaf through it. If I see something I cannot live without, and happen to have some space on my Visa card, I can just pick up the phone, dial a toll-free number, and order it. Why would I want to take the time to log on to Prodigy—or any other service—to place an order online?

It doesn't make sense. Yet each of the Big Five online services has some kind of shopping feature, and some even have "online malls." Only two explanations occur.

First, it may be that many people shop online as part of an entire online session. They may not go online specifically to buy things, but since they're there and it's easy, they do. Second, I suspect that the prices for participating in online malls and the like are kept low and that all parties still view online shopping as an experiment.

Online Banking and Bill Paying

Wouldn't it be great to be able to do your banking online? It could be 3 A.M., and you could go online to move money from one account to another and verify that some deposit had cleared. And what about arranging to have your bank automatically pay your mortgage and utility bills on a date you specify each month?

Of course you can't cash a check online—unless, of course, you have plenty of high-linen-content, red-threaded paper and an exceptionally fine graphics printer—but the convenience of automatic or on-demand bill paying, and being able to check the status of your accounts at any time of the day or night, is certainly attractive.

On the other hand, if you're like me, you know there's never any money in there anyway, so why bother to check? For this and many other reasons, online electronic banking has been a colossal flop, so far at least. There was a time when everyone was in on the act, and all the country's major banks were floating programs, either on their own or in connection with an online service.

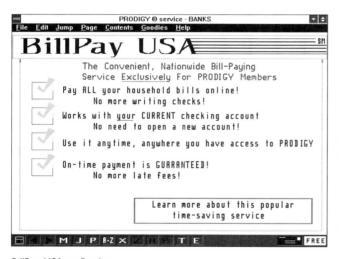

BillPay USA on Prodigy.

Today, among the Big Five, only Prodigy offers online banking. And only Prodigy, CompuServe, and GEnie offer online bill-paying. The reason, I believe, is that the customer is not willing to pay the rates that must be charged to make it worthwhile for a bank or bill-paying service to offer these features.

As you can see in the figure "BillPay USA Subscription Fees and Savings," BillPay USA on Prodigy charges $9.95 a month for up to 30 monthly payments. The CheckFree service that's available on other online services, in contrast, charges $9.95 per month for the first 20 payments. Both services charge $3.50 after that for each batch of ten payments (or portion thereof).

When you can use a program like *Quicken* on your Mac or PC—or Emily's favorite, *Andrew Tobias's Managing Your Money*—to track your accounts and pump out your checks, why would you pay $9.95 a month to BillPay USA or CheckFree to be able to make 20 or 30 electronic payments? (Both *Managing Your Money* and *Quicken,* incidentally, offer CheckFree interfaces, so you can use them to pay electronically, if you want to.) Once again, the online option just doesn't make sense, at least not to most people.

BillPay USA fees.

Time Out for Travel

And speaking of making sense, why would anyone spend the time required to master the arcane commands of the Official Airline Guide or Eaasy Sabre, the two leading databases of airline flight information? They're available on the Big Five, to be sure. But why wouldn't you just pick up the phone and call your favorite travel agent—someone who has been trained to search these databases to get you the flight you want at the lowest possible price?

If it cost you more to use a travel agent, that would be one thing. If you don't have a travel agent you trust, that would be another. But the cost is the same, and most towns have as many travel agents as they do real estate salespeople. Finding a good one should not be a problem.

Unless you're a control freak or someone with a lot of time to kill, searching out the best flights and the best fares yourself is about as senseless as trying to repair your own VCR. Indeed, if the truth were known, most online services originally offered the OAG, Eaasy Sabre, and the like for the same reasons that they first offered newswires: because they already existed and could be plugged into the system relatively easily.

So What *Does* Make Sense?

Only you can judge, but in my opinion, there are two online transactional features that do indeed bring something new to the party, something you cannot do as easily any other way. These are online stock trading and Shoppers Advantage Online (formerly known as Comp-u-store), a service that lets you *search* for products with the features you specify and that guarantees you the lowest possible price.

Online Stock Trading

There is probably no industry more dependent on computers than the financial industry. There is no way, for example, that the New York Stock Exchange could handle today's huge trading volumes were it not heavily computerized.

So using your personal computer to buy and sell stocks and securities is a natural, provided, of course, you know or can convince yourself that you know what you're doing.

I am a great believer in using the telephone—especially the toll-free telephone. When there is something I want to do or have done, I've found that it is often much quicker in the long run to talk to a real human being instead of trying to accomplish the same task by going online. (Since I use a telephone headset, being put on "hold" doesn't bother me—my hands are still free to keep using my computer keyboard as I wait.)

But if you have investments, it can be much easier in many cases to go online and issue buy and sell orders than to try to get your personal stockbroker on the phone. That's especially true in times of financial crisis, when most brokers tend to take calls only from their best clients. But with an online trading account, you can place an order any time of day or night, and it will be executed, by computer, as soon as possible.

Imagine, for example, that a particular company whose shares you hold announces some bad news Friday evening after the markets have closed. Imagine the telephone logjam at a local brokerage office come Monday morning. But, with an online account, you can place your buy or sell order Friday night, and it will be executed automatically at the opening bell on Monday morning.

Now, *this* makes sense! Add to it the fact that all online brokers are discount brokers like Charles Schwab or the Pershing Division of Donaldson, Lufkin, and Jenrette, and this application looks even better. Further add all the financial news and information you can get from most online services, to help you decide what you want to buy or sell, and you've got a real winner of an online application.

After all, whatever you might pay to an online service to research a stock or an industry, it's likely to be far less than you'd pay to a full-commission broker with a lot of fancy research reports from the home office in New York.

Shoppers Advantage Online

Another online transactional service that makes a lot of sense is Shoppers Advantage Online, a service old online hands used to know as Comp-u-store. The reason Shoppers Advantage is worth your while, and many online mall stores are not, is that this feature lets you search a database of over a quarter of a million products for the one unit that has the features you want at the price you want to pay.

Prices typically range from 10 to 40 percent—and occasionally 50 percent—off the manufacturer's suggested retail price. And, should you see the identical item advertised at a lower price elsewhere within 30 days of your purchase, Shoppers Advantage promises to pay you the difference. Just send them the ad and a copy of your order's paperwork.

Anyone can browse the service, but the best savings and benefits are available to those who become members. The cost at this writing is $3.50 per month ($42 per year), and you can cancel your membership at any time.

The savings are quite real. After years of using only an internal, dedicated fax modem, Emily and I finally decided to buy a dedicated fax machine that would let us fax newspaper and magazine articles instead of just computer-created text files. We checked the most recent review of fax machines in *Consumer Reports*—not online, but in the box in our attic where we keep past issues.

Then we marched into Staples and bought a wonderful Panasonic fax machine with a built-in answering machine. We paid $400 for it, plus sales tax. In the course of researching this chapter, however, Emily discovered that the identical fax machine could have been ordered from Shoppers Advantage for $40 less!

Of course, we would have had to pay at least one month's membership fee ($3.50) and might have had to wait for two to three weeks, but here was a real-life, hands-on example of the savings that are possible through Shoppers Advantage. You will find Shoppers Advantage on most services, and you do not have to join to be able to search for products of interest. My advice is to give it a try. It is the only implementation of online shopping that really makes any sense!

Conclusion

There will almost certainly come a day when you can see the great actress Faye Dunaway on TV and say, "Geeze, she was really good in *Network,* I think I'll punch that up and watch it tonight." You will key in a few numbers on your TV's remote control, and the movie will be downloaded to your set-top box immediately, at a cost just slightly higher than you would pay at your local video store.

That's another transactional service that makes a lot of sense. In the meantime, "keyboard commerce" is pretty much limited to the offerings of the Big Five. The most charitable thing one can say about most of these offerings is that they are "experimental." But, as we've seen, some of the transactional, keyboard commerce features available today do indeed make a lot of sense. The trick is in finding them, and I hope this chapter has helped.

cookbook

Introduction

Welcome to the kitchen! Throughout The Little Online Book *I have deliberately avoided cluttering things up with a lot of boring commands. That's because commands and mouse clicks are merely a means to an end. After all, the most important thing to grasp at first is the concept of a wonderful, light, fluffy soufflé. Otherwise, how would any of us ever decide whether it was worth taking the steps needed to create one?*

Now it's time to put on the aprons and roll up the sleeves. It's time to thrust your hands into the dough and do a little kneading. It's time to learn what you've got to learn to make the wonders of the electronic universe come true for you. No one's going to bring it to you on a silver platter. You've got to go online and get it yourself!

But, with this Cookbook open on your desk, it won't be hard. And the coupons at the back of this book will help ensure that it won't be expensive. In short, you'll have a ball.

There are just a few key points worth mentioning:

- This Cookbook covers the Big Five consumer online services and the Internet.

- For each, it gives you the most important basic commands and concepts and includes a "Beginner's Best Bets" section right up front to help you wisely spend your coupon-generated free time.

- This Cookbook will be a big help, but you bear the bulk of the responsibility. I can get you started, and I can give you the commands and tools you need to get more information and help. In short, the Cookbook will point you in the right direction. But you're the one who has to follow up and go exploring on your own. And I promise you, you'll love it!

- Each online service is different. So instead of imposing a rigid, brittle format on the Cookbook entry for each, I have adapted things as necessary for each. You will simply have to trust that the information you really need to get off to a good, quick start with each service is covered in its Cookbook entry.

- The customer service hours given in each service's section are the times when you will be able to speak with a human being. However, all services have voice mail or phone-based menu systems. This means you may be able to get the information you want or make a request even when no human being is available to take your call.

- Finally, one thing I feel is truly worth emphasizing in each case is how to send e-mail to and from different services using the Internet as the intermediary. Here you will find all the information you need to do just that.

Quick Reference

Customer Service: 800-827-6364

Weekdays: Noon to 11 P.M., EST

Weekends: Noon to 9 P.M., EST

Beginner's Best Bets: Take the tour! When you first sign on, play around to get a sense of the system. Then key in Ctrl-K to pop up the Keyword box, and key in `tour`. The tour shows you important features and even lets you "get off the bus" to sample them. When you leave such a feature, you'll be back on the bus and ready to go to the next destination. Also, don't miss the Discover AOL section (keyword: `discover`) and the What's Hot icon you will see on the Discover menu.

Note that you can do all of the following things using the drop-down menus and icons in your America Online software. But holding down your Ctrl key and striking a letter or number is usually faster.

Main Menu: Key in Ctrl-D to go to "Departments."

Index: Click on the Go To menu and mouse down to Directory of Services. Or click on the flash bar icon showing a magnifying glass looking at a disk to "Search Directory of Services."

Mail: Key in Ctrl-M to compose mail; Ctrl-R to read mail.

Billing: Use the keyword `billing`.

Access Numbers: Use the keyword `access` or `9600` to go to the "9600 Baud Access Center."

Sign Off: Click on the File item of the menu bar, mouse down to Exit, and click.

How to Get Help

If you need help before you go online, click on the Help selection of the menu bar. You'll find that the help information built into the AOL program is quite extensive. By searching it *before* you connect with the service, you can save connect time. To tap into the equally extensive online help that's available, use the keyword `help` to get to the Members' Online Support screen shown in the figure "Your Free Online Help Center."

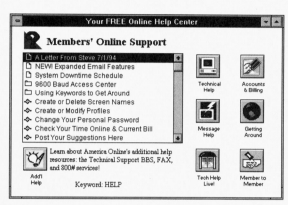

The AOL Members' Online Support screen. Get here with the keyword `help` or by clicking on the big red question mark icon that appears on the AOL Departments screen.

AOL Free Technical Support BBS: You can use this board to find local AOL access numbers, modem setup commands, and other connecting and troubleshooting information. Dial 800-827-5808 using any communications terminal program (not the AOL front-end software). The Technical Support BBS handles speeds of up to 14.4 Kbps. Set your comm program for 8/N/1. If you're using a Macintosh or the Windows Terminal program, remember to choose "No" when asked if you can display ANSI graphics.

AOL's Free Fax Response System: America Online provides information via fax on various technical support issues. To receive information by fax, dial 800-827-5551 from a Touch-Tone telephone. You will be connected to an automated voice system that will prompt you for your fax number and the selections(s) you would like to receive.

Tech Help Live: Lets you use AOL's chat feature to talk directly to AOL support personnel. Available Noon to 1 A.M., Eastern time, seven days a week.

Members Helping Members: A free message board where America Online members can assist and get assistance from other members. Keyword: `mhm`.

Lobby Guides: Guides are on duty from Noon until 6 A.M. Eastern time during the week, and all day on Saturday and Sunday. These are experienced America Online members, available to answer your questions. Keyword: `pc`.

AOL Newcomer's 8-Pack: Send a nice letter requesting the 8-Pack to the following AOL address: AFL SandyB. Geared to the beginning and intermediate user, it provides detailed help on downloading, viewing graphics, and decompressing files. It includes information on Help Sources online, and it "offers a warm hand to hold if you're lost!" Includes an AOL text map listing all Forums and Departments and a handy dandy chart with Forums and the times of their live conferences and chats.

How to Move Around

The easiest, most intuitive way to move around AOL is to just use your mouse to click or double-click on things. Once you've explored the service, however, you'll probably want to use keywords to zap yourself to a given feature instantly. Just hold down your Ctrl key and hit K for "Keyword." A box will pop up letting you specify a word. Notice that the box includes a button to take you directly to the "Keyword List."

For even more detailed information on the various ways to navigate the service, go to the Members' Online Support screen. Then click on the "Getting Around" icon. That will

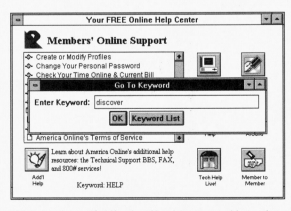

When you key in Ctrl-K, a box like this pops up. Notice that you can click on a button to go to AOL's Keyword List.

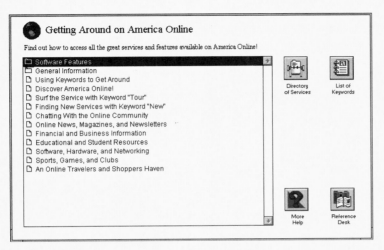

All kinds of help "Getting Around on America Online"!

lead to a screen like the one shown in the figure "Getting Around on America Online." Notice that one of the articles is "Using Keywords to Get Around."

How to Get a Master List of Keywords

The quickest way to get a list of AOL keywords is to key in Ctrl-K to pop up the Keyword box. Then just click on the Keyword List button. Alternatively, you can click on the flash bar icon that shows a big red arrow swooping into a disk.

The Keyword List on AOL is divided into Departments, so to get the complete list, you will have to get the list for each Department. The thing to do is to click on a Department name, let the text flow in, then click on the File icon on the flash bar. The service will prompt you for a file name and, when you enter it, will record the keywords in that file.

Using E-Mail and Finding Addresses

Electronic mail on AOL is so easy and intuitive to use that there's really only one point to make. After you key in Ctrl-M to go create some mail, you'll see a screen like the one in the figure "Compose Mail." The only trick is that hitting your Enter key will not move you from one box to the next. Use your mouse to move among boxes instead.

As for reading mail, the service will tell you if you have letters waiting when you sign on. Just click on the Mail icon. All you have to know here is that you can print or copy letters to disk by clicking on the File option of the menu bar and then clicking on Save or Save As. Or you can click on the File or Print icons on the flash bar.

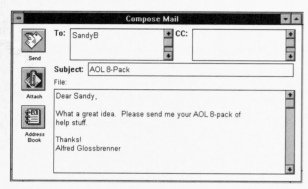

AOL mail couldn't be simpler.

To find the AOL e-mail address of another member, click on the Members item on the menu bar. The drop-down menu that will then appear will let you search the Member Directory, edit your own profile, send an instant message to a user, and so on. Remember that profiles are voluntary.

How to Send Mail to Other Services

To send mail to any of the services listed below, you'll need to know the person's user ID or address on that service, and you'll need to add to it some special routing information.

For example, to send mail to Amy Fowler, whose address on GEnie is a.fowler4, you would use the address `a.fowler4@genie.geis.com`.

To send mail from AOL to a CompuServe subscriber, be sure to substitute a period for the comma that typically separates the fifth and sixth numbers in a CompuServe address.

Sending mail to:	*Enter this at the "To:" prompt:*
CompuServe	`71234.5678@compuserve.com`
Delphi	`address@delphi.com`
GEnie	`address@genie.geis.com`
Internet	`userid@company.org`
Prodigy	`address@prodigy.com`

Sweetalk, WTG, and YGM

These are three shareware programs you can download from the AOL software library. YGM is a mail handler that lets you prepare messages offline and generally manage your mail. WTG and Sweetalk are programs for users of the AOL chat services. Among other things, they let you:

- Send a sound (or a .WAV file) to "say" something to your online friend.
- Prepare and save phrases you want to send ahead of time and then send them with a single mouse click.
- Save e-mail and messages to a file with the click of a button.
- Notify you automatically about which of your friends are online (and where they are) each time you yourself sign on.

Sweetalk also has a "snapshot" or "camera" feature that lets you save any Windows AOL window—whether it's e-mail, a posting in one of the Windows AOL folders, or even a conversation in the chat rooms—just by clicking on one button. The window is saved to a file that you can read or print later. You will need VBRUN300.DLL for Windows to use Sweetalk. It, too, can be downloaded from AOL.

CompuServe

Quick Reference

Since there are over 20 different front-end programs for CompuServe, including the company's own Information Manager and Navigator programs, what you'll find here are command-line commands. You can issue these from *any* program, though there may be an icon or a drop-down menu in your front-end software that will do the same thing.

U.S. Customer Service: 800-848-8990 or 614-457-8650
Weekdays: 8 A.M. to Midnight, EST
Weekends: Noon to 10 P.M., EST

Beginner's Best Bets: Take the tour. It's free and it offers a nice introduction to the service. Open your comm program's capture buffer or otherwise begin logging to disk and key in `go tour`. You should also key in `go practice` to get to the Practice Forum (SIG), where you can learn to use a SIG at no extra charge. The command `go new` will take you to the What's New menu that greets you the first time you sign on each week. All of these options are free of charge.

Main Menu: Key in `top`. (No "go" is needed for this one.)

Index: Key in `go ind`. Get the entire index as a file you can search offline with your word processor. This is the master list of keywords for CompuServe. Also consider producing a file containing the names of all CompuServe Forums. Just use `forum` as your search word. You may also want to try keying in `find` to get to the index search function directly.

Mail: Key in `go mail`.

Rates: Key in `go rates`.

Billing: Key in `go billing`.

Access Numbers: Key in `go phones`.

Chat command summary: Key in `go cb` to get to the chat feature. Pick a channel. After you're connected to a channel, key in `/help`.

Escape Hatch: Key in Ctrl-C once or twice, as needed, to stop a process and get yourself back to a menu. Or use whatever key combination tells your comm program to issue a true "Break" signal.

Sign Off: Key in `off` or `bye`.

How to Get Help

Key in `help` at any prompt for a brief command summary. Then key in `find` and specify `help` as your search word. (Your capture buffer should be open, of course.) You will then see a multi-page menu offering 40 or more help features, including the following free features and corresponding keywords:

Feature	Keyword
CIM Support Forum	CIMSUPPORT
Command Summary	COMMAND
Commonly Asked Questions	QUESTIONS
CompuServe Help Forum	HELPFORUM
CompuServe Magazine	OLI
CompuServe Mail Help	MAILHELP
Feedback to Customer Service	FEEDBACK
Mac CIM Support Forum	MCIMSUP
Member Assistance	HELP
Member Directory	DIRECTORY
Practice Forum	PRACTICE
Quick Reference Word List	QUICK
Review Your Charges	CHARGES
User Profile Program	TERMINAL
WinCIM Information	WINCIM
WinCIM Support Forum	WCIMSUPPORT

How to Move Around

You can get anywhere on CompuServe by following the menus that branch off the main or "top" menu. And you can always return to the main menu by keying in `top`. But after you've had some experience, you will want to use keywords and page numbers.

You can reach any feature with a keyword. Keying in `go ppp`, for example, will take you to the Peachpit Press feature. Within that feature, you will find page numbers like PPP-26 and PPP-34. Once you know what the page number is, you can "go" there directly as well. Keying in `go ppp-34`, for example, would take you directly to that page.

When using menus, keying in `m` at a prompt will usually take you to the previous *menu*. Keying in `p` at most prompts usually takes you to the previous menu item.

Using E-Mail and Finding Addresses

If you're operating from the command line, key in `go mail` to get to the following menu:

```
CompuServe Mail  Main Menu
 1 READ mail, 1 message pending

 2 COMPOSE a new message
 3 UPLOAD a message
 4 USE a file from PER area

 5 ADDRESS Book
 6 SET options

 9 Send a CONGRESSgram ($)
Enter choice!
```

You can read mail by selecting 1 or by keying in `read`. After a letter has been displayed, you'll be prompted as to what you want to do with it. If you key in `reply` at that prompt, you will be able to compose a reply on the spot. When you're finished composing, key in `/exit` on a fresh line, all the way to the left. More prompts will follow, allowing you to approve the sending of a letter. If you do not want to reply, key in `delete` after you've read a letter. The CompuServe mail system always insists that you take some action (delete, forward, file, etc.) on a letter after you have read it.

The only other trick you need to know is that you should use the "Upload" option only when you want to send a graphic image or other binary file to someone. If you have prepared a plain text letter on disk that you want to send via CompuServe mail, select the "Compose" option instead. (If you use the CompuServe Upload option, your recipient will have to download the message using a protocol—a waste of time for most text messages.) When the "enter text" message appears, simply tell your communications program to do an ASCII upload from your disk, and key in `/exit` when it is done. (See your software manual for the necessary command.)

To find the e-mail address of another CompuServe member, key in `go directory`. This is a free service. You will be asked to specify name, state or country, interests, etc. But as long as you specify at least one item, there's no need to specify others. If you want to be listed in the CompuServe directory, you must go there and add your listing. A listing is purely voluntary.

Sending Mail to Other Services

To send mail to any of the services listed below, you'll need to know the person's user ID or address on that service, and add to it the prefix `>internet:` along with some special routing information.

For example, to send mail to Albert Robertson, whose Prodigy user ID is abcd05a, you would use the address

>internet:abcd05a@prodigy.com.

If you're sending mail to an AOL subscriber, be sure to remove any spaces from the user address.

Sending mail to:	Enter this at the "To:" prompt:
AOL	>internet:address@aol.com
Delphi	>internet:address@delphi.com
GEnie	>internet:address@genie.geis.com
Internet	>internet:userid@company.org
Prodigy	>internet:address@prodigy.com

How to Get a "Sense of the SIG"

CompuServe has over 600 SIGs, which it officially calls "Forums." To get the current list, key in `go ind` to get to the index feature, open your capture buffer, and opt to search on the keyword `forum`. After the display has scrolled out, close your capture buffer, sign off, and review the SIG list at your leisure.

When you've found a SIG of interest, sign on to CompuServe and open your capture buffer. Then key in `go` followed by the SIG name. The SIG "Announcements" will usually appear. When you get to the main SIG menu, be sure to join if that is an option. There's no cost, and all you have to do is key in your name as prompted. If you don't join, you will not be able to download files.

The two most important things to do next to get a sense of the SIG are to opt for "Libraries" on the main, or "top," SIG menu and then to pick "Message subjects" under the "Messages" heading on the same menu. Here's the menu from the IBM New User's Forum, the library list, and the message subject list:

IBM New User's Forum+ Forum Menu

1 INSTRUCTIONS
2 MESSAGES
3 LIBRARIES (Files)
4 CONFERENCING (0 participating)

5 ANNOUNCEMENTS from sysop
6 MEMBER directory
7 OPTIONS for this forum

Enter choice !

IBM New User's Forum+ Libraries Menu

0 General [0]
1 Download Help [1]
2 Library Tools [2]
3 Adventures [3]
4 Music [4]
5 Fun Graphics [5]
6 Gen Fun & Games [6]
7 Ask the Sysops [7]
8 Word & Card Games [8]
9 Sports & Chance [9]
10 BASIC Workshop [10]
11 Demo Programs [11]
12 Windows Fun [N]

IBM New User's Forum+ Sections Menu

Section names (#subjs/# msgs)
0 General [N] (125/313)
1 Download Help [N] (20/63)
2 Library Tools [N] (9/21)
3 Adventures [N] (3/12)
4 Music [N] (6/10)
5 Fun Graphics [N] (9/17)
6 Gen Fun & Games [N] (13/49)
7 Ask the Sysops [N] (68/239)
8 Village Inn [N] (13/25)
9 Word Games [N] (1/1)
10 BASIC Workshop [N] (5/16)

Enter choice(s) or ALL !

Quick Reference

Customer Service: 800-544-4005 or 617-491-3393
Weekdays: 8 A.M. to 11 P.M., EST
Weekends: Noon to 8 P.M., EST

Beginner's Best Bets: Delphi has scores of wonderful features, but full Internet access tops them all. From the main menu, key in `int` to get to the Internet SIG, and from the Internet SIG menu key in `gopher`. The Delphi Gopher offers menu-driven access to many of the best resources on the Internet. It will show you what's available and then actually go get it or take you there. If you're feeling really adventuresome, key in `use` from the Internet SIG menu to get to Usenet newsgroups. One word of advice: Select the Delphi newsgroup reader, not "nn," when that choice appears.

Main Menu: Key in `main` at any prompt, or keep entering Ctrl-Z to back up until you get to the main menu.

Index and Master Keyword List: Key in `us ind`.

Mail: Key in `mail mail`. (That's right, two "`mails`" in a row.)

Rates: Key in `using rates`.

Billing: Key in `using rev`.

Access Numbers: Key in `using access`.

Escape Hatch: Ctrl-Z.

Sign Off: Key in `bye`.

Getting Help and Moving Around

Delphi's user interface is more than a decade old. But, until the company finally produces its graphical front-end program—or completely rewrites its software—we're all stuck with it. The key thing to understand about moving around on Delphi is that you can issue a "gang" command that includes the name of the menu you want to go to, the item on that menu you want to use, and the name of the item on the sub-menu then produced.

You can thus get to the Mail feature by keying in `mail` and waiting for that menu to appear, and then keying in `mail` to select that feature from the Mail menu. Or you can just key in `mail mail` to zap yourself directly to the identical location.

The other thing you need to know is that Delphi uses Ctrl-Z for just about everything. Each time you enter it from a menu prompt, you will be taken back to the menu from which you came. The Ctrl-Z command is also used to signal to Delphi that you have finished composing a letter and wish to send it.

As for getting help, the most important command to key in is `main using` to get to the Using Delphi menu. That's the menu that has all the help options and files on it:

```
USING-DELPHI Menu:

Access Information               Profiles/Stories
Advantage Plan (20 hours for $20) Romance Stories
Announcements                    Rates & Billing Policy
Future Forum                     Review Bills/Invoices & Usage
Guided Tour                      Service (Forum)
Internet Register/Cancel         Settings (Profile)
Manuals & Documentation          T-Shirt (Orders and Graphics)
Member Services/Feedback         Tips on Using DELPHI
New Member SIG                   9600 & 14,400 bps Access
Press Releases                   EXIT

USING-DELPHI>(Please Select an Item)>
```

Using E-Mail

The best advice I can give you regarding using Delphi e-mail is *don't*—if you can at all avoid it. It is a truly terrible system. If you've no other choice, however, key in `mail mail`, and when the "MAIL>" prompt appears, key in `send`. Respond to the resulting prompts. Type or do an ASCII upload of your letter. When finished, key in Ctrl-Z to send the letter.

For more on Delphi mail, key in `help` at the "MAIL>" prompt. To easily send mail via the Internet, go to the Delphi Internet SIG and key in `email`. To find the Delphi e-mail addresses of other subscribers, key in `member` at the main menu prompt.

Sending Mail to Other Services

To send mail to any of the services listed below, you'll need to know the person's user ID or address on that service. When specifying the address, begin with the prefix `internet`, followed by the person's user ID and Internet domain name in quotation marks.

For example, to send mail to Katie Meyer, whose address on CompuServe is 71234,5678, you would use the address

```
internet"71234.5678@compuserve.com"
```
(The comma in CompuServe addresses is always changed to a period when sending over the Internet.)

When sending mail to AOL, be sure to remove any spaces in the address before adding `@aol.com`. The address AFL johnc thus becomes `AFLjohnc@aol.com`.

Sending mail to:	Enter this at the "To:" prompt:
AOL	`internet"address@aol.com"`
CompuServe	`internet"71234.5678@compuserve.com"`
GEnie	`internet"address@genie.geis.com"`
Internet	`internet"userid@company.org"`
Prodigy	`internet"address@prodigy.com"`

Quick Reference

Customer Service: 800-638-9636

Weekdays: 8 A.M. to Midnight, EST

Weekends: Noon to 8 P.M., EST

Beginner's Best Bets: The GEnius RT (the GEnie Users RoundTable), run by Mark Hiatt, is your best source for help, friendly advice, and candid tips on what's good and what's not. Just key in `genius`. You might also try keying in `practice`, to get to the free GEnie Practice RoundTable.

If you're a bit more advanced as a computer user and if you enjoy games, try keying in `rscards` to get to the spot where you can download the RSCARDS software needed to play casino games with other GEnie users in a highly graphical, full-color format.

I know this sounds like a promotional announcement. But while GEnie has a lot to offer, it is among the more complicated services to use. If you're interested in really learning to use GEnie, and doing so as painlessly as possible, get my McGraw-Hill book on the subject. As discussed in the "Glossbrenner's Choice" section following this Cookbook, the cost is $25, and the book includes the latest version of Aladdin and a $12 usage credit.

Main Menu: Key in `top`.

Index: Key in `index`.

Mail: Key in `mail`.

Rates: Key in `rates`.

Billing: Key in `bill`.

Access Numbers: Key in `phones`.

Escape Hatch: Hit your "Break" key. (To set your "Break" key, type `set`, choose "Genie Setup Script," and follow the instructions.)

Sign Off: Key in `bye`.

Getting Help and Moving Around

To get help, just key in `help` at any prompt.

The two main ways to move around GEnie are keywords and page numbers. To get to the GE Mail menu, for example, you may key in either `mail` or `m200` (for "move to page 200," the page that contains the GE Mail menu).

How to Get the Master List of Keywords

When you key in `index` to get to GEnie's Index of Products and Services, you'll be given the options of getting the list with short or long descriptions and in alphabetical or page number order. Your best bet is to get the short descriptions in alphabetical order.

Once you have this list, you can use your word processor to search it. Any entry with "RoundTable" or "RT" in the description is a Special Interest Group (SIG).

Using E-Mail

Key in `mail` to get to the GE Mail menu. For very short messages, choose Option 6, "Compose and Send GE Mail Online." You'll be prompted to enter the address, "carbon copy" recipients, and subject. Then type your message in the message area.

To send your message, key in `*s` and hit Enter. To look at your message before sending it, key in `*l` (for list) on a line all by itself and hit Enter. To exit without sending the message, key in `*x`.

For longer messages, it's best to create your message offline and save it as a plain ASCII text file. In that case, choose Option 7, "Upload a Text Letter." Enter the address, "carbon copy" recipients, and subject when you are prompted to do so. Then use your comm program to upload your message. Issue a "Break" signal when you are finished.

To find an e-mail address of another GEnie user, select Option 8 from the GE Mail menu and follow the resulting prompts.

Sending Mail to Other Services

To send mail to any of the services listed below, you'll need to know the person's user ID or address on that service, and add to it some special routing information. The last part of the address will always be `@inet#`. That tells GEnie to send the message over the Internet Gateway.

For example, to send mail to Richard Keller, whose user ID on AOL is rich k, you would use the address `richk@aol.com@inet#`. (Note that the space in the AOL address has been removed.)

To send mail from GEnie to a CompuServe subscriber, be sure to substitute a period for the comma that typically separates the fifth and sixth numbers in a CompuServe address.

Sending mail to:	Enter this at the "To:" prompt:
AOL	`address@aol.com@inet#`
CompuServe	`71234.5678@compuserve.com@inet#`
Delphi	`address@delphi.com@inet#`
Internet	`userid@company.org@inet#`
Prodigy	`address@prodigy.com@inet#`

Quick Reference

Customer Service: 800-776-3449
24 hours a day, 365 days a year

Beginner's Best Bets: Key in Ctrl-J to pop up the "Jump Word" (key-word) box, and then key in `let's explore` to take a pleasant tour of the Prodigy service. You will also want to click on the square labeled "Member Services" on the main Prodigy "Highlights" screen that greets you each time you sign on. You'll find the square to the right of the main Prodigy logo near the top of the screen.

Main Menu: Click on the yellow Highlights screen icon to the far left of the toolbar at the bottom of the screen. Or jump to `highlights`. If you jump to `main`, you will get a list of the main cover pages for each major category of the service.

Index: Click on the "A-Z" tool at the bottom of the screen. For an index of bulletin boards, jump to `boards a-z`.

Mail: Jump to `mail`.

Rates: Jump to `service information`.

Billing: Jump to `billing`.

Access Numbers: Jump to `phone numbers`.

Sign Off: Click on "E" in the toolbar at the bottom of the screen.

How to Get Help

Prodigy offers tons of help to users. But you don't have to go online to get most of it. That's because it's built into your Prodigy software. (Even when you request help while you're connected to the service, the information often comes from your own software.) So load the software

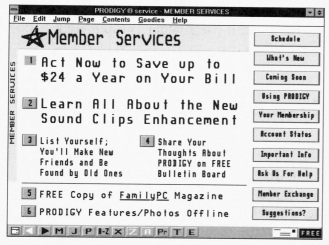

Prodigy's crucial Member Services screen.

without the AutoLogon option and click on Help in the menu bar.

When you *are* connected to Prodigy, jump to `for new members` to get to a master list of help information. Consult the A-Z index for help on using specific products. And consider jumping to `member services` to get to the screen shown in the figure "Member Services." Notice the Using Prodigy button, fourth down in the column of choices. Click on that for extensive information.

How to Move Around

There are more ways to move around the Prodigy service than you can count, but until you discover some favorite places, you're probably best off clicking on things with your mouse. Later, you'll probably want to use jump words (keywords) and macros. Jump words are often drawn directly from the screen names. But many different phrases will take you to the same place, as you will see once you get the complete jump word list.

There are three ways to pop up the Jump Word box. Click on "J" in the toolbar at the bottom of the screen. Click on Jump on the menu bar at the top of the screen. Or key in Ctrl-J. When the box pops up, key in your jump word and hit Enter.

You'll find the macro-recording option on the Goodies drop-down menu on the menu bar. The concept is that you tell the software to start recording every keystroke or mouse click; you do your thing; then you stop recording and write the results to a file. Next time you want to duplicate those keystrokes, you "play" the macro file.

Macros are most effective if they consist of a jump word procedure. Also, once you've recorded a macro, you can use Toolbar Setup to add it to your own toolbar. From then on, you can play the macro by clicking on it.

How to Get the Master List of Jump Words

To capture the list of Prodigy jump words to a disk file, start by clicking on "T" in the toolbar. Select Print Options from the menu that will appear, and opt to "Send to File." (See the figure "Mailbox," which deals with printing e-mail, for an example of the "Send to File" option.) You will be prompted for a file name.

Close the Tools menu and click on the A-Z index option. When the index appears, click on "Pr" in the toolbar to print. You will be given the option of printing a single page or a range of pages. Go for the whole thing. There may be 265 pages or so, but they're small, and despite what the prompt will say, it does not take a long time.

Using E-Mail

The best way to use e-mail on Prodigy is to get a copy of the Prodigy Mail Manager. Assuming you do not yet have a copy, and you want to save one or more letters to disk, follow the procedure discussed previously to send printer output to a disk file. Bring up the Tools menu and change your print option to "Send to File." Then display the letter and "print" it.

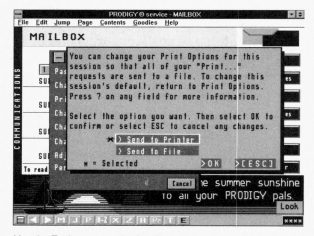

Use the Tools menu and select Print Options to redirect printer output to a disk file. Then display an item and "print" it.

Prodigy's Mail Manager screen.

Once you've had some experience with Prodigy mail, you'll want more features and more power. That's when it's time to download a copy of the Mail Manager package. (The cost to download it is $4.95.) Jump to `about mail manager` to learn about all it offers: preparing letters offline, sending to Internet addresses, filing your mail on disk, sending faxes, and so on.

Follow the instructions provided in the README.TXT file to get the package installed. Then sign on to Prodigy, jump to `mail`, and click on the Mail Manager button. You will then see a screen like the one shown in the figure "Mail Manager."

Finding Service IDs and Sending Mail to Other Services

To get to the feature that will let you search for the e-mail addresses (Prodigy calls them "Service IDs") of other members, there are at least three jump words you may use: `list of members`, `locate members`, or `member list`.

To send mail to any of the services listed below, you'll need to know the person's user ID or address on that service, and add to it some special routing information. For example, to send mail to Mary Kelchner, whose GEnie address is m.kelchner, you would use the address `m.kelchner@genie.geis.com`.

To send mail from Prodigy to a CompuServe subscriber, be sure to substitute a period for the comma that typically separates the fifth and sixth numbers in a CompuServe address.

Finding Service IDs and Sending Mail to Other Services [cont.]

If your correspondent is on AOL, remember to remove any spaces from the AOL address before adding `@aol.com`.

Sending mail to:	Enter this at the "To:" prompt:
AOL	`address@aol.com`
CompuServe	`71234.5678@compuserve.com`
Delphi	`address@delphi.com`
GEnie	`address@genie.geis.com`
Internet	`userid@company.org`

Everything You Ever Need to Know to Use the Internet

The Internet, as you know from the chapters of this book, is the damnedest collection of computers and networks and downloadable files, information, and services the world has ever seen. Created during the Cold War as a means of facilitating, yet de-centralizing, information and communication functions, Internet access became available to us—we of the great unwashed masses—shortly after it was determined that the Cold War had indeed ended.

Those of us who had been "playing with" consumer online services for more than a decade—but could never get access to the Net—were astounded at what we found. On the one hand, there was this incredible, delightful jumble of features and information. On the other hand, there was the clear sense that the software that runs the Net had not progressed much beyond the early 1980s. For many an old hand, tapping into the Net is "déjà vu all over again."

Even the online world, as sluggish as it has traditionally been, has moved far beyond the plain-text, non-graphical displays and bytehead UNIX commands used by Net masters.

But here it is, take it or leave it. And, if you heed my advice, you'll take it, since, for all its computeristic orientation, the Internet—or more properly, the computer systems and networks it connects—has a great deal to offer even the greenest of new users. Here are the main Internet features presented in this Cookbook. These are the ones most people find most useful most of the time:

• E-mail
Send a message anywhere on the planet in seconds.

• Newsgroups
Read and contribute questions, answers, and information on any topic you can imagine.

• Mailing lists
Like newsgroups in breadth of topic, but everyone on the list gets every contribution.

• Archie

Find files on the Net by searching a master directory on the basis of file name.

• File Transfer Protocol (FTP)

Transfer the files, once you find them, to your location.

• Telnet

Log on to a remote computer to search library card catalogues, explore information systems using menus, and so on.

• Gopher and Veronica

Each Gopher menu at each site is different. But all let you locate and obtain files and Net resources or go to Net locations using a menu system. Veronica, in contrast, lets you search all Gopher menus at all sites at the same time.

A Waste of Time: WAIS and WWW

If you want to do some serious time wasting, then plunge into the Wide Area Information Servers (WAIS, pronounced "ways") or the World Wide Web (WWW or W3). These two high-concept Internet features get a lot of press because they're sexy and because the layman's press doesn't know any better.

Unlike Archie, Gopher, and Veronica, which deal in file names and menu items and their descriptions, WAIS lets you search the actual text of the documents at a site. For its part, the World Wide Web not only lets you search for a document, it displays the actual documents you find, complete with hypertext hot-links to *other* documents.

Unfortunately, neither feature is ready for prime time. And WAIS probably never will be, since its creator has stopped supporting it on the Internet. WWW certainly has potential, but before that potential can be fulfilled, tens of thousands of documents on the Internet will have to be reformatted to include hypertext hot-links.

In light of all this, you will not find either WAIS or WWW covered in this Cookbook.

What are the Options?

There are essentially five ways to get connected to the Internet. Not all of them are practical for ordinary people, but here they are:

1. Install a digital phone link able to transfer data at 45 million bits per second.

That's about four and a half *thousand* times faster than your average 9600 bits per second modem. The cost of such connections are in the thousands, too. Per month. Great for businesses and universities. Not so great for Mom-and-Pop operations.

2. Become a student or take a course at a college or university that has an Internet connection.

This is the best deal going. It costs you nothing—or next to nothing—and you can tap in from the computer center, via the personal computer in your dorm room, or from anyplace else where you can reach your college's computer by modem.

    If you're already a student, ask around to find out what you must do to tap in. It has been said that one of the reasons some people become perpetual students is to avoid losing their free Internet access.

3. Go to work for a company that allows its employees to use its Internet connection.

I'm not sure you'd want to make free Internet access a condition of your accepting the job. Then again, it wouldn't hurt to ask the interviewer something like, "And I assume that Vandelay Industries is on the Internet? I wouldn't want to be without the productivity resources it brings to bear . . ."

4. Sign up with a company that offers you full dial-up access to the Internet for between $20 and $200 a month.

These are called "PPP" or "SLIP" connections. They are the kinds of connections you've got to have if you want to run Mosaic, Lynx, Cello, and the other graphical front-end programs you may have read about. But you also have to install this and other software yourself, which can be a major hassle.

The Internet

Since PPP and SLIP connections are dialed up via your modem, the data can't flow any faster than your modem's top speed. And then there's the fact that, regardless of the service provider you choose (and there are tons of them), each can offer only so many connections. You should not be surprised if you have difficulty getting connected to your service provider during normal business hours.

A connection like this does offer the status of making you or your company your own "domain," however. Thus I would no longer use the address Alfred@delphi.com. I could be Alfred@firecrystal.com.

5. Get a subscription to America Online or Delphi Internet Services.
It will cost between $8.95 and $13 for between four and five hours of access. Or consider looking for a BBS that offers Internet access to its paying members. (I should note here that CompuServe is rapidly moving to fulfill its promise of full Internet access also.)

What Should I Do?

You should get your feet wet first is what you should do. Use the free time provided by the America Online and Delphi coupons at the back of this book to explore each service's Internet offerings. Then, and only then, should you even think about going through the hassle and expense of setting up a PPP or SLIP connection. As you read this, it is possible that the others in the Big Five will offer full Internet access. Or not. Meantime, here's what to do on Delphi and on AOL:

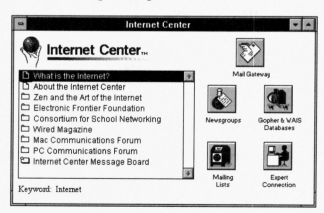

The Internet Center on America Online.

- On Delphi, key in `internet` or just `int` at the main menu. That'll take you to the Internet SIG. Unlike Internet SIGs on other services that are limited to merely talking about the Internet, the Delphi Internet SIG is your gateway to the Net itself.

- On America Online, your best bet is to key in Ctrl-K to pop up the Keyword box, and then key in `internet center`. That will take you to the screen shown in the figure "Internet Center."

Which Should I Choose?

The Internet Center looks pretty good, doesn't it? At this writing, America Online is clearly the leader in offering an attractive, graphical, mouse-driven interface to the Internet. It is a joy to use! But there are other factors to consider.

AOL is considerably cheaper than Delphi. Assume you spend about ten hours online during a month. As long as those hours are in the evenings and on the weekends, your cost on AOL would be about $27, while your cost on Delphi would be $37—a difference of $10.

If you were to spend the same ten hours during *business* hours, your cost on AOL would be the same $27, while Delphi would bill you $127—a difference of $100! That's because of the $9 per hour surcharge for accessing Delphi during the working day.

Wow! No contest, right? We should all sign up with AOL. Not exactly. There are also these four key considerations:

1. AOL does not offer you *full* Internet access—yet.
You can read newsgroup postings and mailing lists, but you cannot transfer files from the Net via FTP, and you cannot Telnet to another system to do things like search the Library of Congress card catalogue. (See the FTP and Telnet sections of the "Cookbook" for more information on these features.) The company has plans for offering FTP and Telnet features, however, and they may be available as you read this. (Click on the Expert Connection icon on the AOL Internet Center screen to find out.)

The Internet

2. AOL does not give you access to all Internet newsgroups and mailing lists.

As a test, I decided to compare the number of alternative (alt) newsgroups you can read on AOL versus Delphi. Right now, there are close to 950 alternative newsgroups available on the Net. You can access them all with Delphi. But America Online offers you only about a third of them.

I can well understand why AOL would want to be so selective. There are many, many newsgroups that no one under the age of 18—18? heck, 21!—should be exposed to, and AOL is a family service. Besides, most AOL subscribers will never know the difference. But now *you* do.

In addition, your AOL mailbox is limited to 550 pieces of mail. That sounds like a lot, but it is a consideration when you're subscribing to mailing lists. Delphi gives you unlimited storage capacity, as long as you delete items within 48 hours, presumably after you have downloaded them to your own computer system.

3. AOL has had capacity problems.

As I write this, the total number of subscribers to America Online has just topped 1 million. Almost exactly a year ago, it was at the 350,000 mark. That's an incredible performance, and they deserve every bit of their success.

On the other hand, in the course of writing this book, I have had considerable trouble logging on to AOL. I connect to the service, but when I try to log on, I am told that "No connection can be made at this time; please try again later."

These problems may very well have been solved by the time you read this. But it is only fair to say that, while Internet access via Delphi is more expensive, and while Delphi's current user interface is ugly, at least you can get on the service whenever you want.

That is not something one can honestly say about AOL—at this writing. My experience has been that to be sure of getting on AOL, you should call very late at night or very early in the morning. That's bound to change. But it is the truth today.

4. A major revamping of Delphi is in the offing.

All indications are that before the end of 1994, Delphi will roll out a totally revamped service, complete with mouse-driven graphical interfaces and software for Windows and Macintosh machines. Delphi will have to run long and hard to catch up with AOL's wonderful graphical interface. But then, Delphi has the power and deep pockets of Rupert Murdoch's The News Corporation behind it, so there's no telling what will happen.

Conclusion

Bearing in mind that all things change, but they tend to change more rapidly in the computer and communications industries, my advice at this writing is to use the coupons at the back of this book to sample both Delphi and America Online. (But keep an eye on CompuServe.) Either or both may be just what you need. And, to quickly find out what you're missing on AOL, you may want to take a look at the Internet Newsgroup Essentials disk available from the "Glossbrenner's Choice" section of this book, since it includes a complete list of the currently available Internet newsgroups.

The Internet

"At-dot" What?

Though not understood or appreciated by the new online user, the single most important feature offered by the Internet is e-mail connectivity. I'm on MCI Mail; you're on AOL; yet we can exchange messages, thanks to the Internet. My message to you will show up in your AOL mailbox, just as yours to me will show up in my MCI Mail mailbox.

Simple. Logical. Common-sensical. But *impossible* prior to the interconnection of most commercial services to the Internet. You'll find more information in Chapter 28 of this book. But basically, once you know your correspondent's address on any service, you can almost certainly exchange electronic mail. The key steps are these:

1. Find out if the service you are using can send and receive Internet e-mail.

2. Make sure you know what your own Internet e-mail address is.

3. Find out the address of your correspondent on the other service. You will read about the Internet Network Information Center (InterNIC) and its "master" directory of Internet user addresses. But believe me, it's much easier to just phone your correspondent and ask for the correct address.

Getting Your Name Listed

I don't have much hope that InterNIC's national White Pages directory of e-mail addresses will truly succeed. But it is certainly worth taking the time to get yourself listed, particularly if you are a businessperson.

If you want to get your name listed in InterNIC's national White Pages, the best thing to do is to send an e-mail message to `admin@ds.internic.net` and ask about getting added to their White Pages directory.

Resources

InterNIC Information Services
General Atomics
P.O. Box 85608
San Diego, CA 92186-9784
800-444-4345, 619-455-4600 (voice)
619-455-3990 (fax)
info@internic.net (e-mail)

4. Consult the service-specific portion of the "Cookbook" to learn the proper format to use when addressing Internet mail to some other service.

5. Just do it! Uh-huh! Send a test message to your correspondent, and request that he or she do the same to your address. Having someone send you Internet mail is sometimes the easiest way to discover your own Internet address.

6. Take notes. Or at least do not let all this work evaporate. If you have discovered the correct procedure for sending messages from your service to a friend's service via the Net, write it down. That way you won't have to reinvent the wheel next month.

What are the Main Newsgroup Categories?

Usenet newsgroups, as you know from Chapter 35, are among the most popular and numerous features on the Net. Anyone, anywhere, can post anything to a newsgroup. It's even possible to post anonymously. And new newsgroups are not that difficult to start. When you consider that the Internet girdles the globe, newsgroups are truly "the world's bulletin board." The only limitation is that no message can be longer than 64K.

At this writing, there are nearly 10,000 newsgroups. To make it easier for people to find what they're looking for, newsgroups are divided into major categories. Each main category is further divided, and the result is often divided again and again, as areas are created for discussions of ever-greater specificity.

The main topic categories of Usenet newsgroups at this writing are:

Name	Description
alt	Alternative newsgroups. Pretty much "anything goes." Examples: alt.atheism.satire, alt.comedy.british.blackadder, alt.comedy.firesgn-thtre, alt.spam.
bionet	Biology, of course. Examples: bionet.jobs, bionet.journals.contents, bionet.molbio.aging.
bit	Articles from Bitnet listserv, automated mailing lists. Eliminates the need to subscribe to these lists yourself. Examples: bit.listserv.gutnberg, bit.listserv.hellas, bit.listserv.hindu-d. (Bitnet is a network of largely academic institutions that, for technical reasons, cannot handle newsgroups.)
biz	The accepted place for advertisements, marketing, and other commercial postings. Examples: biz.books.technical, biz.dec.decnews, biz.comp.telebit.netblazer.
clari	ClariNet is a commercial service offering AP and Reuters newswire feeds, newspaper columns, and much more. Since the site offering ClariNet must pay a fee to subscribe, it may or may not be available at your site. Examples: clari.biz.economy, clari.biz.market.report.asia, clari.feature.miss_manners.

Name	Description
comp	The "computer" topic. Examples: comp.robotics, comp.security.misc, comp.simulation.
ddn	Defense Data Network. If you have to ask, you don't need to know.
gnu	As in "gnu is not UNIX." The Free Software Foundation and the GNU project.
ieee	Institute of Electrical and Electronic Engineers.
k12	Topics for teachers of kindergarten through grade 12. Examples: k12.chat.teacher, k12.ed.art, k12.ed.life-skills.
misc	Miscellaneous, of course. Examples: misc.handicap, misc.headlines, misc.health.diabetes.
news	Not world or national news, but Usenet network and software news. Examples: news.admin.misc, news.announce.conferences, news.announce.important.
rec	The arts, hobbies, and recreational activities. Examples: rec.arts.books.marketplace, rec.arts.fine, rec.aviation.home-built.
sci	Sciences and research. Examples: sci.research.careers, sci.research.postdoc, sci.space.shuttle.
soc	Social issues and socializing. Examples: soc.culture.africa, soc.feminism, soc.singles.
talk	Debate-oriented. Tends to feature long discussions.

Where Can I Find a Master List of Groups?

With nearly 10,000 groups to choose among, if you are to have any hope of finding the group that covers a given topic, you *must* get a complete, current list of the newsgroups that are available. You must also have access to an online service or system that subscribes to the group in question.

The master list to get is the one started by Gene Spafford and now run by David C. Lawrence. It comes in four parts: two for the alternative (alt) groups and two for all the others. There is one line per newsgroup, so you get the newsgroup name and a brief description. Your best bet is to get all four parts and then use your word processing program to search for topics of interest. When you find what you want, write down the name of the newsgroup. On Delphi, at least, you can specify the group you want to read by name.

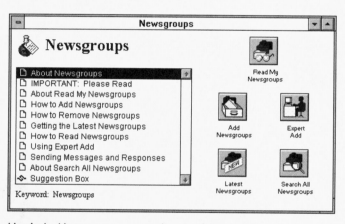

Here's the Newsgroups menu on America Online.

The complete Lawrence list is available from the "Glossbrenner's Choice" section of this book (on the Internet Newsgroup Essentials disk). Or you can get the components via FTP (see the "How to 'GET' Files by FTP" section of the "Cookbook") or newsgroup postings. Here are the places to check:

- FTP to `ftp.uu.net`
  Path: /usenet/news.answers/alt-hierarchies/
  Path: /usenet/news.answers/active-newsgroups/

- Newsgroups:
  news.lists
  news.groups
  news.announce.newgroups
  news.answers

The Most Crucial Groups

If you are a new user, you won't want to miss the following groups. With a little digging, they can tell you anything you want to know about the Internet and how to use it:

Name	Description
news.announce.newusers	A series of articles that explain various facets of Usenet.
news.newusers.questions	The place to ask questions about how Usenet works.
news.answers	Lists of Frequently Asked Questions (FAQs) and their answers from many different newsgroups. Don't miss this one!
alt.internet.services	The place to ask someone where to find a particular item on the Net.

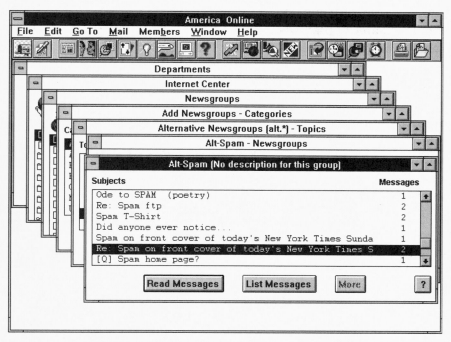

And here are the cascaded windows indicating how I got from the AOL Newsgroups menu to reviewing the message topics in a newsgroup devoted to Spam.

What's a Mailing List?

As you know from Chapter 35, an Internet mailing list is exactly that: a group of people who have asked to receive articles prepared and uploaded by other members on the list. Here are the key points you need to know:

1. All list subscribers get everything posted to the list.

Articles arrive in your electronic mailbox whether you are interested in their topics or not. (With a newsgroup, in contrast, you can pick and choose which articles or messages you want to read.)

2. Some lists are moderated; some are mechanized.

With a moderated list, all uploads go to a single individual who then decides what material will be sent to the list as a whole. Some moderators go further and, to prevent information overload, transmit digests of the material that has been sent to them. Unmoderated lists, in contrast, are handled by software that automatically mails articles without human intervention.

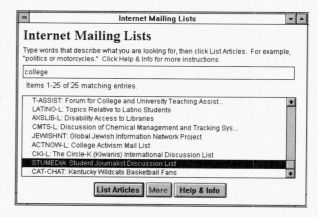

America Online makes it easy to search for mailing lists devoted to a certain topic. Here, I searched for lists with the word "college" in their descriptions.

3. To subscribe to a given list, you normally send a message to the subscription address.

If subscriptions are handled by list-server software, all you have to do is put some specified word in your letter or in its subject line. Although the concept of a mail-robot list-server seems to have originated on Bitnet, you will find these "daemons" throughout the Internet.

4. The subscription address and the article-posting address of most lists is *different*.

Don't make the classic new-user mistake of posting your subscription requests to the main list address.

Is There a Master List of Lists?

Two of the most comprehensive and well-respected "lists of lists" are:

- The SRI List of Lists
  Covers both Internet and Bitnet lists. Updated regularly. Currently is about 1.4 megabytes uncompressed.

- Publicly Accessible Mailing Lists
  Maintained by Stephanie da Silva. Mainly Internet lists. Widely available via FTP and newsgroups. You'll often see it referred to as the PAML list.

Both give you a paragraph or more of description written by the creator of each list. This information typically details the list's purpose, its goals, the creator's hopes for the list, and how to subscribe.

How to Get the Lists of Lists

To get the SRI list, do one of the following:

- FTP to `ftp.nisc.sri.com`
  Path: /netinfo/
  File: interest-groups.Z

- Request it by sending a message to the following e-mail address: `mail-server@nisc.sri.com`. Include this line in the body of the message: `send netinfo/interest-groups`.

To get the Publicly Accessible Mailing Lists (PAML), do one of the following:

- FTP to `rtfm.mit.edu`
  Path: /pub/usenet/news.answers/mail/mailing-lists/
  Files: part1, part2, etc.

- Look for the lists on the following newsgroups:
  news.lists
  news.announce.newusers
  news.answers

Sending Mail to a Bitnet Address

Since so many mailing lists originate on Bitnet, the network that links many colleges and universities, it can be important to know how to send mail to Bitnet addresses. This little excursion would not be necessary if Bitnet used the same "domain name system" used for Internet addresses.

Instead, a native Bitnet address consists of a user name, an "at" sign (@), and a computer name. No .edu or .com or any other "dot" extensions. Thus, if you ever see an address like listserv@tombomb, you will know that it is a Bitnet address.

To convert it to an Internet address, all you have to do is add .bitnet to the end of the address: listserv@tombomb.bitnet. This will work most of the time.

Sometimes you will encounter an e-mail address that contains a percent sign (%), such as biomed-l%ndsuvm1.bitnet@vm1.nodak.edu. The percent sign (%) is always someplace to the left of the "at" sign (@). In most cases, it's used to separate the name of a user from the name of a local computer.

Thus, a message sent via the Internet to the above address would go first to the Bitnet/Internet gateway computer vm1.nodak.edu. Then it would go to Bitnet, and Bitnet would deliver it to the computer called ndsuvm1. That computer would in turn deliver it to the user ID biomed-l.

What's the Big Idea?

Archie is one of the most popular features on the Net because it helps you find all the locations that have copies of the files you want. The concept is simple, especially if you have ever issued the DIR command in DOS or looked at a file directory in Windows or on the Macintosh.

Imagine that on the first of each month, you and everyone you know who uses a computer were to send a copy of their file directories to a central location. Call it the home office in Sioux City, Iowa. (These are just text files containing the various directories of the machines, not the files themselves.)

Now imagine that you were to dial up the home office and search this massive database of file directories for the file name COMMAND.COM. The database software would execute the search and give you back a list of all the computers whose directories show they have a copy of that file. You would then know the computer's name and address and the exact location on that machine where you will find the file.

Getting a Current List of Archie Servers

To get the most recent list of Archie servers, Telnet to any Archie server. (See the "How to Telnet and Why" section of the "Cookbook.") When prompted for a name, log in as `archie`. Open your comm program's capture buffer, and key in `servers` at the Archie prompt. You will get a list of servers. Key in `bye` to log off the system. Then call the server nearest you. It is good practice to help keep Net traffic down by always using the nearest location, if you can.

Most Gophers give you access to one or more Archie servers, so you may want to try that route first. (See the "Gopher: The Best Feature of All!" section of the "Cookbook.") But here is a starter list of Archie servers in the U.S. Telnet to the one nearest you and follow the above instructions:

Server	Location
archie.unl.edu	Nebraska
archie.internic.net	New Jersey
archie.rutgers.edu	New Jersey
archie.ans.net	New York
archie.sura.net	Maryland

The Internet

That's it. That's Archie. There are on the Net a number of sites that operate "Archie servers." It is to these sites that hundreds of Internet locations periodically transmit their file directories. And it is to these sites that you must go to do your searches.

How to Use Archie

The best way to use Archie is to try to find all locations of a file whose name you already know. You may have read that a certain file is available at location X. But when you try to get it, you either can't connect because all slots at location X are filled right now, or you discover that the file is no longer where it is supposed to be.

In almost every case, the same file with the same file name will also be available at sites other than location X. That's when Archie really comes into its own. Here are the steps to follow:

1. Telnet to an Archie server and log in as `archie`.

2. When the Archie prompt appears, key in `set search sub` to tell Archie to look for the string of characters you are about to specify *wherever* they may occur in a given directory or file name.

3. Key in `set sortby time` so that Archie gives you file names from newest to oldest. Not every FTP site can be relied upon to have the latest version of a file or a piece of software. This puts the freshest files up front on your list.

4. Key in `set maxhits 10`. Most Archie servers default to giving you every matching file name or 100 hits (matches), whichever comes first. But you normally only need one.

5. Key in `find searchstring`. "Searchstring" is the name of the file you're looking for or the string of characters you would expect to be part of the directory or file name. (Note that you may be able to use `prog` instead of `find` on some systems. But `find` is the newer command.)

6. Open your comm program's capture buffer to log the results to disk.

7. After the results have appeared, key in `q` to quit Archie.

Here's What You'll See

An Archie search can take a few seconds or a few minutes. So be patient. Here, I searched on the substring "infopop." And Archie delivered results that looked like this:

```
Host knot.queensu.ca    (130.15.126.54)
Last updated 06:58  16 May 1994


  Location:  /pub/msdos/tcpip
    FILE: -rw-r-r— 1297 bytes    00:00   12 Oct 1993   infopop.txt


  Host ftp.utes.edu.au   (131.217.1.20)
Last updated 06:57 25 May 1994


  Location:  /pc/win31/netstuff/tutorial
    FILE: -rw-rw-r— 330578 bytes  04:56  11 Feb 1994   infopop.zip
```

Notice that this information gives you everything you need to FTP the target file: host system, path location, and exact file name. (See the FTP section of the "Cookbook" for more information on how to FTP.)

What's the Key to FTP?

FTP is the Internet File Transfer Protocol. But as far as we're concerned, FTP is the way to get files from a distant computer on the Internet. The concept is simple, but, as you will see, the devil is in the details.

Basically, hundreds of computers connected to the Net offer outside callers access to selected files. You can sign on "anonymously," which is to say, without having an official account on the system. But, of course, you will be limited to just the FTP area of that system.

The files that are available could be anything from the full text of Milton's *Paradise Lost* to the lyrics of all songs recorded by Firesign Theater to the budget of the United States. Or they could be computer programs and shareware software. (The 64K limit that applies to e-mail and newsgroup messages does not apply to FTP transfers.)

You can go poke around at an FTP site, looking for files of interest. But it's more typical for you to learn that a certain file exists at a given site. To get it, you FTP to that site, go to the path location containing the file, and quite literally issue the GET command followed by the file name. The file will be transferred so fast, your head will spin.

It may be transferred to your own personal directory if you are using the Net from a college's computer center or some other location with a high-speed connection. Or it may be transferred to a holding "workspace" area if you are using a SLIP, PPP, or Delphi connection. To get the file into your own personal computer, you must then download it from that location.

What's the Procedure?

The difficulties you will encounter with FTP are twofold. First, if you are a Windows or Macintosh user, you will find yourself dealing with a DOS-like command line. Second, if you thought DOS was bad, wait till you try UNIX, the operating system most FTP sites use. Personally, I'm constantly forgetting that UNIX is "case sensitive." The commands DIR, Dir, and dir are not the same as far as UNIX is concerned. (Indeed, if you try one and get an error message, try the same letters again with a different case.)

The FTP procedure can be mastered, however, and the more you use it, the sooner it will become second nature. So here we go. Let's assume that you want to get the full text of the novel *Anne of Green Gables.* This is just one of thousands of public-domain works that have been keyboarded by the volunteers at Project Gutenberg.

Since, at this writing, Delphi is the only widely and easily available service that offers FTP, we'll assume that that's what you're using. (America Online and others may offer FTP connections as you read this.) Here are the steps to follow:

1. Sign on to Delphi and key in `internet` to get to the Internet SIG.

2. Key in `ftp` and respond to the prompt with the address of the FTP site you want to go to. Hit your Enter key at the "Enter username (default:anonymous)" prompt. Hit Enter again at the "Enter password" prompt.

3. You will now be logged on to the remote system, and some welcoming text will almost certainly appear. Your mission now is to move to the path location containing the file. Let's assume you've been told the path to enter is `doc/gutenberg/novels`.

4. Key in the command `cd "doc/gutenberg/novels"` to change to the directory with that name. The quotes may or may not be necessary, but they never hurt. So get in the habit of using them. DOS users, notice that the slash is the forward slash, not the backslash you're used to entering.

5. Key in `dir` to get a list of files in that directory and thus verify that the target file is there and called by the name you are expecting.

6. Key in `binary` if the file you want is a binary file. This switches the transfer mode from the ASCII (text) default. (This, too, never hurts since both text and binary files can be transferred this way, but binary files cannot be transferred when you are set to ASCII.)

7. Then you key in a command like `get "anne_of_green_gables.z"` `gables.z`. This tells the system to transfer the file to you, renaming it "gables.z" in the process. Renaming is not crucial, but if you are a DOS user, you will find that the long file names used in the UNIX system will automatically be truncated to no more than 11 characters.

8. On Delphi, the file you have just "FTPed" will end up in your personal workspace. Key in `exit` to log off the FTP site and return to the Delphi prompt.

9. Then key in `work` to get to your personal workspace on the system. Do a `dir` to get a list of the file names your workspace contains.

10. Key in `download` followed by the file name you want to transfer from your workspace to your own computer. Or key in `download` and wait for Delphi to prompt you for a file name or series of file names.

Internet Compression and Archiving

In Chapter 41 of this book, you learned about the major techniques used to compress and archive files in the non-Internet world. Some of those same techniques and corresponding file name extensions are used at FTP sites. But over the years, the Net has developed its own way of accomplishing compression and archiving.

Here are the main file extensions you are likely to encounter at FTP sites, what they mean, and the name of the program you will need to decompress or dearchive the file. The DOS versions of all such programs are available from the "Glossbrenner's Choice" section of this book on the Compression and Conversion Tools disk.

File Extension	What It Is and How to Handle It
.gz	Compressed archive requiring GZIP.EXE (GNU ZIP) program from the GNU Project. See also .z.
.Hqx or **.hqx**	Macintosh compression format. Requires the Mac program BinHex 4.0, the DOS program XBIN23, or the UNIX program MCVERT to convert.
.jpg	A file in the Joint Photographic Experts Group (JPEG) format. Can be viewed on any system with a JPEG-compatible viewer program.
.pit	A file created by the Macintosh program PackIt 3.1.3.
.sea	A Macintosh self-extracting archive. Must be run on a Mac.
.shar, .sh, or **.Shar**	A "shell archive" created by the UNIX SHAR program. Use the UNIX program UNSHAR to decompress.
.sit or **.Sit**	A compressed archive created with the Macintosh StuffIt or StuffIt Deluxe programs. DOS users can also unstuff such files with an unstuffing program like Unsit.exe.
.taz or **.tgz**	Shorthand for .tar.z. Use GZIP.EXE first on such files, and then TAR.EXE.
.tar or **-tar**	Short for "tape archive." These files are archives packed into a single file by the UNIX TAR program. Use TAR.EXE to unpack.
.uu or **.uue**	A binary file in ASCII format requiring the UU-DECODE program or a clone to convert back into binary form. UU-CODE programs are available for most computers.
.Z	A compressed file requiring the UNIX UNCOMPRESS program or a clone, like the DOS program U16 or the Mac program MacCompress 3.2.
.z	Case counts! A lowercase "z" usually indicates an archive requiring the free GZIP.EXE program from GNU Project. To reduce confusion, newer versions of the GZIP.EXE program create files ending in .gz instead.

The World's Your Oyster!

The first time I saw the word "Telnet," I assumed it was a misspelling of "telenet." Not so. The Telnet protocol is one of the major features of the Internet, and there is both a lot less and a lot more to it than meets the eye.

Here's the concept: The Telnet protocol is what makes it possible for you to log on to a remote system once you've logged on to the Internet. That's it. After you're on the Internet, you key in a command like `telnet`, follow up with a valid Telnet address, and you're there.

And then, as they say, the fun begins. For what happens next is solely in the control of the software running at the Telnet site. When you use FTP, in contrast, you always know what to expect, regardless of the site, since FTP is strictly for file transfers. But Telnet sites put you into a program of some sort.

For example, if you Telnet to an address in France—

```
metro.jussieu.fr 10000
```

—you'll find yourself in the Subway Navigator, a program that covers most of the subways in the world. Key in, say, `paris` as your departure station and `versailles` as your destination, and the program will tell you how long the trip will take, the station stops along the way, and where you have to change from Line 13 to Line 12.

It'll do the same thing for the New York subway system. I specified Grand Central Station and the Bronx Zoo, and then checked the results on my Flashmaps for New York City. The Subway Navigator got it exactly right.

Or how about searching a database of transcripts from the PBS TV show, *Charlie Rose*? Just Telnet to `pac.carl.org` and select "PAC." Then choose "Information Databases" and "Journal Graphics" on the menus that will appear. You'll have to pay for the actual transcripts, but being able to search the Journal Graphics database is wonderful!

The Easy Way to Telnet

There are at least two ways to Telnet to a given location. You can use a Gopher menu, if one is available on your service. (See the Gopher section of the "Cookbook" for more information.) Or you can use the Telnet command and follow with an address. The only real twist is that it is best to set your own computer's software to "VT-100" emulation.

After all, you're going into a remote system pretending to be one of its terminals, and most systems expect their terminals to be VT-100s or compatibles. (See your comm program's manual for information on how to emulate a DEC VT-100. This is the most widely supported full-screen terminal in the world, so it is sure to be among the terminal types your software can emulate.)

Most of the time, whether you're FTPing or Telnetting or using some other Internet feature, you won't notice that you are technically emulating a DEC VT-100. But setting your *own* computer's software to VT-100 may not be enough. On Delphi, for example, it's important to access the Using Delphi option and the menus it leads to in order to set your terminal type to VT-100. (The default terminal type is "Unknown.")

It's also important on Delphi to key in `/echo host` at the Internet SIG prompt *before* you select the Telnet option. We have found this to be true regardless of whether we are connecting to Delphi via SprintNet or Tymnet.

Also, do not assume that you have to hit your Enter key when you are connected to a remote system. Test by hitting just your question mark key (?) at a prompt and waiting to see if anything happens. If it does, you are on a system that does not want you to hit Enter; if it does not, hit Enter and assume that you will have to do so after typing each command.

Finally, when you see a message indicating that "Escape character is '^]'" assume that the little pointy hat (a circumflex) is the Ctrl key on your computer. So "^]" means that you must hold down your Ctrl key and hit the right bracket to issue an escape. You might use the escape sequence to get the Telnet program's attention, such as when you want to leave by keying in `quit`.

The Internet

The most common escape sequence in the UNIX world is Ctrl-]. But some systems respond to Ctrl-\ (Ctrl combined with backslash). Or they may use something else again. The key thing is to watch the first few lines of text the remote system sends you when you log on. The system will almost always tell you what escape character sequence to use.

Finding the Best Telnet Sites

One of the truly wonderful things about the Internet is the way various people have assigned themselves the task of producing and continually updating guides to Net locations and resources. It reminds me of nothing so much as the Ray Bradbury novel *Fahrenheit 451,* in which dedicated individuals memorized and "became" classic books to prevent them from perishing from the earth.

There are lots of outstanding guides, but one of the most famous (with good reason) is the "Yanoff List." Its author, Scott Yanoff, calls it "Special Internet Connections." It covers FTP sites, e-mail, and Gopher and Telnet locations.

You can order a copy of the current Yanoff List from the "Glossbrenner's Choice" section of this book; it's on the Internet Must-Have Files disk. But you can also get a copy by FTPing to `ftp.csd.uwm.edu` (Path: /pub/inet.services.txt). Or check the newsgroup `alt.internet.services`. Or log on to the Gopher site `csd4.csd.uwm.edu` and select "Remote Information Services."

What is a Gopher?

A Gopher is a menu system that takes you by the hand and helps you locate Internet resources of interest. The single most important thing to remember about Gopher is that every Gopher menu at every site is *unique.* The software that makes Gopher menus possible was developed at the University of Minnesota. It is available to any system administrator who wants it. But it arrives as an empty shell.

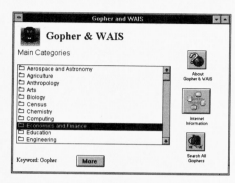

It is up to the system administration staff to fill in the blanks. This is what gives each Gopher its own focus and unique personality. The Gopher at a small liberal arts college might feature literary items on its menu, while the Gopher at a medical school would almost certainly be heavy on medical and scientific items.

Here's the Gopher on America Online. A truly great graphical interface. I eventually scrolled to the topic "Government" and clicked.

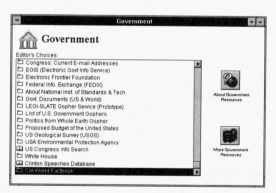

The AOL Gopher then showed me its Government menu. Notice by the slider bar that I'm at the bottom here. And I'm about to pick "CIA World Factbook."

The next most important concept to grab and hold on to is that a Gopher menu can incorporate all aspects of the Net. It is definitely *not* a mere directory to the files stored at a single site. Thus the Gopher at a liberal arts college might include a selection labeled "Shakespeare—Complete Works." Select it, and you will be instantly transported to a location where you can FTP files, each of which contains one Shakespeare play.

Another item on this same Gopher menu might read "Search Library of Congress." Select it, and you will be Telnetted to that site where you can search for an author like, oh, I don't know, try "Glossbrenner."

The Internet

What is a Gopher? [cont.]

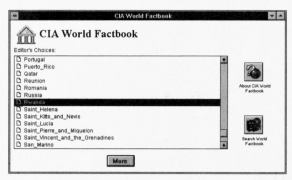

Now that I'm connected to the CIA World Factbook, I keep clicking on the More button until I get to Rwanda.

Notice that not only do these things appear as menu items, but when it comes to "getting" them, there is no need to remember or key in an FTP address or the address of a Telnet site. The Gopher menu does it all for you.

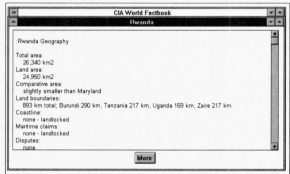

Here I've just clicked on Rwanda in the CIA World Factbook. And, as you can see from the slider, I'm at the very top of the file. There is a lot more information to be displayed, printed, or copied to a file.

How to Tap a Gopher

If you have a college or university connection to the Internet, ask your system administrator if the system has a Gopher. If it does not, get a copy of the Yanoff list, described in the Telnet section of the "Cookbook," by FTPing to `ftp.csd.uwm.edu` (Path: /pub/inet.services.txt). You can then Telnet to one of the Gopher sites Yanoff singles out and use the Gopher located there.

And Veronica and Jughead?

The file name searcher Archie is named Archie as a pun on "archive." But that name started a craze for mining the old Archie comic strip for other names. Hence, Veronica and Jughead, the comic strip Archie's girlfriend and best pal, respectively.

Fortunately for us, all three of these software programs search some kind of database for something. So they at least have a broadly similar function.

Archie searches a database of file names and file directories. Jughead searches the contents of a *single* Gopher menu system. And Veronica searches all the Gopher menus in the world! (Or just about; in Netspeak, Veronica searches "Gopherspace.") Unfortunately, just as Archie is available only on certain Archie servers, Veronica and Jughead may or may not be available on your particular system. And, frankly, Veronica does not always work the way it should. But when it does work it is fantastic, so give it a try!

Help, Info, and Bookmark Commands

The commands used by the Gopher software are very straightforward. Key in `help` or `?` at your Gopher's prompt for a summary. But you will want to pay particular attention to the Info and Bookmark commands.

The Info command forces any given Gopher to reveal all its secrets. Thus, if you key in `info 5` when you want to learn more about Item 5 on a Gopher menu, Gopher will tell you the name of the FTP or Telnet site or whatever it is set to access when you select that item. (On other Gophers, the Info command may be an equals sign (=). On such systems, move your pointer to the target item and enter `=`. Macintosh Gophers use Command-I for this purpose.)

The Bookmark command is called "SAVE" on Delphi. It may have a different name on other systems. But the purpose is the same. When you find a particular item on Delphi's Gopher menu that you think you will want to use again, you can add it to your own "Personal Favorites" list with the SAVE command. On other Gophers, entering `a` adds the current item to your Bookmark list, while entering `A` adds the entire menu. The Bookmark commands, in effect, let you create your *own* Gopher menu, which can be a great timesaver since it eliminates the need to work your way through the menus to get to a particular item.

Grab the Gopher Jewels!

Cross your fingers in hope. Then check your Gopher menu for a feature called "Gopher Jewels." (If your system has Jughead software, search on your Gopher for the word "jewels.") Created by the Gopher Jewels Project under the leadership of David Riggins, this feature celebrated its first birthday on June 1, 1994.

The concept behind Gopher Jewels is simple: Collect the Gopher menus from many leading Gopher sites, then go through them all, *clas-*

sifying—yes, *classifying*—each menu item by subject. When you're done, rearrange all the items into a new master Gopher Jewels menu in which everything is presented by subject.

This is a truly marvelous resource. So make a special effort to check it out. I promise you that you will not be disappointed. I have not verified the fact, but it certainly looks to me as though the America Online "Main Categories" Gopher guide, shown earlier in the figure "Gopher and WAIS," is based on the Gopher Jewels. And the other figures in this chapter show how easy it is to wend your way to the CIA World Factbook.

Accessing Veronica

The only way to get to Veronica is via a Gopher. If your local Gopher does not offer a Veronica feature, use Gopher to go to the server at `gopher.micro.umn.edu 70`. Choose the menu item "Other Gopher and Information Servers." Choose "Veronica" from that menu.

If you don't currently have access to a Gopher, you can Telnet to one of the Telnet-accessible anonymous Gopher sites:

Host Name	Log In As
consultant.micro.umn.edu	gopher
gopher.uiuc.edu	gopher
panda.uiowa.edu	panda
info.anu.edu.au	info
gopher.chalmers.se	gopher
gopher.ebone.net	gopher

appendix

Shareware and public-domain software are probably among the most important creations of the personal computer revolution. Not that "free" programs haven't always been available for computers of every size and sort. But when you've got tens of millions—even hundreds of millions—of computers out there, something reaches a critical mass, and things just explode.

The Problems with Shareware

Since the explosion takes place underground, as it were, most people are not aware of it. Shareware authors don't advertise, and very few magazines carry regular features devoted to the subject. So, not surprisingly, the vast majority of computer users have no idea what shareware is or what it can do for them.

That's one problem. The other is that there is so awfully much of the stuff. There are so many shareware word processors that, assuming your time has value, you will be ahead of the game if you just go out and buy the leading word processing program for your machine—instead of spending the hours needed to examine, evaluate, and select the *best* shareware program.

The Essence of Glossbrenner's Choice

That's why Emily and I created Glossbrenner's Choice, a small collection of shareware that includes only what we feel are the very *best* programs in each category. These are the programs we like and use ourselves. They're the ones that transform our computers into extensions of our hands and brains. And, like all the best works of art, they are handcrafted, reflecting the vision of a single individual, not some development committee. We're happy to share them with you.

All of the programs are on 3.5-inch, high-density (1.44MB), DOS-formatted disks. If you do not yet have a drive that can handle 1.44MB disks, you ought to get one. Your local computer store has them for as little as $40, and they really are the future as far as magnetic media is concerned.

If you're a Macintosh user, you will be able to use all of the Internet disks marked "Mac-readable." These disks contain only plain MS-DOS format ASCII text files that you can easily import as Macintosh format files using the Apple File Exchange software you will find on one of the Utility disks that came with your machine. No need to worry with any "translator" modules. Check your Reference manual for an appendix titled "Exchanging Disks and Files with MS-DOS computers."

The cost is $5 per disk, plus a small charge to cover shipping ($3 to U.S. addresses, $5 outside the U.S). Visa, MasterCard, and phone orders are cheerfully accepted. Indeed, we hope you will treat Glossbrenner's Choice as a convenience. It is our hope that you will use the knowledge gained in this book to locate and download the pro-grams you want. From long personal experience, we know how much fun it can be to search for a program that will perform some function, find one, download it, unZIP it or whatever, print the documentation, and *run* it!

But we also know that there are times when a system is heavily loaded and so slow to act that you just can't bear it. Or you may get knocked offline if you forgot to disable Call Waiting and a call comes in. Or a platoon of thunderstorms trooping through your area may cry havoc and let slip the dogs of persistent transmission errors. That's when ordering a program on disk makes a lot of sense. It also makes sense when the program is quite large, and you'd rather not spend your connect time twiddling your thumbs as you wait for the download to finish.

A Quick Summary of the Disks Offered Here

Many of the programs on the disks described here were cited or discussed in the text of this book. But here's a quick summary:

BBS Access (FirstClass and TeleFinder)

As you know from Chapter 22, bulletin board systems (BBSs) are becoming more and more "graphical." Graphics are great, but to benefit from them, you often need to call a board using a special program. Two of the most popular programs in this category are the FirstClass and TeleFinder "client" programs used to access BBSs that run the matching "server" programs. Both the FirstClass and TeleFinder client programs are on this disk.

Communicator's Toolchest

Most comm programs suffer from "featuritis," but they often lack a few of the features real people really use. For an active communicator, it's a nuisance to be forced to rekey all of the entries in your current comm program's dialing directory when switching to some other package. That's why this disk includes CVTT, a Windows program to convert among ProComm, ProComm Plus 1.0, Telix, and text dialing directories. It also has DIRCOPY to convert among Telix, Qmodem, ProComm, ProComm Plus, Bitcom, and text formats. In addition, the disk includes the programs needed to add Zmodem and CompuServe B+ support to almost any DOS comm program.

CommWin Communications Program

Our current favorite comm program for Windows is Gerard E. Bernor's CommWin program. It's quick, clean, intuitive, and beats the Windows terminal program all hollow.

Compression and Conversion Tools

Here are all the programs a DOS or Windows user needs to decompress or dearchive the various files available online, plus a Glossbrenner-written quick-start manual to show you how to use each one. Forget the tons of useless features and go for the heart of the matter! To wit: How can I get this darned file extracted? Extraction programs included range from those for .ARC and .ARJ files to .Z and .ZOO.

D-Lite for Delphi

If you regularly use Delphi mail and SIGs, this DOS program can save you money. D-Lite lets you do all of your thought work offline, signing on only to pick up messages, mail, and files, or to blast them into the service. It's really a must for any heavy Delphi user.

Encryption Tools

Want to encrypt a text or binary file so that *no one* will be able to read it without the "key"? Then this is the disk for you. Among other things, it includes Philip Zimmerman's famous Pretty Good Privacy program that's driving the FBI nuts!

Games Disk (*Adventure* and *Wolfenstein 3-D*)

This is a sentimental favorite. *Adventure* and *Wolfenstein* represent the alpha and omega of public-domain and shareware gaming so far. In my opinion, your life won't be complete until you play each of them. They are quite different. But both are absolutely splendid!

GEnie Aladdin

If you're a DOS user, the most economical way to use GEnie is via Aladdin, a program you can use to prepare messages and RoundTable postings offline, transmit what you have prepared, and capture messages and mail addressed to you. Aladdin can also be used to download files you want.

Internet FTP Essentials (Mac-readable)

Internaut Perry Rovers has written an excellent FAQ on how and where to use the Internet's FTP feature to get files. He also maintains a list of FTP sites that's about as comprehensive as you can imagine. Both documents are supplied on this disk. Updated monthly, Rovers's FTP list gives you the site address, country, time zone (number of hours plus or minus Greenwich Mean Time), and date of last modification for the site; source of the most recent information for the entry, aliases, administrative address, organization, e-mail server address, and hardware and operating system; and any general comments or restrictions, types of files, archives, or mirrors available.

Internet Just the FAQs (Mac-readable)

This disk contains the gigantic 100+ page FAQ Index that lists all of the FAQs currently available on the Internet. The FAQ Index includes precise file names to help you locate the files via Archie. In addition, you will find a selection of FAQs, tutorials, and files, including Compression FAQ; Pictures FAQ; Find-Addresses FAQ; IRC FAQ, Primer, and Tutorial; MUD FAQ; Gopher FAQ; and Veronica FAQ.

Internet Mailing List Essentials (Mac-readable)

This disk contains two gigantic lists of Internet and Bitnet mailing lists, plus the LISTSERV REFCARD command summary to help you communicate with mailing lists. It includes the SRI List of Lists, which covers both Internet and Bitnet lists, and Publicly Accessible Mailing Lists (PAML), which are mainly Internet lists with a dozen or so Bitnet lists.

Internet Must-Have Files (Mac-readable)

This is a disk of plain ASCII text files that contains a huge amount of what you need to know to use the Internet effectively. Included are the best FAQ (Frequently Asked Questions) files for new users, recommendations on Internet sites to explore, and timesaving resource guides. The disk also includes a DOS tutorial that does a wonderful job of distilling the essence of the Internet.

Internet Newsgroup Essentials (Mac-readable)

Newsgroups are a world unto themselves. This disk includes current information on all the newsgroups available on the Internet, including the popular "alternative" newsgroups. At this writing, all of the groups on the disk are available via Delphi and CompuServe, but AOL offers only a sanitized selection. At the very least, this disk will show you what's available and what you may be missing. Also included is the ROT-13 program you will need to read some of the raunchier jokes in newsgroups and UU-CODE, the program that converts pictures uploaded to newsgroups as text files back into viewable binary graphics files.

Internet Telnet Essentials

For DOS and Windows users only, this disk contains Peter Scott's remarkable Hytelnet package, which has a gigantic database of Telnet locations that includes at least one screen per location describing what you'll find there. For ease of use, the entire thing is organized as a hypertext-style menu system. Also on this disk is Bruce Clouette's optional Subject Guide to the main Hytelnet menu, as well as a Windows front-end (WINHytelnet).

Megahost BBS Package

If you want a simple—yet powerful and easily installed—bulletin board for your business, office, or home, Megahost fills the bill. It's the simplest, easiest bulletin board to set up. This is not the program you want if you plan to become a sysop for fun and profit. But it's great for serving as a message board and file transfer point for a small business or work group.

Qmodem Communications Program

At this writing, Qmodem is simply the best shareware communications program for DOS available anywhere. As *Computer Shopper* said, it's "a true powerhouse."

TAPCIS for Compuserve

TAPCIS makes it easy to handle electronic mail and get the most out of CompuServe Forums. If your main way of using CompuServe is mail and SIGs, TAPCIS can save you a bundle on connect time.

Wildcat BBS Package

Wildcat is a zippy, feature-filled bulletin board system with tens of thousands of loyal users. If you want to run a *real* BBS, open to all comers, this is the program to start with. If you like it, you can easily make the transition to the commercial version of the product. And Mustang Software, its creator, offers great support.

Glossbrenner's Quarterly

For the past several years, Emily and I have produced an on-disk publication we call *Glossbrenner's Quarterly.* It began as a means of providing readers of Glossbrenner books with the latest articles from the Microsoft KnowledgeBase (available on GEnie and Compu-Serve). Readers of *DOS 5*, *DOS 6*, and *Power DOS!* were interested in getting the latest Microsoft information on those software products. The *Quarterly* still contains that information. But it has evolved into something more: short essays, opinion pieces, cool software—the jack-o'-lantern Windows wallpaper and spooky .WAV sound files we did for a fall issue around Halloween were a really big hit—and more. Basically, if you like the books that Emily and I write, then you will probably like the *Quarterly.*

Order Form

You can use the order form on the next page (or a photocopy) to order Glossbrenner's Choice disks and subscriptions to Glossbrenner's Quarterly. Or you may simply write your request on a piece of paper and send it to us.

We accept Visa and MasterCard, as well as checks or money orders made payable to Glossbrenner's Choice (U.S. funds drawn on a U.S. bank or international money orders). Please allow one to two weeks for delivery.

Resources

Glossbrenner's Choice
699 River Road
Yardley, PA 19067-1965
215-736-1213
CompuServe: 70065,745
Delphi: ALFRED
GEnie: GLOSSBRENNER
Internet: alfred@delphi.com

Glossbrenner's Choice Order Form
for Readers of *The Little Online Book*

Name _____

Address _____

City _____ State _____ Zip _____

Province/Country _____ Phone _____

Glossbrenner's Choice Disks:

___ BBS Access (FirstClass and TeleFinder)
___ Communicator's Toolchest
___ CommWin Communications Program
___ Compression and Conversion Tools
___ D-Lite for Delphi
___ Encryption Tools
___ Games Disk (*Adventure* and *Wolfenstein 3-D*)
___ GEnie Aladdin
___ Internet FTP Essentials

___ Internet Just the FAQs
___ Internet Mailing List Essentials
___ Internet Must-Have Files
___ Internet Newsgroup Essentials
___ Internet Telnet Essentials
___ Megahost BBS Package
___ Qmodem Comm Program
___ TAPCIS for CompuServe
___ Wildcat BBS Package

___ Total number of disks, 3.5-inch HD ....($5 per disk) _____

Books and Newsletter:

___ *Internet Slick Tricks,* 288 pages ....($16 each) _____

___ *Glossbrenner's Master Guide to GEnie,* 616 pages,

includes Aladdin and $12 GEnie account credit ....($25 each) _____

___ *Glossbrenner's Quarterly,* one-year subscription, 3.5-inch HD disk .....($20 each) _____

TOTAL: _____

Pennsylvania residents, please add 6% sales tax _____

Shipping ($3 to U.S. addresses or $5 outside the U.S.) _____

GRAND TOTAL ENCLOSED: _____

Payment: ☐ Check or Money Order payable to **Glossbrenner's Choice**

☐ Visa/MasterCard # _____ Exp ____ / ____

Signature _____

Mail to: **Glossbrenner's Choice**
699 River Road
Yardley, PA 19067-1965
215-736-1213 (voice)   215-736-1031 (fax)

GEnie®
The most fun you can have with your computer on.

No other online service has more cool stuff to do, or more cool people to do it with than GEnie. Join dozens of awesome special interest RoundTables on everything from scuba diving to Microsoft to food and wine, download over 200,000 files, access daily stock quotes, talk to all those smart guys on the internet, play the most incredible multi-player games, and so much more you won't believe your eyeballs.

And GEnie has it all at a standard connect rate of just $3.00 an hour. That's one of the lowest rates of all the major online services! Plus -- because you're a reader of *The Little Online Book* -- you get an even cooler deal.[2] When you sign up we'll waive your first monthly subscription fee (an $8.95 value) and include ten additional hours of standard connect time (another $30.00 in savings). That's fourteen free hours during your first month -- *a $38.95 value!*

You can take advantage of this incredible offer immediately -- just follow these simple steps:

1. Set your communications software for half-duplex (local echo) at 300, 1200, or 2400 baud. Recommended communications parameters 8 data bits, no parity and 1 stop bit.
2. Dial toll-free in the U.S. at 1-800-638-8369 (or in Canada at 1-800-387-8330). Upon connection, type **HHH** (Please note: every time you use GEnie, you need to enter the HHH upon connection)
3. At the U#= prompt, type **JOINGENIE** and press <Return>
4. At the offer code prompt enter GAC225 to get this special offer.
5. Have a major credit card ready. In the U.S., you may also use your checking account number. (There is a $2.00 monthly fee for all checking accounts.) In Canada, VISA and MasterCard only.

Or, if you need more information, contact GEnie Client Services at 1-800-638-9636 from 9am to midnight, Monday through Friday, and from noon to 8pm Saturday and Sunday (all times are Eastern).

1 U.S. prices. Standard connect time is non-prime time: 6pm to 8am local time, Mon. - Fri., all day Sat. and Sun. and selected holidays.
2 Offer available in the United States and Canada only.
3 The offer for six additional hours applies to standard hourly connect charges only and must be used by the end of the billing period for your first month. Please call 1-800-638-9636 for more information on pricing and billing policies.

Effective date as of 7/1/93. Prices subject to change without notice. Offer limited to new subscribers only and one per customer.
©1994 by General Electric Company   Printed in the U.S.A.

CompuServe.

The difference between your PC collecting dust and burning rubber.

No matter what kind of PC you have, CompuServe will help you get the most out of it. As the world's most comprehensive network of people with personal computers, we're the place experts and novices alike go to find what's hot in hardware, discuss upcoming advances with other members, and download the latest software. Plus, for a low flat-rate, you'll have access to our basic services as often as you like: news, sports, weather, shopping, a complete encyclopedia, and up to 60 e-mail messages a month. And it's easy to begin. All you need is your home computer, your regular phone line, a modem, and a CompuServe membership.

To get your free introductory membership, just complete and mail the form on the back of this page. Or call 1-800-524-3388 and ask for Representative 449. Plus, if you act now, you'll receive one month free unlimited access to basic services and a $15 usage credit for our extended and premium services.

So put the power of CompuServe in your PC — and leave everyone else in the dust.

CompuServe®
The information service you won't outgrow.™

Put the power
of CompuServe
at your fingertips.

Join the world's largest international network of people
with personal computers. Whether it's computer support,
communication, entertainment, or continually updated
information, you'll find services that meet your every need.

Your introductory membership will include one free month
of our basic services, plus a $15 usage credit for extended and
premium CompuServe services.

To get connected, complete and mail the card below. Or call
1-800-524-3388 and ask for Representative 449.

Yes! I want to get the most out of my PC. Send me my FREE
CompuServe Introductory Membership, including a $15 usage credit and
one free month of CompuServe basic services.

Name: _____

Address: _____

City: _____ State: _____ Zip:____

Phone: _____

Clip and mail this form to: CompuServe
P.O. Box 20212
Dept. 449
Columbus, OH 43220

EXPLORE the INTERNET
——— FREE! ———

DELPHI is the only major online service to offer you full access to the Internet. And now you can explore this incredible resource with no risk. You get 5 hours of evening and weekend access to try it out for free!

Use electronic mail to exchange messages with over 20 million people throughout the world. Download programs and files using "**FTP**" and connect in real-time to other networks using "**Telnet**." Meet people from around the world with "**Internet Relay Chat**" and check out "**Usenet News**," the world's largest bulletin board with over 10,000 topics.

If you're not familiar with these terms, don't worry; DELPHI has expert **online assistants** and a large collection of help files, books, and other resources to help you get started. After the free trial you can choose from two low-cost membership plans. With rates as low as $1 per hour, no other online service offers so much for so little.

5-Hour Free Trial!
Dial by modem, **1-800-365-4636**
Press return a few times
At *Password*, enter LITTLE

Your Road Map For The Information Superhighway— America Online®

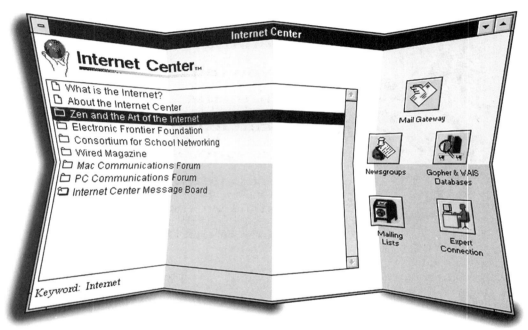

Start Your Test Drive Today!

Before you can exchange ideas with people around the world, you have to learn your way around the information superhighway. No problem. Just go to our Internet Center—your road map to the Internet. You'll find we've made it as easy to handle as America Online. With a point and click, you can access newsgroups on hundreds of topics, send e-mail to other online services or overseas, access information on everything from home brewing to NASA news using Gopher and WAIS databases— and more. Plus, check out America Online's software libraries with over 100,000 files to download. Multi-file downloading and 9600 baud modem access make it fast and easy. You can even talk with other members in live conversations, conferences, and classes. All on the most "clickable" online service there is. So hit the information superhighway and head for America Online. It's easy. Simply call 1-800-827-6364, Ext. 4455, to order today!

AMERICA Online®

1-800-827-6364, Ext. 4455

Get Connected-Free.*

Join the millions of PRODIGY® members who have discovered how easy it is to get more from their computers. More value. More use. More information. More fun. More savings.

FREE!
10 hours + 1 month trial

World Class Service. Friendly and informative help 24 hours a day, 7 days a week.

Hot off the wire. News, weather, ESP-NET™ sports and more.

Connect with people. Exchange ideas on thousands of Bulletin Board topics, hold conversations online in real time, and link up directly to *America's Talking*™ on Cable TV.

Manage your money better. With one-stop investing —databases, ideas, analysis and discount trades. And get online with your own bank and our time-saving bill payment service.

Give your kids the learning edge. Make homework fun and play educational. They'll reference a 33,000 topic encyclopedia, experience interactive NOVA, National Geographic and Sesame Street℠ and much more.

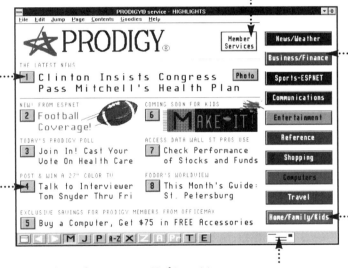

Great graphics and sound. For Windows™ and Macintosh® users.

Mail is waiting. Send and receive E-mail from friends and family. Plus Internet.

PRODIGY®
Service

Take an Additional 10% Off PC Connection or MacConnection's Already Low Prices on any Zoom/Modem, FaxModem or Voice FaxModem!

PC Connection, MacConnection and Zoom Telephonics have teamed up to provide purchasers of *The Little Online Book* with an unbeatable deal on the hardware you need to access the Internet. You can take 10% off of the PC or MacConnection price on any Zoom Telephonics product. This offer is limited to mail-in purchases only. Your order must be accompanied by this original coupon. Only one modem, faxmodem or voice faxmodem may be purchased with each coupon. We cannot accept copies of the coupon. *This offer expires 9/95.*

Send in this coupon, along with your order and payment by check, MasterCard, Visa, American Express or Discover Card. Mail to:

PC Connection®

6 Mill Street, Marlow, NH 03456
For information or a catalog, call 1-800-800-0005
Source Code: ZOOMP1
Shipping Charge: $5 for your order, which ships overnight via Airborne Express
Sales tax: Ohio residents should add applicable tax.

MacConnection®

14 Mill Street, Marlow, NH 03456
For information or a catalog, call 1-800-800-0002
Source Code: ZOOMM1
Shipping Charge: $3 for your order, which ships overnight via Airborne Express
Sales tax: Ohio residents should add applicable tax.

Index